EVANGELISTICALLY
YOURS

Raymond Fung

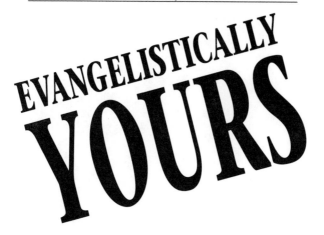

EVANGELISTICALLY YOURS

Ecumenical
Letters on
Contemporary
Evangelism

WCC Publications, Geneva

Cover design: Rob Lucas

ISBN 2-8254-1045-4

Printed in Switzerland

Contents

Introducing Myself   *Raymond Fung*   vii

1. Listening — and Speaking

    Emilio Castro / John Stott dialogue on listening to the cry of the
    oppressed or the cry of the lost... We must listen rather to the
    cry of the sinned-against... People don't cry out because there
    are no listeners... If you listen you must also speak... to people,
    not about issues... Why radical Christians make ineffectual
    evangelists... Concern for the re-evangelization of Europe . . .   1

2. Mission among the Young

    Youth participation in ecumenical organizations cannot build or
    rebuild a strong youth movement... Wanted: missionaries to go
    among the young and find out what God has done... Conversa-
    tion with Catherine... A plan of action by women students in
    Africa   19

3. Good News to the Poor

    Concern for world evangelization has to include concern for the
    poor... The solidarity of the eucharist needs to be vindicated by
    the solidarity of the secular table... Of faith healing and Bible
    studies... What proof do we have to say that God is just?... The
    covenantal event... Biblical justice has nothing to do with
    power or equality... It has a lot to do with accountability and
    answerability... God is just because he keeps his word... Justice
    as accountability in practice   45

4. Dialogue with People of Other Faiths

A dialogue colleague writes to a young man on bearing witness to Christ among Hindu neighbours... Letter to Ranjith stimulates substantive responses... Plea for a high view of other faiths and for inviting Muslims, Hindus and Buddhists to follow Christ 64

5. Trends in World Evangelization

Faith healing... Crisis in youth evangelism worldwide... A mission encounter with American Christians... Does bringing third-world evangelists to the West help?... Why people become Christian in China 92

6. Debate with Donald McGavran

McGavran proposes a Giant Step in Christian mission... Inviting global debate... Churches in six continents respond... Fung and McGavran draw conclusions 127

7. Perspectives on Proselytism

Discussions on proselytism of a general and theoretical nature have limited value... Focus on alleged proselytizing circumstances... A series of exchanges and input from Protestant, Catholic, Orthodox, Pentecostal and Jewish sources... Concluding survey 188

8. In the World Council of Churches

Ecumenical report on Korea presumes opposition between church growth and human rights... Genesis of "Mission and Evangelism: An Ecumenical Affirmation"... An evangelism defence of the *Reader's Digest* attack on the WCC... A midterm assessment of evangelism in the WCC... Evangelism breakthrough in the San Antonio world mission conference... The World Council in assembly in Canberra 224

Introducing Myself

Dear Friends,

When I took up the job of secretary for evangelism in November 1981, Emilio Castro reminded me of the *personal* nature of this monthly letter. I take it to mean that the letter is an ongoing, unfinished, reflective piece. I do not take it to mean "intimacy". That would be rather embarrassing, in the case of a stencilled letter going to more than 6,000 addresses! I think the idea may approximate a Chinese expression: friendship as clear as water. A friendship not based on mutual dependency, or on being together, but one based on common commitment to something other than ourselves. In this case, to the communication of the gospel of Jesus Christ to people in our immediate setting and all over the world. With this understanding, I can afford to be open and a little vulnerable, banking on your giving me the benefit of the doubt.

The letter format, I believe, is going to suit me fine. I am no good at producing theological writings of a formal nature. I am a lay person, and I bring to this task remembrance and gratitude: my decision to be a Christian twenty-two years ago; participating in Bible study groups on a university campus; teaching Sunday school in my local church; seeing my aged parents too confessing Jesus Christ in baptism. And then there were the twelve years of urban industrial mission among labourers in Hong Kong. The latter experience, of being friends with the poor in situations of naked injustice and indignity, has disturbed me profoundly. Here, Paul's longing finds echo, an imperfect echo, in me: "that I may know him and the power of his resurrection, and may share his sufferings... not that I have obtained this... but I press on to make it my own, because Christ Jesus has made me his own" (Phil. 3:10-12).

But I hope I do not only bring remembrance and gratitude. I hope to bring through this letter new stories, fresh insights, and more fruitful

ways of understanding and doing evangelism, from churches across the
nations. From you, wherever you are.

Yours in Christ,

Raymond Fung
November 1982

Chapter 1

Listening — and Speaking

1

Going over the back issues of the monthly letter, I came across the Emilio Castro/John Stott dialogue on listening. John Stott criticized the WCC for listening only to the cry of the oppressed and not to the cry of the lost. My feeling is we should listen to the cry of the sinned-against. The forces which oppress people are sinful forces, and not simply social, economic, political or military forces. Human beings are lost in sin which violates both God and the human person. Every human being, oppressed or lost, is both the object and the subject of sin. Evangelism must address the question of sin, its reality, the horror of its impact on human lives. Of the many forms of Christian ministry, evangelism is the one which must deal with sin head on. Let us not be naive or shallow in this regard. I have come by a little understanding of this while working with labourers in Hong Kong and reading the scriptures in their midst.

On the evangelistic significance of listening, Castro and Stott have no doubts. This, I hope, will be developed and driven home. Too many of us pay lip service to it. But we don't listen. I have a theory as to why many evangelists, or Christians generally, do not listen to people. We do not listen to people because we do not hear people crying out to God. How can we listen if there are no cries? So we say Christ is the answer, not knowing what the question is. Or the more sophisticated among us would go for market research and audience analysis as substitutes for listening. But why is it that the people do not cry out? This is contrary to our theological dogma about the human situation. My theory continues: people do not cry out because there is no one there to listen. People came to realize their real needs and exposed them to Jesus because they knew they could depend on his listening to them. There is first the listener, only then comes the human cry. Herein lies the evangelistic nature and significance of listening. It follows, then, that the listener and the act of listening are much more than a means of evangelism. They are part of the good news to the person who does not cry out but who, on encountering the listener, does then cry out. Therefore not to listen is not just bad evangelism. It is not evangelism.

November-December 1982

2

One of you wrote to me: "I am not sure if you are quite right to say that if only we would listen, there are plenty of cries; is it not one of the real blocks in a society like ours that many of the relatively affluent do not cry out, except perhaps to protect the affluence in which they have come to trust so much?" Well, I did not actually say that there are plenty of cries if we would only listen. But let that be. Plenty of cries or no cries? Let us share our experience of listening. You've listened to the cry from the relatively affluent. It is a cry to protect their affluence. But do you think that the same can legitimately be understood and formulated differently? For example, as a cry to preserve an adequate income to pay one's mortgage, to prepare for the day when one gets old and cannot work? A cry to provide for children so that they can go to college? A cry to be somebody? In short, a cry of fear? I believe it can, for you know and I know that we are not talking about the super-rich, or even those whom we call rich, but about the relatively well-off, the middle class, the people in our churches. The sector of the community of whom most of us are part.

The cry of the middle class may well be a sinning cry — protecting the affluence in which they have come to trust and, if I may add, ignoring the poor in the process. But it is no less a cry of the sinned-against, fearful of failure, anxious about loss, uncertain of the hand which holds their future. Such are the signs of their sinned-againstness and, at the same time, the reasons for their sins against the poor. In this upside-down world of ours, noble human hopes and desires — individual and family well-being — can be turned into instruments of injustice and oppression against the vast majority of the world's people who aspire to the same.

Someone once said: "The dynamics of the haves are to keep. The dynamics of the have-nots are to take." I recognize and accept this as a simple factual statement. But if we go a step further, we will find that the goal of the middle class among the haves is exactly the same as that of the poor, namely, personal and family well-being. The haves want to keep on having it. The have-nots want to have it for themselves. The hope of the middle class is the hope of the poor. This in itself does not make them friends. It does put them in the same boat.

So we listen to the reality of the middle class. We need to affirm their desire for personal and family well-being, if only to be honest, if only to point to the sinfulness of having it, and treasuring it and yet denying it to others. For those of us who work among the middle class not only in the first world but also in the third world (third-world congregations are poor in comparison with those in the first world, but in most cases are far from poor in their own respective contexts), I feel we should take their sinned-againstness seriously. Sinned-againstness can be the common ground for the middle class and the poor. On this common ground of shared experience, there is a chance for empathy to develop and real ties to be forged. Hence, the middle class and the poor are no longer donors and recipients, but fellow sinned-against, sharing not only in material resources but in suffering also. Not only learning to heal each other's wounds, but also struggling together against the forces of sin.

This, I hope, is good theology. The question remains whether it is good economics and good politics: do we have the kind of economic and political analysis which shows that the interests of the poor and that of the middle class do not necessarily conflict, that the poor and the middle class have reason to work together in the pursuit of their common aspirations? In short, that the relatively affluent are not sinned against by the poor and their struggles for well-being? That the bad guys are somebody or something else? I think we have that kind of analysis. But even if we don't, awareness of middle-class sinned-againstness would at least make us better persons and better Christians. It is not only the crimes of the middle class that sin against the poor; their very virtues do. Herein lies the sinned-againstness of the middle class. The good news, coming into this reality, both judges and affirms.

I received another response, this time from North Africa: "The insight that folks don't cry out because they know no-one is listening ... I think is true. Though I have long been concerned with the poor ... and have lived with them for a decade, I am distressed that they do not cry out. I am also distressed that the church here has done so little to help them voice their hurts."

One of the things I have learned about the art of listening is to see the other person as a brother or a sister. Not as a client whose role is to be weak and to generate guilt. Nor should we, in our listening, treat the other person as being so different from ourselves or so full of wisdom that we let ourselves be overwhelmed and lost for words. When we listen to persons, we listen to our brothers and sisters, people with all their sins and sinned-againstness, all their faults and goodness, and — and this is the important point — their absolute claim to be listened to and spoken to, because of the family blood-tie between us, or theologically, our shared parentage deriving from the Creator God. This family relationship does not commit all those involved to agreement on issues and values, or even to peaceful togetherness. But it does commit everyone concerned to something like "we are in this all together".

In the family, there are rich brothers and poor brothers, rich sisters and poor sisters. And each lives his or her own life. But regardless, the ties are always there. So the notion of seeing other people as brothers and sisters, be they poor or middle-class, is no mere sentimental notion, because the brother-sister relationship is no sentimental relationship. What it does is to turn people from being "they" to being "you". This way, there is no escape. This way, we would find it easier to hear the cries and find the word, and be more free to speak of a deeper brother-hood and sisterhood in Jesus Christ.

One of you really has helped me with this elaboration. Commenting positively on my belief that listening is not simply a precondition for evangelism, but is part of the good news, she wrote: "If we try to look at things from the point of view of, say, the non-believer, it is obvious that the good news is this listening person." So it is in solidarity with people that we can speak. Proclamation is to take place in community.

We have discussed the concern of listening in evangelism more or less in individual terms. How does a local church listen? Well, a local church is a gathering of Christian people, so the listening must be done by them. In most cases, even in situations of much population mobility, members of the congregation do have some knowledge of their larger community, the people, their problems and hopes, because they are in the community and part of it. Very often the problem is, Christians assume that their listening to people in the community has nothing to do with the business of the church, and therefore they do not share such concerns in congrega-tional life. As it is, the leadership concludes that the church is alienated from the community — which, of course, becomes true by self-fulfil-ment. But it is an alienation resulting not so much from failure as from failed perceptions and failed opportunities. Once it is recognized that the local church is Christian people, and that through them the church is already in the community and is part of it, then there need be no doubt that the local church can indeed listen. It can then go on to encourage, teach, plan so that the Christian people can listen more carefully, and together struggle to find and speak God's word.

From these premises, appropriate evangelistic methodologies can be worked out. Pastoral visits, for instance, should no longer be the sole province of the pastor and those chosen at the beginning of each year. Visits should be made by those in the congregation to whom the ones to be visited are more likely to be responsive. One may soon find visits to non-believers outnumbering the rest.

April 1982

3

Of all Christians, those with ecumenical convictions ought to be among the best listeners. The WCC world mission conference in Melbourne in 1980 began with a prayer, "Your kingdom come". This calls for listening. The conference found its answer in the direction of a church in solidarity with the poor. Almost at the same time, the Pattaya consultation [on world evangelism, in 1980, sponsored by the Lausanne Committee for World Evangelization] focused on the question "How Shall They Hear?" This calls for speaking. The conference ended with strategies to reach the unreached. In Pattaya, the good news is essentially understood as words, a series of propositions, to be spoken to the unreached who will then hear. In Melbourne, the good news is primarily understood as community or kingdom, to be experienced in the solidarity encounter of the church and the poor. For Pattaya, the evangelistic process consists of separate and distinct elements: the evangelist, the gospel to be communicated, and the recipient. For Melbourne, the evangelist or the church reaching out to the poor in solidarity is already a part of the gospel. In Pattaya, the rest of the world are "they" who must be persuaded to hear. For Melbourne, the rest of the world are "you" with whom the church must be in solidarity.

So it seems that there is every reason for Christians with ecumenical convictions to be good listeners. But does the same augur well for our being good speakers too? For the two functions must come together. After the listening, there is the speaking. Otherwise the other person might as well have a piece of stone as listener. That which makes us credible listeners also makes us credible speakers. Or we have no right to enter into a trusting relationship at all. Of course, the reverse is also true. That which discredits us as listeners also discredits us as speakers. But once we have credibility as a listener, we are obliged to speak. Obliged to speak to that person in that given situation, in the same way we have listened.

This, it seems to me, is the important thing. We do not speak words, generalities, abstractions divorced from life. Our prayer should be: "God, what is your word for that person, for us, in our situation today?" There are many possible Christian messages, many Christian words. "All have sinned and have come short..." "Come, all you that are weary and heavy-laden..." "Behold my servant whom I uphold, he will bring forth justice..." "Awake and keep watch..." "Repent, the kingdom is at hand..." "In my father's house, there are many mansions..." And so on, and they are all beautiful messages. But which is the message for our situation today? What is God's word for us now, the word which cuts through the complexities and ambiguities of a given human situation, allowing light to come through?

This is risky business — listening to people; praying, "God, what is your word for us this day?"; finding it; speaking it. It is the risk the prophets took. Nathan finding the right word and giving it straight to David: "You are the man." And the evangelist — John daring to declare the profoundly simple truth: "The word became flesh, and dwelt among us, full of grace and truth." And the Lord — Jesus receiving his puzzled disciples with "come and have breakfast".

I hope I do not sound romantic to you. At the back of my mind is the experience that for the first five years of our involvement among the poor in Hong Kong, my colleagues and I were not able, and did not dare, to engage in evangelism among working-class people. We were not able to, because there was no audience. The Christian church at the time had no base of support among the working class, and no credibility. We did not dare because we were afraid that instead of preaching the gospel of Jesus Christ, we might be preaching an "opiate to the masses", violating both the gospel and the poor. Our university and middle-class background, for which no apology was required, did not qualify us to be evangelists among the poor. It made us aware of the need to listen. So we did. We listened to the men and women working in the textile mills and electronics plants. Then we were able to speak to them about one another, about friends and families, about visiting those injured at work, about the city's injustice, the need to organize for power, about Jesus. And what message did we find for the factory workers in Hong Kong? What is God's word to them in their situation? What were we speaking to them as we listened to them? Essentially, in our case, it was the word of Jesus: "Take up your cross and follow me. I have heard you. I know you. I am with you. But I have a task, a tough and costly task. Come, join me. Let us go together." An abundant statement, speaking to people in their weakness and in their strength.

Before I left for Geneva, a question was raised by my Hong Kong colleagues: whether we as a group waited unnecessarily long before we were able to begin relating the story of Jesus to the story of the poor. Amazingly, it was the workers who had recently become Christian who thought we had waited too long. In a way, I was happy to hear that; but I still am not sure. The poor know from experience that there is no free lunch. I know from experience that there is no short cut. But I am listening.

So I hope we learn to listen, and struggle to speak. For those of us who are only too aware of the cheapness, the hypocrisy and the hollowness of empty words, maybe "struggle to speak" is the right expression. Like the dumb speaking for the first time. Or like my Korean friends who said no to human rights violations when they were supposed to keep their mouths shut. What comes out is no mere words. It is action.

At this point I would like to share with you a sad story. About two years ago there was an ugly industrial accident in Hong Kong in which six workers were killed. It occurred at a construction site. A cable broke and an elevator plunged down from the eighth floor, crushing the six men inside. There was a mass funeral. Several hundred workers were there, including us, who had been convening a coalition of some sixty labour unions to fight for better safety regulations. Two persons spoke: a union official, and a pastor, as one of the six victims was a Christian. The union man spoke briefly. He pledged the union to the task of changing the law on compensation and safety. He urged the families to "go on living bravely". Then it was the pastor's turn. He spoke for about twenty minutes. There is a door in heaven. It matters a great deal which side of the door one is at. He urged the audience to repent. He talked about Adam and Eve and how sin came into the world. I was boiling inside. At the very moment when Christian witness was best expressed by solidarity, a commitment to be together, this Christian man chose to divide us. After the ceremony I was too ashamed to join the crowd. But a Christian worker caught up with me. He appeared to be in the same boat, muttering in great frustration: "I wished Jesus had been there to speak for himself." And I remembered Jesus at Lazarus's funeral. How I wished that story were told.

Finally, there must be occasions when one listens but cannot speak. What comes through may be so awesome that the spoken word — any spoken word — becomes a joke. A Dutch Christian has written to the Commission on World Mission and Evangelism (CWME): can we "go on confessing and writing as if Auschwitz had not happened?" I can understand this, but I must confess I do not really grasp the full impact. At the Netherlands Missionary Council recently, where I was invited to discuss a CWME draft statement on "Mission and Evangelism: An Ecumenical Affirmation", I met a happy old man with a broken body, broken by hard labour under the Japanese at the River Kwai, on the Burmese border of Thailand, during the second world war. We spent a whole day together, roaming in the Saturday market. His has been an experience far, far beyond articulation and verbal response. Yes, there must be occasions when we listen but cannot speak. Then we can only pray. We can only pray that God would do the speaking, both to those to whom we listen and to us who listen. For after the listening comes the speaking. Romans 8:18-27 may be saying something to us in this vein: "Likewise the Spirit helps us in our weakness; for we do not know how to pray as we ought, but the Spirit himself intercedes for us with sighs too deep for words."

March 1982

4

Reading the many church statements on various issues confirms me in this belief: that in trying to communicate the gospel, Christians and churches must have our faces turned towards the people to whom we wish to communicate. In other words, evangelism requires that we listen and speak direct *to* people, that we always regard people as "you", not as "they". This, it seems to me, is an evangelistic posture. The church has other legitimate postures, such as speaking *on* issues and celebrating *among* ourselves. But until we turn our faces to people, hear their sighs, read their grins, and have them face us likewise, we are not yet into a relationship of sharing what means most to each other. Many of our churches have spoken on the issue of unemployment. But *to* whom are we addressing ourselves? The government? The federation of employers? The trade union congress? The church? Fine. But what about the unemployed? Why do we not say something to them direct? Our message to the many unemployed would not be the same as our statement on the issue of unemployment. Probably, we could use more or less the same analysis and argument. But certainly we would put them differently, and include other words as well. I have the feeling we are not very good in speaking to people. That's why we'd rather speak about their problems, the issues. Or we'd rather tell people what they should believe. Telling people is very different from speaking to people. Here we come to the heart of our evangelism concern. What is the content of the good news? A CWME commissioner was very insistent in one of the meetings that the central question of evangelism is *what*, not *how*. What is the good news to those to whom we wish to communicate the gospel? That's tough to answer. But as we turn towards the people, and learn to face each other, and have them solely in our mind and in our love, not caring too much what others think, then perhaps we are on our way to finding the word.

June 1982

5

The assembly of the Church of England Evangelical Council took place last week. It was a three-day event, with business to be conducted like the election of officers, the passing of resolutions, etc. The Council is a quasi-synodical body within the Church of England which seeks to promote causes dear to evangelical Anglicans. It was my first exposure to the group, and probably it was also the first time they had a WCC staff person address them. To be frank, I was aware that to some evangelical Christians, I as a WCC staff person would be starting with three or four points minus on their score card. That induced in me a sense of ambivalence as to approach. Should I play diplomat and build bridges? Or should I play advocate and expose differences? In reality, there is of course no real choice. My two mental options are essentially caricatures. We are fellow believers who feel an accountability to each other towards greater maturity in Christ and greater effectiveness in mission. There can be no other way. Nevertheless, I must admit a feeling of ambivalence as I prepared for my involvement. As it turned out, the problem was resolved for me by the high degree of acceptance the organizers first and then the assembly accorded me. I took part freely in the preparation. I was listed as one of over two hundred participants. I was invited to participate as a Christian brother who is secretary for evangelism in the World Council of Churches to share with them what I know. I think I did. There were moments of tension. Recalling the criticism Dr John Stott directed at the

WCC at the Nairobi assembly in 1975 — that the WCC has listened to the cry of the oppressed rather than to the cry of the lost — I decided to be provocative. A sheep without a shepherd, a sheep that has gone astray: Jesus' classical image of human lostness. I put to the plenary: how do we account for this human lostness: the sheep has sinned? Or the sheep has been sinned against? I then offered the conclusion that human lostness is *primarily* human sinned-againstness. That created a stir. After many comments, questions and exchanges, Dr John Stott, who was the out-going chairman of the Council, intervened. He started by observing that my insistence on primacy polarized the discussion. He pleaded with the group "to accept what Raymond Fung has tried to tell us", and he pleaded with me "to accept that human lostness is human sinned-againstness *and* human sinfulness". In the final session when I was given the privilege to make my reflection on the assembly, I shared with the group that I accept totally John Stott's plea that we hold both realities together in our understanding of sin. I recognized that any assumption and discussion of primacy rests on the acceptance of both in the first place.

In this particular discussion, there was a challenge that has since driven me back to the scriptures. Responding to my thesis of human lostness as human sinned-againstness, a participant asked me how I would deal with the parable of the prodigal son in Luke 15. On the spot, I responded that the lost son recognized his own sinfulness. "I have sinned against heaven and against you, I am no longer worthy to be called your son." The older brother, too, insisted that his brother had sinned and was sinful. But the father's assessment was different. Explaining to the self-righteously angry elder son, he said: "This brother of yours was dead and is alive again; he was lost and is found." What is this young man's reality in his father's eyes: sinner or sinned-against? Or that it did not really matter except that he was his son? On such questions and what they mean for evangelism, I am still searching.

The next concern follows logically. If human lostness is, or consists of, substantial elements of human sinned-againstness, what of individual responsibility? With that, I was able to share what I have been sharing in the pages of the monthly letter. I suggested that the good news could be understood along the line of Jesus' invitation to take up one's cross and follow him. Half of the world insists that an individual is not responsible, in order to control. Big brother knows better. And the other half of the world insists that an individual is indeed responsible, in order to condemn. You are unemployed because you are no good. But Jesus, by his invitation to, and offering of, community, takes the matter of individual responsibility away from the realm of law, and puts it in the realm of grace. With Jesus, each person is and can be individually responsible for his or her life, and that of others. This is good news...

I hope there is no self-serving element in this report. It is not easy to report on such an encounter, and yet I feel I must try. For me, it was a rich learning experience.

February 1985

6

Some time ago in these pages, I put word to a thought which had been with me constantly. Why are "radical" Christians ineffectual evangelists? I put the word "radical" in inverted commas because, in this context, I could not, and cannot, give a precise definition of it. But what I have in mind is clear. I am thinking, for instance, of congregations with strong community outreach programmes to people in need, but with very few noticeable evangelistic consequences. The ministry appears holistic in terms of its range, but the effect on people's lives seems fragmentary. I am thinking of the phenomenon of the poor, the refugees finding their spiritual homes in "reactionary, fundamentalist" churches which preach other-worldly sermons, rather than finding their spiritual homes in "mainline" churches which are in solidarity with them on issues of human rights, legal protection, jobs and schools. So I ask why "radical" Christians make such ineffectual evangelists.

I admit the formulation is woefully inadequate and could be unfair. Such generalization is practically impossible to prove or disprove. Nevertheless, I believe the concern is real, the question legitimate. I have since received much encouragement from "mainline" ecumenical Christians and "radical" evangelicals, to develop the discussion. Let me approach it on a personal, spiritual and theological level in the general setting of a local congregation and a local community.

Probably the most likely first answer to the question is the most obvious: time, or the lack of time. Christians with heavy community involvement are busy people. Even more so if you are a pastor. You have many many meetings to attend. Meetings of the various committees of your congregation. Citizens' committees. Neighbourhood committees. Support committees for many worthy causes. Meetings to ensure funding. Meetings to prepare for meetings. And if you belong to a "mainline" church, you would also be sitting on a number of committees and task forces at a higher jurisdictional level. And if you are "ecumenical", you believe in doing things together. That probably means more committees and meetings with your fellow clergy and church workers. You spend your days rushing from one meeting to another. You are so busy you have no time for people. And if you have no time for people, you can forget about evangelism.

The solution lies, of course, in reducing the number of committee meetings, in setting priorities, in becoming less busy. But the real solution is spiritual in nature: that in our busyness, we are "disturbable", and that people know we are "disturbable". If we are able to get across this feeling of "disturbability", people would be that much more ready to seek us out, to invite us out for a walk, for instance.

Secondly, "radical" Christians in their dealing with people in the community tend to be shy about words such as "salvation" and "Jesus", probably for very good evangelistic reasons. If this is merely a matter of being sensitive to others, there is no problem. But if it is a matter of unwillingness or inability to speak about faith in Jesus Christ to other people, there is. And our neighbours and people in the community can certainly tell which is which. Should they come to the conclusion that we are uncomfortable talking about personal salvation in Jesus Christ, they would understand and would not embarrass us with the subject. It takes a lot of courage for people to approach a Christian with personal religious questions. When they do make the approach, they expect sympathetic, intelligent and clear responses. If they are not sure about that of us, they would simply not bother us with their questions in the first place. They could not afford the embarrassment, to say the least, of getting responses like "I don't know", "it doesn't matter", "do what you think is right", "I'll have my pastor call you".

The solution does not lie in adding a few more religious terms to our daily vocabulary. The solution lies in our being fired with a strong desire to see many more people come to faith in Jesus Christ, and being "ready to give an account of the hope that is in us". As this expectancy becomes a part of our total being, it will find natural expression in our daily actions, behaviour, relationships and indeed conversations.

Many "radical" Christians are ineffectual evangelists because their desire that others may also come to believe is not strong enough. They send out mixed signals. People outside the church are confused by these signals and do not know what to expect if they take the first hesitant step.

Thirdly, there is in many "radical" theological orientations an "absolutist", "totalitarian" or "fundamentalist" streak which does not make much sense to the average person. And if this streak is lived out in the life of a "radical" Christian, such a person will have much difficulty identifying with the people and, more damaging, the other way round. When there is no identification, there is no evangelism.

I would describe the streak as utopian expectation (which is not necessarily damaging) plus (and this is highly damaging) contempt for the very imperfect human efforts that seek to operate in the world as it really is. Simply put, I am describing a person with utopian commitments who despises small achievements by way of immediate or intermediary solutions. To thinking people, such a person makes little sense. Certainly not to the poor with their prayers for daily bread.

I remember a "radical" theologian addressing a gathering of migrant workers from an Asian country, who serve as domestic helpers away from home. He gave an analysis of how the migration had hurt the social fabric of their own country. He attempted to show his solidarity by citing cases of unfair dismissal and sexual harassment. He thundered against their US$300 monthly wages as exploitative. All the women present lowered their heads. There was complete silence. The theologian might have well been right in what he said. But he had only added to the women's shame. He had no good news to offer. He succeeded only in humiliating them.

There was the occasion of my visit to the churches in the Netherlands. At a press conference I was asked how I felt about Dutch society. I said I could easily make a list of their hundred sins, but as a Christian from the third world, I thought it was a pretty good society worthy of respect. The fact that people from poor countries knock on their doors proves it. "You have a good society," I said, not good enough, I am sure, by your own higher human standards, or by Christian standards. And you should keep working on it. But you do have something good to show and to share. I urge you to reach out to share what you have. The next day, it was given prominent coverage. My host told me many in the churches were grateful that I said what I said. He added: "But if it was I who had said it, it would have been dismissed as the ravings of a reactionary."

Now this is very serious for evangelism in the Netherlands, if my friend was not just joking. His remark suggests to me that a clear if limited affirmation of Dutch society is controversial in the Dutch church. Whether this is simply the idiosyncratic tradition of the Dutch intellectual elite or a reflection of Reformed utopianism is beyond me. What I am quite sure of is that without a fundamental affirmation of people and community, the Christian church is not in a position to evangelize.

A corporate refusal by the church to say yes to one's society will eventually be read by men and women, old and young, as a no to their individual efforts and aspirations in community. Only if the church first says a big YES can it, when the time comes, say a big NO later. I am thinking of the way that people in the streets feel whether the church is with them or not with them. If they somehow come to feel in their daily existence that the church is not with them, that it does not understand them or even care to do so, that the church's attitude is one of permanent judgment, and a kind of self-righteous pitying, then the church is not good news.

Fourthly, the question why "radical" Christians make ineffectual evangelists boils down to a matter of having understanding of and respect for persons and peoples. The "radical" Christians' favourite word is "issues". In the ecumenical movement, locally and internationally, when Christians and churches get together (apart from celebrating our faith, which we do joyfully, thank God), the first question is always "what are the issues?" and then much later, if ever, the second question, "who are the persons who should be involved?" This may be a good way to engage in ecumenism or in justice (I would doubt even that). It is surely not a good way to engage in evangelism. We are also very strong with "people" rhetoric, but I am reasonably sure we are much more comfortable with "issues".

Let me cite a revealing incident. When the recent East German poll was over and the votes went heavily for the conservatives, a North American friend of mine said with a tinge of sad annoyance: "They (the East Germans) voted for blue jeans and McDonalds." Her remark was not unique. I have since heard and read similar remarks in the ecumenical movement, many from North Americans, and a few from West Europeans, and a lesser few from third-world people. The most offensive remark is "they voted for their stomach". Such remarks are not in themselves problematic. There is nothing wrong with voting for one's stomach, especially when food shelves are empty. There is nothing wrong with voting for blue jeans and McDonalds, especially when local products and services are few and far worse. People have always voted like that everywhere, North America and Western Europe included. What is offensive is the tone of haughty dismissal. And what is truly problematic is that those who make such remarks are supposed to be persons who respect peoplehood, who believe in the poor, the marginalized and the oppressed. But now that a whole people have exercised their free choice and made their will known, our "radical" Christians feel let down, because the people don't think the way they should. They don't think the way our "radical" Christians think. When our respect for persons is conditional upon their agreeing with our ideological positions, it is not respect. And where there is no respect, there is no real understanding.

Probably the most useful thing "radical" Christians should understand about people, most people anyway, both rich and poor, but especially the poor, is that they are tired. They are tired in the body and tired in the soul. If you do not understand, accept and respect that, you'd have a hard time being their friend and being effective in whatever you do with them, evangelism included.

To conclude, the problem with "radical" Christians is we are not radical enough. We have not thought things through. We have not done enough soul-searching of ourselves. We have not spent enough time with the poor. We are too comfortable in our little ghettos, with our "radical" rhetoric. Which is a great pity. For "radical" Christians have at their disposal some of the most useful elements to make good evangelists. They affirm the world and the people in the world. Their convictions lead them to work with people outside the churches rather than simply talking to Christians all day long. They do not have much respect for pietistic religious jargon. If only they can put their acts together!

So much for this piece of polemic. If you think I am totally off the mark or wrong at some points, let me know and I will give you equal time in these pages.

Let me share a quotation. It is useful for evangelism, particularly among the poor. From Dom Helder Camara:

> If we don't press the absurd claim of being the best, if we present ourselves as brothers and sisters for others, we shall be astounded to discover what a lot of people of good will there are about. Some of them may perhaps be rather timid, others will be so situated that they can't see things in the same light as we do. But once they come across somebody who speaks from the heart, not seeking to impose anything on them or humiliate them, and not with the conviction of being any cleverer or holier, then they are affected and also join the march. *

July 1987

---

* *Through the Gospel with Dom Helder Camara*, Orbis Books, Maryknoll, 1986, p.109.

7

I have been doing a lot of travelling and speaking lately, also a lot of listening and thinking. As I went along, I tested ideas and formulations with people I met, soliciting their reactions, quietly pushing limits in the existing framework of understanding. There is an idea I have tried out on several different occasions. The uniformly positive reception has given me confidence that it may be important for evangelism. I am still working on it, but I want to share it now with you in case it makes sense to you and you may wish to explore it in your context.

I begin with a concern about the evangelization of Europe or, as some would put it, re-evangelization. I am concerned that easily eighty to ninety percent of the people seldom, if ever, grace a pew. This is the case in the cities as much as in the villages. Secular men and women, young and old, have better things to do than go to a worship service. How does the church deal with the problem? In broad terms, there is, as far as I can tell, one main response. Outreach. Christians reaching out to the community, proclaiming and serving as individual persons in daily witness, in small groups, or corporately through local congregations and ecumenical efforts. In the process, we share with people the gospel of Jesus Christ. Some Christians do it aggressively. Others less so, lest they offend. But reach out, the churches all seek to do, in one way or another. I am excited by this mission consciousness, and with it the effort to re-equip the clergy for evangelization, to train the laity, to encourage the participation of youth and women, the involvement in social and economic and human rights issues, and the formation of small fellowships and action groups, and the occasional bringing together of thousands upon thousands of Christians for the celebration of their faith. Will this dynamic of reaching out evangelize Europe? More accurately, will it put the churches in a position to evangelize Europe?

The idea I have been trying out, however, suggests a different dynamic. It does not, I am sure, contradict the dynamic of the church reaching out. It can make more effective Christian outreach if we are mature enough in our understanding and appropriation. But it is nevertheless a different dynamic.

I refer to the dynamic in the parable of the prodigal son (Luke 15:11-32) as a model for the process of evangelization in Europe. We are all familiar with the story. Here is a man at the height of his physical vitality who decided to collect his share of the estate and go his own way. He turned away from home and began to serve mammon in a new situation.

Finally, he came face to face with the hollowness of his new god. It no longer satisfied him. He wanted to return. And in his disillusionment, he was prepared for total submission. He asked to be accepted as a servant in his father's house.

People awakening to the realization that secularism is a false god — there are signs of this everywhere. When this happens, it will be crucial for evangelization whether the Christian church behaves like the father in the parable or like the elder son.

The obedient, long-suffering and self-righteous elder son, who has not left home, who has served faithfully in his father's household, is prepared to accept his brother home on the latter's own terms as a servant. "You can be part of the household, indeed you are welcome, if you follow our rules." There is no question about it. But just as surely, this would result in the younger son leaving home again in the end.

The good news is that this is not the father's way. He has been waiting for his son's return. He sees his son coming a long way off. He runs to him. He embraces him. He accepts the disillusioned young man back into the household as a son, not as a servant. If the Christian church behaves like the father, the evangelization of Europe, in my reckoning, will have taken a significant step forward.

Let us take a closer look at the father, who he is and what he does. He rejects the overtures of both his sons. He rejects the self-righteousness, however justified, of his elder son. No less, he rejects the total surrender, however justified, of his younger son. He states his condition openly in no uncertain terms: "This young man does not come home as a servant. He can only come home as a son, with all the privileges and duties, all the freedoms and accountabilities, all the comforts and all the toil."

That the father can say this, or that he is in a position to communicate this message, and indeed that his lost son can find the courage to come back to him in the first place, must be due, I suspect, to the transparency of his hope. He did not go out in search of his son and induce his return by whatever means. But neither was he resigned to the loss. Jesus described him as waiting in compassion, ready to act at a moment's notice, ready to see the signs at a distance, to run, to embrace. This is not passivity. This is active waiting. The kind of posture which communicates not so much expectations directed at the conversion of another person as a buoyant expectancy that God will do wonders and one should be ready to play one's part.

This, then, in a very preliminary way, is how I see the relevance of the parable to the evangelization of Europe. The dynamic is not so much the church reaching out. The dynamic is secular men and women seeking to return to God. And the church evangelizes not so much by humbly serving the world, according to the world's felt needs, or by confidently offering promises of power and security, as by a compassionate openness to the search for God of secular men and women, an openness made transparently inviting by active waiting and buoyant expectancy. To wait and yet not be passive, to live in evangelistic expectancy, but not expectation, is a mission spirituality we need to cultivate.

In the dynamic of the parable of the prodigal son, may I suggest we see the possibility of the re-evangelization of Europe. And perhaps not just of Europe. Perhaps also in situations of desperate want or tension, or where religious liberty is restricted, perhaps in a multifaith setting, perhaps in societies where God-talk has become cheap.

December 1987

Chapter 2

Mission among the Young

8

When I use the term "youth" or "young", I have in mind people in their late teens and early twenties. The WCC is committed to the revitalization of an ecumenical youth movement. An entire morning was devoted to this agenda in the last meeting of the WCC central committee. This excites me. I would like to do my part, especially from an evangelism perspective.

I think we need to differentiate between the goal of building, or rebuilding if you like, an ecumenical youth movement and the goal of youth influencing the ecumenical agenda. In theory, the two goals overlap, each has a cause-effect impact on the other. In practice, given the present state of our situation, they do not overlap. And if we confuse the two by somehow thinking that they are one and the same thing, whatever efforts we make will remain futile. I am afraid that today this confusion does exist. Our stated goal is the building of an ecumenical youth movement. What we are actually concerned with is how youth can better influence the ecumenical agenda.

The proof is found in the dominance of the concept of "youth participation" as an ecumenical principle. As it works out, this means quotas on committees and conferences, youth events before or alongside important ecumenical assemblies, and youth gatherings and visits on ecumenical issues. This is an appropriate strategy for the goal of influencing the ecumenical agenda. (Its effectiveness is a different matter.) When young people are physically present, and as a group, they have the opportunity to exert influence. This is however not a strategy to build a movement, and it is not meant to be. And if those who are given the specific task of building or strengthening the movement on the international, regional and national levels spend most of their efforts advocating youth participation in ecumenical structures, meetings and agenda, valuable as it is, they are not working on the stated goal.

I hope you will not take me as being critical of the principle of youth participation. I am eager to see it happen. But unfortunately I do not see it happening. That is because the ecumenical youth movement, or whatever is left of it, is weak, to put it mildly. And if one is weak one has no influence even though one is allowed to sit on boards and committees and given platform time.

The strategy for the building of a movement is not so much to "get in" as to "get together". Not so much to seek participation in the existing structure and its agenda as to seek to organize and multiply the people into a movement of their own, which will in that process decide on its own agenda and how it should make its presence felt. The builders of a movement are not those recognized by the established order as leaders, but those recognized by their peers as such. The church has often bureaucratized its understanding of a leader as someone who speaks and debates well or someone who occupies official positions. We have often forgotten that a leader is fundamentally somebody who has a following, articulate or inarticulate, position or no position. Programmes for leadership-training or development do not produce leaders. They seek to, and can only, impart leadership skills to people who already have a following at home.

I was deeply moved at the central committee session on "youth" by a senior churchman who testified how his life had been transformed by ecumenical exposure because, when he was young, his church saw fit to give him such opportunities. But the demise, or the near-demise, of the ecumenical youth movement today is due not to the absence of or decrease in such opportunities. It is due to the collapse of the base from out of which leaders of the young, not in the bureaucratic sense but in the sense of persons with a following, can emerge and benefit from the equipping opportunities offered by the established order.

At this point, I must pause to ask myself, am I not depicting the two goals and their respective strategies in too starkly polarized a framework? Can we not work on both together? After all, there is such a thing as division of labour. Let some, especially those at the grassroots, work on strengthening the movement, and others meanwhile work on opening up the WCC, denominational headquarters, etc. Many people are involved, and many levels and types of activities are going on. But, for the same reason, we must have clarity of goal and consistency of strategy so that all those who are involved in youth and student work in different parts of the world and on various levels can move in the same direction. As far as I am concerned, the decisive choice still has to be made whether the goal is to build or rebuild an ecumenical youth movement or to seek more youth participation in the present ecumenical structures and agenda. I have no doubt that in this day the urgency and importance of the first supersedes by far that of the second. And anyway, if there is a vigorous worldwide ecumenical youth movement, the "influence" concern will take care of itself. The organized churches and ecumenical organizations will then have to follow (as used to be the case). Meanwhile, a choice has to be made.

So far, I have painted the options in strategic and political terms. And I do not apologize for that. But the choice is in fact very much of a spiritual and theological nature. The choice is not, I am happy to say, a choice between good and bad. The choice is between the good and the better. But it does have consequences which, if we are serious and logical about it, bear on how we, corporately and individually, live out the Christian faith.

On the premise that the building of an ecumenical youth movement is our call to mission, then the following, for example, should be obvious:

— The wellbeing of youth (indeed, people) is more important than the wellbeing of institutions.
— It is youth who must determine their ecumenical agenda, and not the other way round. (In the latter case, it would inevitably look awfully small and insignificant, I am afraid.)
— Undergraduates are more important than graduates and post-graduates, including seminary graduates.
— An old woman on a pension who gathers ten neighbourhood young people in her flat is more important than a professional youth worker who cannot.
— Spending time with youth is more important than haggling with church bureaucrats over youth participation in the established structures.
— Getting youth workers back into school compounds and college campuses is more important than getting them on to church boards and ecumenical commissions.
— Pro-youth is more important than anti-middle-age (or anti-anything).
— If you are youth, when protest against the established order is called for, it is preferable to protest at a moment convenient to you and your

fellow youth and in a way effective for your purpose, rather than protest at a set hour in a slot generously provided for by the ones you want to protest against.

— The non-youth are not youth, and have no business making decisions for youth. The non-youth are, however, former youth, and have, or should have, a lot to show. Let them lay out their wares before the present youth if their wares are any good. The worst thing that could happen in this scenario is that the former youth have no wares that the present youth can buy or reject.

I can go on, but I must stop. The above are not simply hints for building an ecumenical youth movement, they are no less ingredients in the make-up of a spirituality and an evangelizing character which will communicate to the young. I mean singleness of purpose, holy indifference to secondary matters, consistency of belief and action, and refusal to play institutional games.

Generally the churches' work with youth and students is in a bad shape. It is high time, if it is not already too late, for a radical reorientation of mind and spirit, in defiance of the conventional wisdom and mind-set which has contributed to the weakening of the ecumenical youth movement in the past twenty years or more. I am not so much concerned about the health of institutions and organizations. I am concerned that young people everywhere have a chance to come to know the good news of Jesus Christ, to share their faith, to strengthen each other, and to contribute to the worldwide fellowship of churches in the ecumenical movement. For this, we need a strong ecumenical youth movement.

July 1987

9

I have a few things to share about evangelism among youth — some observations and experiences of gospel outreach to young people.

• Not so long ago, a young woman sent us a long, impassioned letter. She had been working on an ecumenical youth event for a few months. The event was over and in the letter she was reporting back. The whole thing must have cost her a great deal.

She began by telling us that "young people resist all forms of paternalism and patronizing". My immediate response: "Yes. Of course. I agree. We in the WCC have learned, or are learning, the lesson. We do not tell you what is best for you. We realize we cannot. And if sometimes there are signs to the contrary, we are ready to be corrected."

She then advised that we must "be prepared to let go". My immediate response: "Yes. Of course. I agree. You are speaking to the converted. We have let go a chunk of power. You and your fellow young people had control over the content of the event, over budget and schedule and most other things. You and your colleagues are your own free agents as much as anybody can be free these days. We have let go. And we are not unhappy about that."

And then, came her conclusion: "Therefore you will have to commit yourself to maintain the sharing between generations." I had no immediate response. I was not prepared for such a conclusion. It did not seem to make sense. I reread her letter with care. There was no mistake. That was truly her conclusion. Then I began to see.

The young woman was telling us: "Don't patronize us. Let go of your control. But don't leave us alone in benign neglect. Listen to us. Speak to us. Walk with us."

Whether in personal evangelism or in the rebuilding of a Christian youth movement in our churches, this message has fundamental importance.

• A personal testimony. I have a son who is 19 years old. In his studies and social life, he has developed well. My wife and I are happy about his independence and the environment he has chosen to surround himself with. About three years ago, we noticed in him a sense of alienation. He spoke much less to us. He became very critical of the church. We attributed the change to the normal and inevitable process of growing up. Whether the diagnosis was right or wrong, it did not help of course. We felt helpless.

Then one day I had an idea. I announced that from now on we would spend a little time around the supper table for intercession. We would pray for each one in the family, for our friends and for the world. Instead of saying grace, which usually lasts ten seconds, we would intercede for a minute or two. We would pray for the children's studies, their life in school, their safety on skiing trips, their friends whose parents are divorced, classmates who are on drugs. For our health. For our relatives back home. For Hong Kong and China. For the Philippines. For many suffering lands. Just a brief period of intercessory prayer around the supper table. These daily one-two minutes since then have altogether changed my son and our relationship. I can tell it is something he looks forward to, and we look forward to.

My wife and I have been wondering why it has worked with our son and with us. One answer is the whole thing is brief, and it is not very religious. My own educated guess is that it has worked because the moment of intercession is a moment in which the whole family let one another know that we all have needs. That despite outward appearances, each has fears and anxieties. As we acknowledge our weakness and our needs in prayer, the alienation among us disappears and we become strong together. I suppose in my son's eyes I have seemed strong and successful. I fly around the world. I lecture in universities and seminaries. I speak to large crowds and important groups. My articles appear in learned journals, and my pictures in popular church magazines. In his eyes, I am a can-do person. I have no needs of others. This must have been difficult for him to cope with. Regular family intercession, even if it's only for a couple of minutes, has changed all that.

In modern society, certainly in cities like Geneva or Hong Kong, no one can afford to show weakness. If you are weak you are despised. So we all pretend to be strong. We declare to the world in one way or another that we have no need of others. I understand this and am sympathetic. Acknowledging need and confessing weakness are dangerous. One may be rebuffed. One may be manipulated. But in the context of prayer and of worship, in the conscious presence of God, it would be easier to confess. And what is more, such a context will not permit us to wallow in our weakness; it helps us to emerge strengthened together. At least it has been the case with my son and with my family.

• One of my intellectual and, to some extent, spiritual struggles in communicating the Christian faith is finding responses to the kind of human suffering which apparently makes no sense. Needless loss. Needless pain. Needless violation. Needless dying. I am not sure if young people are more prone than adults to raise the question. This is of course not the place to deal with the problem of suffering. There are many good and wise books on the subject, and we are acquainted with a variety of possible Christian responses, ranging from "yes, it is God's will", through "no" and "I don't know", to a silence which struggles to reach out. Much depends on the circumstance of the encounter and who that person is and who you are.

In a recent encounter with some university students, mostly not Christians, in a group setting, in an atmosphere totally un-solemn but apparently serious, I was asked to respond to the question of human suffering individually and as a people. I felt it appropriate to try out what I had been struggling with myself for some time. "You don't want a general answer. You want a specific one. I think we should all ask God directly for an answer. Whisper, shout, whatever. Try the scriptures by yourself or with friends. By the time you arrive at heaven's gate, if you still do not have an answer from God that you can accept, you should refuse to go in. I would. My suspicion is you would have got an answer by then."

I believe I have Job's approval and quite a few biblical prophets', and hopefully St Paul's (Rom. 9:1ff.). I know I have the students'. Several have become friends since then.

• However, the young woman who has access to the WCC, my son, the university students, they are one thing. Quite another matter is the young people who are heavily marginalized, anywhere in the world: the long-term unemployed, the drug addicts, the school drop-outs, the casual labourers, the homeless. Those whom you find loitering around railway stations and market squares. People who have a 14-, 16-, or 20-year old body but whose soul is easily 40 years old. How can the church reach out to them?

In a previous reflection in these pages I said that in my opinion an institutional approach is unlikely to help. "These young people have been so severely wounded that nothing but a full-scale, long-term missionary movement will do. I mean the church sending out their best, young or old, it doesn't matter, who feel the call to be brothers, sisters, fathers and mothers to them. The church letting these missionaries do what they want, giving them no job descriptions and no deadlines, only assuring them of the church's good will and their readiness to listen to the missionaries reporting back. Then, maybe, in the midst of sharing and acceptance, some way may be found."

Since then, and after many exchanges with friends old and new, I have gained a more specific set of ideas. Once again, I mix idealism with pragmatism. It is not going to be a total solution or strategy. I seek a significant, do-able, strategic entry into the world of these young people. The idea is that we look for missionaries among church-going adult Christians who live a reasonable Christian life. We encourage a movement of Christian people, men and women, lay and ordained, single and married, homemakers and job-holders, in their thirties and older, towards a very simple and specific ministry: that within one's life time, each person will seek out and befriend at least one marginalized youth in one's own environment. Find a way to indicate an absolutely clear commitment to be a friend. Be ready to go very far within one's human capability and Christian understanding, ready to say a clear yes and a clear no if need be.

Depending on circumstances and the response, the relationship may or may not involve giving advice, connections, shelter, money. It will certainly involve giving time, sporadically or in an ongoing way. It is a ministry of commitment and availability on the part of an adult Christian to a young person.

There is a catch, though. A Christian catch. The missionary in his or her involvement "imposes unilaterally" the hope, expressed in the manner of a clear but gentle wish, that when this young person grows up and life is back in shape, he or she would reach out to another marginalized youth with the same commitment and availability. We are not talking about contracts and covenants. We are talking about the sharing of a hope, and the nurturing of a memory, which cements the friendship between two persons because it embraces many more.

This catch is all-important for the effectiveness of this missionary movement among marginalized youth. It would save it from being merely charity. It would reduce the dangers of paternalism and manipulation. It would turn the missionary and the young into genuine partners. And they are. The adult will benefit just as much. At least a chance to be less selfish with one's time and an inducement to get out of one's comfortable shell. And if there is some institutional recognition, encouragement and help from the church — say, your local pastor bringing together several similar missionaries from the same congregation to compare notes or, more ambitiously, a national coordinating office sharing stories of Christian people (homemakers, farmers, carpenters, teachers, workers, nurses, doctors, politicians, accountants, salespersons, bankers, policemen and women, pastors, secretaries, retired persons) breaking through to the world of the deeply alienated youth — why, we may even find ourselves bona fide members of a great and visible movement doing missionary work without having to leave home, and enjoying it. I am optimistic about a ready response from our lay people to this kind of missionary call, maybe even some of the more "frozen" of God's people who seem to have a particular preference for the pew at the back of our churches.

Of course we need to remind ourselves that an adult is not necessarily an adult — a mature person — and it is no secret that church-going Christian adults are not free from problems of their own. Who are they to want to be missionaries to the young, especially people who have been heavily marginalized? One answer lies in help and empowerment from people with experience and expertise — pastors, elders, theologians, professional counsellors, and others. This must be made available. And obviously there are many Christian people who could not make it, and shouldn't. Another answer is that one of the beauties of Christianity is the belief that witness is not the exclusive domain of gurus, of persons who have already attained a high degree of enlightenment and perfection. Christian witness is to be borne by the wounded, fallible human persons. And that the important thing in evangelism is to be ready to give an account of our hope, the not-yet we are striving towards with all our being, and not an account of the success we have already achieved.

Well, how does the whole thing look to you? An immediate response from a friend: this sounds so middle-class! I told her I got the idea from Africa and Central America. In an African household, we often find children and young people who are not children of the head of the household. They may be distant relatives, or friends of relatives. They may have left their home for school or work, or they simply have lost their homes. So they come here, and they are taken in for a year, two years, many years. No big deal. As for food and bed space? "Well," the adults say, "things are short. They eat what we eat. There is room for one more body. We will worry about things when we need to worry about them. Meanwhile, this is home." And from Honduras and Guatemala, the same type of story but with a sharper edge. Peasant households and urban families taking in children and teenagers who have no homes, some of them very disoriented and disturbed, because they have witnessed the slaughter of their parents and relatives. No, this is not a middle-class thing. But if it does speak to middle-class Christians in affluent societies, why not?

- As I allowed the concern of youth and evangelism to dominate my thinking and prayer in recent months, I came across something which seems like a perfect concluding piece for this reflection. Craig Dykstra was writing about an emerging religious search that he observed happening in the United States, a search which does not seem to be merely "a nostalgic revisiting of a safe, comfortable, sentimental religiousness".

> If a fresh awakening is taking place and if I am right about its character, pastors and theologians need to be prepared. Many of those who are searching may be coming in our direction. They may turn to us for help, wanting to see if there is any food left in the cupboards of religious institutions they long ago may have left. They may even come with a sense of hope and anticipation. But they will be testing us to see if we know what idols are — including religious ones — and to see if we are willing to call them by their names. If they sense we do not and will not, they will go away again, perhaps more cynical than before. If they sense we do and will, they may become interested.

But even this is not enough, for they are asking for something more. The deepest question they are asking — and may not yet dare to ask out loud — is this: Do you know God? If they sense we do not, again they will go away — perhaps this time more sadly than cynically. And if they sense we do, it will not be because we *say* we do. It will be because they see it in the way we live, in the manner of our speaking, and in our willingness to listen and to search. They will see it in the freedom this knowledge provides and in what this knowledge commits us to.

All this is true not only of the "thirtysomething" crowd who may have been reading the paper and buying bagels on Sunday mornings instead of going to church. It is true as well of people of all ages who populate the pews from week to week or spend their money on religious books and magazines. They want to know theological things. They want to know God.*

With this, we are encouraged and warned.

August 1989

10

Catherine is a young Swiss woman who had been working with me for some time in the office. Among many things, she typed the monthly letter and saw to it that it got produced and distributed. Every time she got the letter ready I would ask her if it made any sense. If it did to her, I'd feel assured. Occasionally, she would raise questions with me or with the translation, and we would sit down, sometimes with the professional translator, to make sure.

Catherine came to work every day on her bike, spent weekends building a boat with her friend. She had spent a year on her own in India and Nepal. She does not eat meat. And she does not vote. We got along well.

After nineteen months with us, Catherine announced she'd be leaving by the end of the year. She needed to devote more time to building her boat. (Noah's boat, she calls it.) The idea took hold of me that I should interview her for the monthly letter before she left, something I never did with former colleagues, and am not likely to do again. I broached the idea with her. She accepted. So one morning we sat down and talked. Here then is a record of our conversation. I am grateful Catherine was willing to let her views be printed. This monthly letter could well turn out to be one of the more important pieces for our Swiss readers.

---

* Craig Dykstra, "A Fresh Awakening?", *Theology Today*, July 1989, Princeton, pp.127-128.

A CONVERSATION WITH CATHERINE

Raymond: Catherine, tell me why you don't go to church.

Catherine: I don't go to church. Should I? I believe in God. God is not especially found in a church. God is found everywhere. I know there are people who feel the need to worship in a church. There are people who feel the need to be with other people to pray and meditate. I do not feel the need. Sometimes I enjoy sitting in an empty church.

Raymond: So it is the people who go to church who bother you!

Catherine: Maybe, but I simply just do not feel the need to attend church. If I feel like praying and meditating, any place would do, especially among natural scenery. And why a church? Isn't our body a temple created by God! Many people go to church out of habit, or because that's the place where they feel right for meditation, or to celebrate together with friends and other people. Some go to church to show they are better than others. Some are hypocrites. They don't live their faith.

Raymond: How do you know this to be the case? You have not gone to church for quite some time. This is just a feeling on your part, isn't it?

Catherine: I've not met a lot of people who go to church or to the temple. But among them, some are ... "BLAH"! Or should I say the evil in them stinks. After my family moved from our village to Geneva, a friend and I decided to go to church, to do something by ourselves and look to new horizons. We went a few times, then we stopped. It was boring and there was nothing to do. I was twelve.

Raymond: I remember your telling me, while you were roaming around India, how you were chased out of a Christian church compound, but were received in a Hindu temple. Does this experience not have an effect on you?

Catherine: All experiences have an effect in one way or another. This story is true and shows that real faith goes beyond religions. Many Hindu temples are closed to non-Hindus and outcasts too. In general, yes, churches tend to want to protect themselves. It is true in India as it is in Switzerland. They are afraid of strangers. So the church develops institutions and bureaucracy to ensure that people behave themselves, to control, to impose, to make sure things run smoothly. I don't feel the need to be part of anything like that. It is myself and God. If I do bad things, I do bad things. I face God. I don't want others to answer my questions. Someone said: "I don't want a master who influences me but a master who teaches me not to be influenced."

Raymond: I am from Asia. From this perspective, I must say I have good things to say about Swiss churches. They have reached out to our part of the world in times of need. I also know, living in Geneva, how many lonely old ladies derive comfort and joy from the little communal parish.

Catherine: I do not disagree with you. And I do not disagree with these old ladies who find parish life meaningful. But being helpful is a difficult thing. It does not necesarily touch one's life. And aren't we escaping our own selves by wanting to help others! I came from a large village. My grandparents went to church. It was the proper thing to do. I am sure my grandfather liked it. He loved singing. He and all his friends went to church. There, he was recognized, he was somebody. He felt important. And for a man in a village context, that means a lot. My father didn't go but he wanted all his children to go. My sister resisted. There would be a crisis in the family every time we went to my grandparents' place.

My Christian heritage has not come from the church, but from little things. My grandmother had cards with Bible verses printed on them. There were those religious pictures. There was one with two children perching dangerously on the edge of a cliff, plucking some wild flowers. A kindly and strong guardian angel hovered over them, giving them protection. So all was well. I loved the Don Bosco stories. Don Bosco is a little orphan boy. He roams about, working in a farm one day and a circus the next. He is a little saint. These little things made up my Christian heritage. They are meaningful to me.

Raymond: Tell me about young people in Geneva.

Catherine: I don't want to talk, and don't have the right to talk for others. What I can do is give you an idea of how I see it. You find some of them actively participating in and enjoying the products of the society without thinking very much and very far. You also find some of them in the English garden, a beautiful part of Geneva, on the lake front and the town centre. These young people gather, many from families with problems like divorces, alcohol, or simply disharmony, lack of love. They are open. They like to discuss things. People from the Mormon church and Jehovah's Witnesses spend time there, talking, showing their scriptures. I and my friend sometimes join our young friends there. Some of them are on drugs and we talk with them about drugs and life in general. In Zurich, the authorities are liberal about drugs. They have organized distribution. But I don't think this is going to help. These people are on a search. They have no hope in "our" superficial, square society. According to the Bible, they are the last who will be the first. For the young people, money is not a taboo as it is and was for the older generations. We are born with it. We live in abundance, so it is taken for granted. And if there is no money, that's no problem. The shops are full of goods. So why not help ourselves. It is a sin to steal but to tempt others is a sin too.

Raymond: The churches are getting serious with work on justice, peace and the integrity of creation. Does this not mean anything to young people? Do such themes speak to them?

Catherine: No, young people are not impressed. The church should have been engaging in such things anyway a long time ago. North American Indians, for instance, were living in this spirit and the church is only now talking about it, after having participated in their destruction! The church merely follows the world. Justice and peace talk is in the very air we breathe nowadays. Even right-wing politicians talk aloud of love and peace and meanwhile the world is getting worse. If the people want to hear it, they get to hear it. Mother Teresa lives Christianity. She is saving the reputation of the church among the young. Still her action is considered her own and not so much that of the church. Young people think of the church as part of the past. They think of the church the same way they think of their fathers.

Raymond: That is a very hard judgment on fathers in this land.

Catherine: I know. This is of course a generalization. But I know I am talking about many fathers. Authoritarian figures. Do-what-I-say-but-not-what-I-do figures. Intelligent but possessing no understanding. Self-sufficient but not seeing. Men who believe they have nothing to learn from their children. And they show it. I once read a book about Jesus. It is a novel called *The Man who Became God* by Gerald Messadié. There he describes an encounter between a priestess and Jesus. She said to him, there were two kinds of men in the world — the fathers and the sons. And blessing Jesus, she told him: "You are a son. And you're going to meet with a lot of hatred from the fathers."

Raymond: That is a powerful story. For the church, does the answer lie in a more feminine orientation?

Catherine: My mother has lived a hard life. Hers is a family of six sisters and brothers. She often missed school because she had to look after the younger ones and help my grandmother who was sick. Often there was no money at home. Not enough shoes for everyone. So she and her sisters and brothers had to take turns to go to church. They had to show up to save the family's face. I love my mother. But like most mothers, she is afraid of losing us. Like society, she is possessive. But children need to be free. To answer your question, I don't have *the* answer. I believe in a feminine orientation or contribution, but not only for the church. I don't believe in matriarchal feminism.

Raymond: The new generation of fathers are somewhat different, aren't they?

Catherine: Yes, some men today are more sensitive. This is hopeful. But in another way, they are losing their masculine qualities. If we women keep getting more masculine and men more feminine it may lead to no more man and woman!

Raymond: This hard judgment on fathers and the comparison with the church: does it have anything to do with the Swiss ideology of neutrality?

Catherine: It has. But I don't think this is specifically Swiss. It's our "occidental" cultural heritage. On the one hand, if you are neutral, you don't take sides. You don't judge. You don't even pretend to because no sides are right. On the other, the only judgment you make is that you are superior to the rest of the world with your neutrality. The truth of the matter is eventually you side with the winner, you always go where the profits are. And yet we think we are good and strong. There is a gulf between my father and I because he sees nothing wrong in any of this. He is proud of being part of this system.

Raymond: I think I understand you. I want to say you are lucky: you are Swiss, so you won't starve no matter what, and you have friends and someone who loves you. But I know it is still hard to put oneself more or less outside. Tell me, where do you get your support?

Catherine: I am Swiss with all that it means because I was born and grew up here. But I am not proud of it. That I won't starve I am not sure. Switzerland is not a star outside the world... I understand myself as a child of the earth among billions. And what makes me get up every morning is the hope that I'd meet and walk side by side with the heavenly Father. If the church isn't there to guide people to their soul's awakening, it has no reason for existence.

Raymond: You have been with the WCC for close to two years now. Has it been meaningful?

Catherine: I was impressed with the worship at San Antonio [the conference on world mission and evangelism]. People coming from all over the world, with an expectant mind and an open heart. It moved me.

As for the WCC from day-to-day, my hope has not been fulfilled. We talk much of love, but we are not too different from the post office, the shops and the banks where I had previously worked. Here there is more focusing on people and on the world. But still it is not too different from the rest. I had hoped for another dimension. I didn't find it. You don't meet saints here. I am looking for examples. But of course, it's not among people that we find them. That's why God exists.

December 1990

You remember my interview with Catherine, a young Swiss woman and a colleague? The one who comes to work on a bike, builds a boat, has a lot of young people as friends? Catherine who shared with us her thoughts about God, the church, Switzerland and Swiss fathers, herself?

Judging from the responses, the interview could have been the best piece to have appeared in these pages. A sample:

> The conversation with Catherine was a wonderful idea. I don't know when I have read in a Christian piece of literature such a straightforward description of what has to be a very large number of Western young people. I have been in on such conversations, but not seen anything like this. It helps a great deal to know the people whom we are trying to reach.

Not only Western young people. Several Asian readers made more or less the same observations for their part of the world. Other church people's responses are affirmative of Catherine and introspective of themselves, painfully so in the case of a retired Swiss evangelist who had a tremendous following among the young in his more vigorous days. I have shared these with Catherine.

Now I would like to make my own response. I do not wish to analyze what Catherine said. You don't analyze friends. Let others analyze if they wish. I simply wish to respond to Catherine and then make a few suggestions to my friends in the Swiss churches who are concerned about evangelism among the young. As for readers who are not Swiss, why don't you just take it as a case study on evangelism?

LETTER TO CATHERINE

Dear Catherine,

Our conversation was a good idea. You have communicated to me and to many others. Our words have built trust between ourselves. And many people have found in our conversation echoes in their hearts. What more can words do?

The last portion of our conversation prompted a few anxious glances in my direction. "Close to two years working in a Christian organization and an evangelism office at that, and Catherine hasn't been converted?" Well, I don't know about that. I am sure I'd be very happy if I were able to report that you have been converted. I must confess I am not too worried about it, rightly or wrongly.

In my friendships and in my own life, I seek dignity more than comprehension. No doubt, on occasions, I feel the urge to share my ideas and insights. (I have been doing the monthly letters for years, haven't I?) But fundamentally I am content to make my separate and private peace. Friendship with Jesus. Salvation in Christ. Commitment to a Christian community. These are matters over which a person must decide for herself. An evangelist understands and respects that, and waits.

Any particular response to you on my part? Yes. If I were to present the gospel to you, I would not want to say it is meant to meet your needs. It does, but let me warn you, too often in a way you don't expect. Instead, I would want to say, "because it is true". I know this is a difficult thing to say nowadays. It sounds so glib, perhaps even meaningless. But that's the best I can come up with. I'd dearly love to invite you to consider the claims of Christ on your life on the ground that the claims are true.

Of course I cannot prove to anyone in propositional terms that the gospel is true. I can only show that *I believe* it is. Truth, like a painting, speaks to you. And when it is indeed the truth, it speaks truth to you and you recognize it. How do we recognize truth? There is no set rule, and it is hard to put into words. I would venture to say with some trepidation and much excitement that truth is often recognized as *light and joy*.

Here I can do no better than to borrow from a wiser pen:

> The fundamental reason people in biblical times said that Jesus was the light of the world was that he showed them so much. The great achievements of Greek philosophy and science were like a candle to the light of the sun when compared to the understanding Jesus gave them concerning the great question of life. What may we believe? What must we do? What may we hope for? In him they also found the Jewish expectations of a saviour raised to altogether new dimensions. This understanding was not achieved immediately or easily. The New Testament clearly shows that Jesus had to make strenuous efforts to overcome frequent and deep misunderstandings by his listeners and first followers. But slowly their understanding grew, and within a few generations Jesus was seen as the crown and culmination of the finest insights of the ancient world. It was precisely because both the heart and mind were satisfied that many ancient people received the benefits that the full wealth of

conviction brings. Jesus becomes our light only when we study his life and teachings and let them illumine the world in which we live, allowing them to show us what is worth striving for and what is reliable and trustworthy. *

As for joy — I mean when truth comes to us, it often brings joy, and we recognize truth this way — I must confess that joy doesn't characterize modern people, inside or outside the church. Nietzsche's most deadly critique of the Christian faith is that Christians have no joy. In the Western church, and elsewhere too, active or passive, yes; indifferent or caring, yes; sombre or cheerful, yes; tired or boisterous, dull or ecstatic, yes. But always there is a heaviness of sorts. And very little joy. I cannot describe joy to you, not in a way which communicates on paper. But I seem to understand Jesus committing his followers to the Father so that they may have the full measure of my joy within them (John 17:13). And the daily invitation to enter into the joy of the Lord (Matt. 25:21).

Light and joy — they help us recognize truth.

Well, that's about it. I wish you well with your boat and your friend. Take it into Hong Kong, the Fragrant Harbour, some day. There is always a welcome for you.

August-September 1991

LETTER TO THE SWISS CHURCHES

Your responses to my interview with Catherine have prompted me to write this short note. Also the encouragement of many European colleagues in the WCC, particularly the quiet ones who normally do not get involved in big theological talk — the "non-theological" people who work in the cafeteria and the cashier's office, and behind computer monitors. When these people give their approval, I know we have done something right. So, if Catherine's interview makes sense, and does speak about the young of Switzerland, what can and what should we do as a church? Allow me to make a few suggestions for what they are worth.

• Sharing the gospel with the young in Switzerland requires nothing less than a full-scale, long-term missionary movement, with the sort of commitment and daring and sensitivity which characterized the best of the missionary movement of the last two centuries. No institutional tinkering and programming will do, and no festivals of faith will suffice. It has to

* Diogenes Allen, Stuart Professor of Philosophy, Princeton Theological Seminary; the quotation is taken from "The Fields are White for the Harvest", in *Evangelism in the Reformed Tradition*, ed. Arnold B. Lovell, CTS Press, 1991, p.16.

be done by the churches sending out their best to where the young people are, who will learn their culture, sing their song, find out what God has done in their midst, and there and then look for ways to build up a people of God.

• A missionary movement could begin with the church calling on its best people and letting them free to do what they want. Look for people, young and old, ordained and lay, male and female, married or single, those skilled with words and those skilled with their hands. People who have a sense of vocation and who enjoy being with the young. Give your missionaries no timetables and no job descriptions. Only encouragement and support. The mandate: go to the young, into their own territories, and then report to the church of what God has done.

It is entirely conceivable that after three years or five years of such missionary engagement, Swiss church attendance may still show no increase. I happen to believe that church growth is an important concern for evangelism, but only at the very end of the process, never at the beginning.

Catherine is right that the church's job is "to guide people on their soul's awakening". Justice, peace and the integrity of creation are a proper and necessary witness of the church. But people do not become Christian for these reasons. They come to Christ for religious reasons.

• Catherine is half right and half wrong when, describing the source of her support, she tells us that "I understand myself as a child of the earth among billions. And what makes me get up every morning is the hope that I'd meet and walk side by side with the heavenly Father." Yes, God is truly like that. But, at the same time, God is also not like that. I shudder to think about walking with God, or, if I may say it, of Catherine walking with God, side by side and every morning. I shudder because of what God's holiness, power, glory, and God's suffering, helplessness, indeed, God's otherness, will show up in myself, in her, in us. God's love, I suspect, will easily floor me if I come so close. (So, Catherine, watch out!) So I propose that the church resist the temptation of telling young people, indeed all people, only what they want to hear, or what we think they want to hear. Let us not present a god made in any human image. We present a God who is godly enough to follow and whose cause is worthy enough of youthful lives.

• Swiss pastors spend a lot of time home visiting. A parish pastor in Geneva wrote recently: "Lots of lonely and elderly people were waiting for their pastor's visit and the very sick at the end of life and the people who had met with accidents were in great need of me..." I'd love to have young people do some of these visits. Theirs may not be pastoral visits. But they will be good visits, bringing comfort and hope and some fun. Not just to those who are shut in, but to the visitors as well. And where, you may ask, do I find these young people? Why, they are in your parish. They may not be in the church on Sundays, but you know their names and their whereabouts. Call them up. See them as partners. Offer them a chance to express their care and their love. And they will respond. Come to think of it, ask Swiss fathers to do visits as well. Catherine described them as intelligent but not understanding. Perhaps getting closer to helplessness and loneliness might help.

August 1991

11

Almost a week ago, I came across a workshop report which does two things to me. It helps me understand the situations and problems of women students in Africa today. The report is so vivid in its simplicity that it radiates truth. And as I read it, the strategist in me recognizes right away realistic possibilities of action for the church to get involved in and to make a crucial difference in many lives in that part of the world.

Not many reports of Christian meetings are like that. Many are written for insiders only. Many are so watered down that they hide rather than inform. Many are so cliché-ridden they are not intelligible, much less implementable. Many show a narcissistic shallowness and mindlessness. But here is one which educates (me) and, when I meet it half way, invites me to exercise my faculty on its behalf. The sense of excitement is still with me.

What I am referring to is a seven-page report of a two-day women's workshop in Entebbe, Uganda, 27-28 November 1989. It was part of a larger consultation on mission and evangelism organized by the Africa region of the World Student Christian Federation. Although neither the nature of the workshop nor its finding is unique, this is something special.

Let me now introduce you to the report. It listed thirteen participants, all young women, from Zambia, Lesotho, Zimbabwe, Kenya, Tanzania, Madagascar, Burundi and Uganda. I presume they are either college or secondary school students (SCMs in Africa work at these two levels). "The majority of the women present were attending such a workshop on women for the first time."

The two days started with a prayer and a chorus called: "You must learn to build the nation now". Participants paired up to get acquainted. An introduction to the WSCF's African women's commission was given. For the rest of the workshop, participants "brainstormed" on problems faced by female students and sought solutions. Prayer, meditation and singing supported the process. The report named "Rock of Ages" as one of the hymns.

Problems faced by female students. I quote this part of the report in full:

1. Female students are not taken seriously by male lecturers and this hinders their academic progress.
2. Teenage pregnancy also cuts off the educational progress of female students; as a result some commit abortions and suicides.
3. Household work obstructs female students leaving them without adequate time for study.
4. Girls are brought up more strictly than boys, they therefore lack exposure and as a result they end up being victims of their own ignorance/naivety.
5. Lack of sex education.
6. Parents prefer to educate boys rather than girls.
7. Female students face sexual harassment by their teachers and sugar daddies.
8. Early marriages — dowry.
9. Lack of career guidance.
10. Lack of involvement in decision-making at home, at school and in church.
11. Lack of leadership training skills.
12. Cultural attitudes.
13. Female health and nutrition.
14. Language barriers.
15. Lack of solidarity and support from fellow women.

Having drawn up this list, the young women proceeded to group the problems and find solutions. Here I quote the substance and use their phrases. I put them in four groupings. I do not intrude.

1. Female students are not taken seriously by male lecturers — sexual harassment by teachers/sugar daddies.

Solutions
— Counselling in churches, schools and homes.
— SCMs to network with groups already involved in this kind of issue.
— Assertive training: girls should not allow themselves to be touched without their consent. They must show that they are not objects of pleasure for men. They have a right to refuse and dictate on what should touch them.
— SCMs should encourage sharing and fellowship: there should be open discussions among members and the leaders should be able to identify a contact person who can help.
— Affected students should be encouraged to come out into the open so that the teachers who engage in this kind of behaviour can be exposed (SCMs should be action-oriented and not passive).

2. Lack of sex education, teenage pregnancy and lack of solidarity and support from other women.

Solutions
— Encourage dialogue between mothers and daughters.
— Sex education at home and in schools for both boys and girls, which should be factual and not negative.
— SCMs should include discussions on subjects such as premarital sex and boy/girl relationship. If SCMs can have an environment that is sympathetic to girls who fall this would in a way discourage abortion and suicide. (A personal objection: "Girls who fall" — that is not Jesus' word.)
— In cases of pregnancy, the girls should be accepted and supported, bearing in mind they are going through much self-condemnation. Some participants felt they should not be accepted because this will encourage them to continue misbehaving. On abortion, all were unanimous that it should be discouraged. They were also agreed that the girls need to continue with their studies in the same ways boys do even though they are responsible for such pregnancies.

3. Cultural attitudes and leadership.

Solutions
— Girls should know they have a place side by side with boys. That they can be priests (ordained), that they can study engineering if they want to. But some parents force their daughters to do courses they do not like. Girls are assumed to be interested in sewing and knitting.

Sometimes this is not so. Girls must rebel respectfully, be firm and stand their ground. The parents should know how they feel.

— SCMs should bring about new cultural awareness by working with associations and the mass media.

— SCMs should have leadership training programmes for women nation-wide. Women should have opportunities to look at contemporary issues. They should participate fully in all the activities of the movement. They should be presidents/chairpersons instead of being secretaries (because their handwriting is good) or treasurers (because they can be trusted with money). They should be given opportunity to be at the top — that will give them the necessary exposure and a chance to learn how to be good leaders.

— Communication needs to be improved. SCMs should encourage members to learn English, French and Swahili. International level exchange programmes should also be encouraged.

4. Health, nutrition, poverty (identified as one of the causes of prostitution).

Solutions

— Women need to take care of their health, nourish their bodies, instead of giving the good food to the men and being content with the left-overs.

— The SCMs should work with relevant organizations to educate women on nutritious ways of preparing food.

— Members should be encouraged to volunteer their services for community work during vacations.

— SCMs should develop income-generating projects in order to help members, such as selling food, making jam, cake sales for weddings and birthdays, mohair weaving, fruit cooperatives. Women should be aware that there is a United Nations body UNIFEM which supports women's projects in Africa.

Enough of quoting from the report. I have done it in order to show its clarity and authenticity, and above all, and because of these qualities, to show how eminently "do-able" the report is. It is a case of so defining a problem that the solutions suggest themselves. And much more than that, it is a case of so defining a problem that an entire outline of mission strategy to and with female students in Africa is revealed. That's why the report excites me.

Here we have a group of young women who describe their situations and spell out their needs and those of their peers. They use their own words, which communicate not only the substance of the problems or felt needs, but also their people's world-view, values, moral expectations, cultural attitudes, and their social ethos and economic parameters. The report does not only describe a set of problems and possible solutions. It carries the everyday hopes and struggles of female students in Africa. And because it is authentic, it identifies precisely what Christian action is called for and the points where it will be met with positive reception.

What then is the next step? The report tells of the existence of a women's commission within the WSCF movement in Africa. The commission has three regional coordinators and an adviser who, I assume, have a natural interest in ensuring institutional follow-up. The resources are scanty, and the magnitude of the task blows the mind. But the structure for something to happen is present. I am glad this women's workshop is part of the WSCF's Africa network.

But the usefulness of this report goes beyond its service as a basis for WSCF action. The organization, the movement, can only do so much. The genius of this report is that anybody and any organization can use it with confidence for a mission among female students in that part of the world. Its clarity makes sense to all people of good will. Its authenticity inspires action because it is so practically oriented. In this case, there is reason to believe that what should happen coincides with what can happen.

A college lecturer or school teacher, a Sunday school teacher, a pastor, a youth worker, indeed a parent with teenage children, any mature person whose daily routines intersect with female students — they can make things happen. You gather a few of the young women you know to share what concerns them the most.

Have them bring their friends the next time round. You do the best you can to get to know them and their situation and gain their confidence. You try to understand their problems first-hand, read up on the subject, identify people and organizations within reach who have the appropriate skills and resources and bring them in. The problems of teenage pregnancy, sexual harassment, sugar daddies, sexism in schools, in job markets and at home, and the problem of poverty, of course, will not go away. But you will have a group of people with you struggling to make a difference in each other's life and beyond. As an individual, your reach is limited. But two or three people like you will quickly make a difference in a congregation, a school, a village. The only resources required are your caring, your thoughtfulness and, yes, the most demanding of all, your time.

If you happen to be a full-time Christian worker, such as an SCM staff person, a youth worker of a denomination or an agency, or a missionary in search of a fruitful role, you can of course do much more. You have time, and you have the possibility of institutional support.

From the perspective of Christian involvement, the most important goal is not so much the elimination of problems such as teeenage pregnancy. The most important goal is the creation of a community environment in which young women can get in touch with each other and with caring adults. An environment of acceptance, encouragement, mutual support and growth into maturity and understanding. It follows therefore that your methodology cannot be one of you and your experts going all out to find solutions for poor ignorant teenagers who get pregnant. It's got to be a common effort — you as a person who cares, the young women who feel the need, the people who have the skill and the resources. Together you can make a difference.

In case I make it sound too easy, let me hasten to suggest that certain skills are necessary to meet effectively the problems and to bring about the solutions described in the report. I propose to name four sets of skills if only to show that they are not extraordinary but ordinary skills, that they are not the privileged tools of the highly trained but are available fairly widely to the churches in the ecumenical movement.

First, whoever wishes to act according to the report must be able to make a reasoned case that God cares for women no less than for men. That our bodies are temples of the Holy Spirit and must not be fooled around with, or neglected and undernourished. Whoever wants to be helpful to these female students must study how Jesus treated women and then behave and live accordingly. By all available standards, this is not too much to ask of any mature Christian anywhere. And you don't need to be a biblical scholar to come to such conclusions. Besides there is a lot of help in the form of Bible studies and theological expositions, from the first world for sure but no less from the third world. If such material is not available in certain parts of Africa, then the churches must make it available. If it remains available only for the upper echelons of the churches, then feminist theologians and Christian educators who present powerful and learned papers on such subjects in international conferences must be told to produce some for the grassroots. As I see it, it is not a matter of money. Only of priority and will.

The second set of skills necessary for the implementation of the report has to do with empowerment, i.e. helping people help themselves. This is now a universally-acclaimed concept in church, government, academic and development circles. Hundreds of training schemes have been drawn up. In my opinion, many of these try to turn themselves into a scientific programme, geared more for the acclaim of fellow professionals than to the need for authenticity and effectiveness on the ground. With the churches, we have some of that too, but there are also many good training resources and occasional events which are theoretically sound, practical and culturally sensitive. There are people in almost every region who can do an adequate training job. In the art and technique of working with people, especially the poor, helping them to stand on their own two feet, my inclination is to demythologize professionalism and its scientific claims. That comes out of my own experience when I used to provide training to urban industrial mission workers in Asia. So if tested training resources and events are available, fine, take advantage of them. If not, don't lament their absence, just go ahead and make your own. Behind the modern and impressive language of training is really an ancient apostolic ministry — the ministry of encouragement. Here two simple ideas might help. One: a sense of personal limits. Christians are neither Santa Clauses nor saviours. We can only do so much. Two: unless the people become involved and start doing things for themselves, we are not getting anywhere. With these, we stand a good chance of getting together an increasingly large number of people to tackle problems of great magnitude, and at the same time having a good time. A ministry of encouragement is healthy physically and spiritually for everyone.

A third set of useful skills is what is generally known as networking. It is the skill to link persons and organizations with similar interests and concerns, to multiply contacts and information, to identify expertise and resources, to build trust and solidarity. In short, a skill to maximize effectiveness. It works well in an urban, industrial setting. I have no idea whether it applies at all in traditional rural settings where functions are undifferentiated and services are personal and more or less integrated. But judging from the report, the situations the female students are in are urban and different services are available. Skill in networking should come in handy.

Later, as the local/national work develops to a degree of maturity, i.e. when you as a local person know what you are doing and have the people to do the job, networking can go international. But not earlier. I am always convinced that a ministry which sustains people and is itself sustainable has to be carried out by local people. Expatriates can help make a strong ministry stronger. They cannot turn a weak ministry into a strong one. But with a strong local team, a time will come when tapping into an international network makes sense.

I have with me, for instance, a notice of a handbook on teenage pregnancy prepared in association with the Baptist Ministers Conference, Washington DC, in the USA. While cultural and ethical norms might differ, if I were working with the group at the workshop, I would certainly want to get hold of a copy of this handbook and study it. These Baptist pastors in Washington DC, most of whom are black, face the same problem of teenage pregnancy in their community. The strategist in me is already sensing the excitement and the benefit of partnership between African churches with the National Baptist and the Progressive Baptists — the largest black churches in the United States. They are members of the World Council of Churches but have not been active. Perhaps here is something that will bring them out, with their talents and their solidarity.

Fourthly, a skill which I regard highly is the skill which enables micro-action to have macro-impact. While I believe Christian mission must be person- and people-oriented rather than issue- or problem-oriented, there is no reason why we should be content with effecting changes only in the lives of a few individual persons and not in a large number of people and in public life. So skill to generate an impact positively disproportionate to limited resources and input is a valuable skill.

This could be described in various ways. It is a matter of positioning. In a chess game, the humble pawn can beat the powerful queen, if placed right. So putting one's scanty resources where they will count the most is a skill or an art worth learning. It is a matter of articulation. You can be a lone voice crying in the wilderness. But yours can also be one that finds an echo in thousands and indeed millions of human hearts. It is a matter of timing. It is a matter of speaking the truth that the emperor has no clothes on. A matter of discernment that the formidably armoured giant has feet of clay. This skill is more difficult to pin down, but I am sure its ingredients are found in the fertile soil of every culture and every people.

Colleagues who know Africa better impressed upon me a sense of urgency. I hope Christians with a deep concern for sharing the gospel among the young will get hold of the practical vision of this report and become involved in a small way or a big way. With people like that, the likelihood of lives transformed among female students in Africa will be that much greater. And who can fight the good fight against sexism and poverty in Africa except young, transformed Africans?

February 1991

Chapter 3

Good News to the Poor

12

I would like to start a serious reflection and discussion on "evangelism among the poor". I believe this is what Jesus wants to see us do. In most parts of Asia, the large majority of the people are poor, and they have not heard the gospel. Therefore, we cannot seriously talk about the evangelism of the world without reference to the evangelism of the poor. "But what about the rich?" someone would say — and quite a few have done — as if I am claiming exclusive grace for the poor. (Unfair! When my own church organized a series of weekday gospel lunches in a luxury hotel to cater to the needs and schedules of business executives, no one thought of saying: "How about the low-paid clerks eating out of their lunchbox in the park?" Perhaps someone should have.) Anyway, I accept the question. Let's talk about it. I cannot claim special insight on the subject of the rich. But I happen to believe that the evangelism of the poor and the evangelism of the rich are related, one capable of shedding light on the other. In my own self-examination, I have sometimes wondered if this evangelism emphasis on the poor would lead to creating a gospel of the poor in the same way that much of the gospel we preach today can be said to be a gospel of the middle class. I believe not. There is but one gospel of Jesus Christ, and this gospel came to us in a manger, not in Herod's palace. I have found that sharing the gospel with factory workers enables me to understand God much better than sharing it with those from comfortable, well-to-do families. I suppose this is what we mean when we say the poor have good news for us, and that, in evangelizing, we also become evangelized.

I am also aware of the "we-may-be-materially-poor-but-we-are-cul-turally-rich" response. I bow to this sturdy spirit. Here I am definitely referring to evangelism among the materially poor — factory workers, slum-dwellers, rural farmhands, for example. I have no quarrel with the claim of cultural wealth, although my experience raises the question how much and for how long cultural wealth can cushion the materially poor from the onslaughts of exploitative forces. But let us proceed. A Christian brother from an impoverished third-world country said with anger as he walked away: "We don't like to call ourselves or our people poor. It is insulting." So let us find another word to describe this human reality to which we must respond evangelistically. Otherwise we get nowhere, evangelically. In recent years, Korean Christians have begun to use the word *minjung*, or people existing in their own right, as distinct from people as the king's subject, or people as the masses, or people as the proletariat. This is an exciting development. I believe we will hear a lot more of it. I hope minjung theology will have something important to say about evangelism. There is indeed room for discussion on terminology. But in general we know what we mean. I remember at one point in the Melbourne world mission meeting, a delegate was asking: "Who are the poor?" My neighbour mumbled to himself: "You know who they are in your country. Or you are in trouble."

My interest in mounting a serious discussion on evangelism among the poor also has a strategic angle. I mean, how else can "ecumenicals" and "evangelicals" have a no-nonsense dialogue in which we can learn from each other and at the same time advance the kingdom of God? A theological debate will not do. How about a friendly competition to see which version of the Christian faith — if I may put it this way — can best serve the God-given task of evangelism among the poor? For me, this is the crucial test for Christians who claim priority commitment to the poor.

At this point, let me declare my interest. I am not the referee. The poor are. I realize I am grossly simplifying now. The competition may well be played inside the same soul. And this analogy cannot be further stretched. The referee may turn out to be the coach after all.

November 1981

13

The ecumenical movement places great importance on the eucharist. I think Christians should not be sentimental about it. It is much easier, for example, for wealthy Christian landowners to kneel around the Lord's table with their peasant hired hands than to sit with them at the bargaining table. The solidarity at the Lord's table has to be vindicated by the solidarity of the secular table. For me, solidarity with the non-believing poor in struggle comes before solidarity with the believing rich in the eucharist. If it comes to such a choice, that is. Because the tie that binds our hearts in Christian love is not, and should not be, the strongest thing in the world. Or because, despite our own feelings, our Christian ties are indeed strong, so strong that we can afford to take them for granted, depending upon their not breaking, whatever challenges Christians pose to each other. I am inclined towards the second. All this is not to take the eucharist lightly, only to give it the seriousness it requires of us. The apostle Paul puts it very bluntly: "Whoever, therefore, eats the bread or drinks the cup of the Lord in an unworthy manner will be guilty of profaning the body and blood of the Lord. Let a man examine himself, and so eat of the bread and drink of the cup" (1 Cor. 11:27-28).

Let me share with you a way in which the eucharist is evangelistic. When a group of factory workers began meeting as a church, the question of the eucharist in Sunday service came up. There were usually some labourers attending the service, most of whom had seldom been in contact with the church before. Both the integrity of the eucharist and the integrity of the community had to be respected. After much discussion and reflection, the Christians hit on the idea of inviting to the table all who were prepared to follow Jesus. From then on, every celebration of the eucharist in that humble church became an evangelistic invitation, arising from the natural worship life of the congregation. Each time, an opportunity is provided for decision-making, to take the name of Christ and participate in discipleship. And, each time, community acceptance is immediate and experiential.

Let me share the testimony of a factory worker:

> I have always been an active labour union member, feeling very much at home with everyone there. After I became a Christian, I continued my involvement with a new sense of meaning. But soon, I began to feel a slight distance between my friends and I. I did not know if my friends at the union felt the same about me. They did not know of my conversion. Was it just a feeling on my part? Anyway, I felt less at home than I had been before. I did not like it. I felt bad. Finally, right after a union meeting, I got several of my friends together for a bowl of noodles, and told them there and then that I had become a Christian. And that I hoped that nothing had changed among ourselves. Everyone smiled in good humour. They slapped my back. It seemed they had known about it. We shook hands. The distance was gone.

Let us face it. The gospel does make a person a stranger in his or her own environment. It creates a difference, a sense of separation. And the difference, the separation, can only be overcome by confessing it, pointing to Jesus who causes it all. In this light, the act of evangelism does not alienate the Christian from his or her neighbours. On the contrary, it does away with the alienation already there, and brings about a sense of reconciliation not experienced before.

To me, the primary characteristic of the person of Jesus Christ whom we communicate is not his saintliness, his miraculous power or his wisdom, but his solidarity with people, especially those rejected by society, those who have no place under the sun. The biblical word is "love". At this point I prefer the term "solidarity" because it yields more methodological clarity. "And *the Word became flesh and dwelt among us*, full of grace and truth." "Became flesh"… "dwelt among us"… these are the dynamics of the person of Jesus, the manifestation of his being. To point to this Jesus requires the method of solidarity on the part of Christians.

May 1982

14

A circular letter from two Christian couples working among the poor in Central America has given me much joy. I must say it is among the best that has come my way. Let me simply share it with you. Ken and Rhoda Mahler and Ernesto and Norma Weigandt of Panama wrote the following.

An event and a movement are working to create interest in the Bible down our way, and a number of us from different churches are up to our elbows in the production of Bible study materials, happy as larks.

The event. In a small chapel next to the road that leads from the Panamerican Highway to our rural centre in Panama's Cocle Province, a picture of Christ that hangs by the altar recently began to perspire, according to worshippers there. Some folks even said that they saw tears roll out of his eyes and down his cheeks. The news got around in a hurry, and people began flocking from all over to witness the "miracle".

Now, this kind of "miracle" is fairly common in our part of the world. The church is, understandably, very cautious! A commission sent by the bishops is investigating the phenomenon. What we are watching is the kind of excitement and interest that such a happening awakes in people. Everybody suddenly becomes either a religious philosopher or a seeker. The peasants among whom Ernesto works are feeling their nerves especially a-tingle because the event is taking place so near them. If the "weeping Christ" turns out to be a real miracle, there is no end to the possibilities for them — healings, secret desires obtained, etc.

There is much discussion, and the opinion of an authority on religion like Ernesto is eagerly sought after. That usually means that the discussion turns to scriptures at some point. Thus, the awakening interest in the Bible, further fired by another matter that we now take up.

The movement. From time to time a pentecostal movement flares up in the countryside, as it often does in the urban poor neighbourhoods. The last year has seen an unusual amount of these spiritual bushfires here in Panama.

Ernesto is especially concerned because the pentecostal folk who are working the neighbourhoods where he ministers are the sort that are convinced going to the doctor shows a lack of faith. It's affecting some of the people we know well. Doña Santos was gravely ill in the hospital, but the pentecostal preacher convinced her children to take her out so he could cure her by prayer. When they saw that she was only getting worse, her family put her back in the hospital, but it was too late. Ernesto had to fetch her dead body back to Miraflores for burial.

A young woman from neighbouring Martillada gave birth, but had post partum complications. After three-and-a-half hours of prayer didn't furnish results, the husband came to get Ernesto to take his wife to the hospital. Just in time! So it goes every few days.

Of course all these cases have folks wondering. Faith healing is so attractive because it is free and uncomplicated. You don't have to negotiate the trip to the town where the hospital is, or spend money on medicine. The preachers talk a convincing line, and they read out of the Bible. This impresses poor people a lot.

So Ernesto is beseiged with questions and wonderings, as are a lot of our clergy friends from other churches. The upshot has been an ecumenical group that is seeking to create and promote Bible study materials that fit the language and thought patterns of the Panamanian poor, i.e. the majority.

The group is working on its first publication, a Bible manual that local leaders can use for helping their people get into the scriptures. When it is ready we will introduce it in a series of seminars in the city and in the country. This first experience will most probably create the need for other materials and other seminars. We are thrilled.

Our group includes Roman Catholic priests, a Methodist pastor, a Baptist layman plus Ken and Ernesto. We would be happy if you would include this project in your prayers of thanksgiving and of intercession.

I am sure you are with me in sensing the joy, the compassion, the determination, the authenticity in all this. No comments of mine can add anything to this report. Let me just use this occasion to share a few thoughts about evangelism among the poor.

As in the slum in Panama's Cocle Province, faith healing is probably the most common means of evangelism among the world's poor, certainly in rural China and rural Africa. Large numbers of people have embraced the Christian faith because they want to be healed. This is easy to understand if you and your neighbours have no money to pay for the doctors and medicine, if there is no clinic close by, and if you happen to be a believer and you care, and what you have, in your near illiteracy, is vivid memories of gospel stories of Jesus, casting out the demons and healing the sick. Most of us in leadership positions are more sophisticated and tend to take a longer-term view, and we do not know how to deal with this phenomenon and the masses' enthusiastic response to it. We can, with valid reasoning, dismiss most faith healing practices *a priori*, but that would mean our spirituality is miles away from the spirituality of the poor. We can, also with valid reasoning, espouse it, but that would be doing the poor an injustice. Ernesto and his ecumenical colleagues did neither. They accept faith healing and its spirituality. They would help arrange an encounter between the Bible and the people. And they are "happy as larks" doing it.

This attitude presupposes a commitment to the poor, period. Not only a commitment to the poor who are politically conscious. It presupposes solidarity with the poor in their mundane daily existence, not only in the moments of exploding crisis. A preferential option for the poor when they are ignorant, stupid, wounding each other, not only when they show their wisdom, their power and their love. Much ecumenical rhetoric tends to project a mission commitment to the poor when the poor conform to our ideological expectation. A lot of theological articulation seems to suggest that the poor are all radical activists, or at least potentially so. Those who are not are defined out of existence. But those who work daily in urban and rural slums year in and year out know better.

My colleague Ana de García, who recently returned to Latin America after three years of service in Geneva, said to me once, when liberation theology was once again being hotly debated: "What those from outside read as elements of class struggle and hatred, those who live in the slums and barrios have experienced as ministries of consolation." If it is not so, then it is no theology of liberation, and woe upon us.

December 1984

15

These days, no international gathering of Christians can do its business without discussing the question of justice. The degree of serious commitment varies, but there is no denying that "justice" has become a fixed item on the contemporary Christian agenda. The Society of Jesus, in its 1985 year book, describes its work as "integrating the service of faith and the promotion of justice". The forthcoming meeting of the policy-making central committee of the WCC in Buenos Aires will base its corporate biblical reflection on the theme of "God's justice — promise and challenge".

Predictably, the concern for justice also divides us. Some time ago, I clashed with some visiting leaders of charismatic groups in Europe and the USA over the issue. They insisted that justice is a consequence of the good news, whereas I, and probably many of my colleagues in the WCC, would insist that it is an essential and integral part of the good news. Obviously, there are deep-rooted differences. The semantic confusion in the translation of the biblical original into either "justice" or "righteous-ness" does not help. It seems to me that biblical translators make their particular choice over the two options at whim. Take for instance the crucial text of Romans 1:17. One translator tells us "in the gospel a righteousness from God is revealed" (New International Version). Another tells us that "the good news reveals the justice of God to us..." (Jerusalem). Yet another has "Here is revealed God's way of righting wrong" (New English Bible). I know what I prefer for myself, but that hardly equips me to have an intelligent discussion with someone who has other preferences, and vice versa.

My point is that (1) Christians today care about justice or claim to, (2) there is serious disagreement over what it is, and (3) for reasons good and bad, "justice" is one of the least-defined words in much of Christian discourse on the subject. The last point may not be a problem when we are in the heat of a struggle resisting evil. But it certainly becomes problematic when Christians want to talk to one another, or when they want to make use of an opportunity to participate in the building of a more just society in this imperfect world of ours. At such a point, a sound understanding of biblical justice becomes vitally impor-tant for our missionary obedience. Whatever the case, I have been reflecting on the subject, talking with many people, and spending time in the library. Let me share with you how I got started and where I am at the moment.

When Christians make the claim that the God we worship is a God of love, we can substantiate it, at least to ourselves. We can point to the incarnation. We can point to the cross. And if one cares to look, every Christian can find demonstration of God's love within one's own experience. But when we make the claim that God is just — the very foundation of our commitment to justice — do we have similar substantiation? What basis do we have for such a belief? What biblical event can we point to? It is not so easy. And if we turn to experience for a clue, not all of us, I suspect, will find something in our own lives which we can confidently identify as evidence of a just God.

To be sure, biblical writers and biblical personalities do not seem to have much hesitation in asserting that God is just (although many do so only in the final analysis). When God announced that the city of Sodom was to be destroyed, Abraham interceded for the just men, on the basis that destroying the just alongside the wicked would be contrary to God's own nature. The psalmists and the prophets of Israel believed in an all-powerful, kingly God. "Clouds and darkness are round about him; justice and judgment are the habitation of his throne." The theme of the saints' songs in John's Revelation is a just God: "Great and just and true are thy ways, thou King of Saints." Such scriptural references are numerous.

But I was not satisfied. Apart from assertions, prayers and doxologies, what concrete event, what historical act can we point to in order to prove our claim that the Christian God is just. There is indeed a biblical event which points unmistakably to the Christian claim that God is just. But this event, or series of events, also seriously challenges certain notions of justice which many of us take for granted. I refer to the covenant that God made with Moses at Sinai.

There a covenant was sealed between Yahweh and the people of Israel. Certain conditions were agreed upon. Yahweh agreed to deliver Israel from Egypt and to set her up in the land of Canaan (Ex. 3:7-10,16 ff.). In return, the people of Israel agreed to worship Yahweh as the one and only God. Yahweh promised aid and protection. The people of Israel promised faithful obedience. Thus was born a relationship summarized by Yahweh's declaration: "You are my people, and I am your God." Pointing to this covenant, I think we are now in a position to claim that the God we worship is a just God. The covenant enables us to say: "God is just because he has kept his promises. He is just because he has kept his side of the bargain provided for in the covenant. He is just because once he has made himself accountable to us, he is faithful to it."

The covenant binds God and humanity together in mutual accountability. From this point on, God is duty-bound to listen to the human cry, or he risks being unjust. Salvation is freely offered because he has promised it to us. For that we can be grateful, but *we do not have to be*. At least not in the manner of beggars towards their charitable benefactors. Instead we lay claim to God's attention in the name of justice: "You have promised." And then, we may see cause for deeper gratitude as we come to understand how God has allowed himself to be held to ransom. For the crux of the matter is that God did not have to come into a covenantal relationship with humankind at all. He could just as well command and exact our adoration and obedience without binding himself. But he did. And once he did, there is no turning back. God is bound to us. From then on, God becomes vulnerable not only to the constraining urges of love, but also to the covenantal demands of justice. Having freely chosen to enter into a binding relationship with humankind, God's dealing with us is no longer, if I may use a bureaucratic expression, discretionary. He has volunteered to subject himself to covenantal control. And he did pay up according to the covenant, all the way to the cross. The apostle Paul put it in those famous words, that Jesus, "though he was in the form of God, did not count equality with God a thing to be grasped, but emptied himself, taking the form of a servant..." (Phil. 2:6-8). God is just because he has kept his promise. By entering into covenant, he has made himself accountable to us. In the sense of accountability, biblical justice is a profound manifestation of biblical love.

As for us, the other party to the covenant, the same in a strange way applies. We are considered just because we have made ourselves accountable to God. "Abraham believed Yahweh, and it was credited to him as justice" (Gen. 15:6). "God reveals his justice at the present time, so that he is just himself and justifies him who believes in Jesus." God, in the very act of making himself accountable to us, makes it possible for us to be accountable to him. In the most concrete manifestation of his commitment to justice, God makes it possible for us to be called just. And if God considers us just, we are just indeed.

This covenant at Sinai is not an isolated event; it was linked with the more ancient covenant with Abraham (Gen. 15) and was renewed subsequently at certain crucial turning points in Old Testament Jewish history. It found fulfilment in the New Testament period as Yahweh entered into a new covenant with a new people, a covenant made more perfect than the patriarchal, Mosaic and Davidic covenants by the seal of the cross. The covenant event dominates all religious thought in the Old

Testament and acquires fullness in the New. I propose that it is this event we can point to in support of our claim that God is just. The biblical centrality of the covenant event puts justice at the very heart of the Christian faith.

I am therefore glad that "justice" is so very much part of the Christian agenda, occupying as it does such a central place in our thinking. Understood as accountability, biblical justice is a profound expression of biblical love. And this expression is helpful to our mission involvement. Love, to be satisfying, requires positive response, but does not enjoy the right to demand it. But accountability, for its fulfilment, does not require reciprocity. One simply does what one has agreed. But accountability fulfilled does give one the right to challenge the other, without threat, without shame: "I've done my part. Have you done yours?" The mission enterprise needs the availability of such challenge — from God to us, among the churches and between ourselves and our neighbours.

But practically, is accountability adequate as a measurement of justice? I believe it is. It gives content to the abstract concept of justice. It judges and challenges each and every structure with the question "Is it accountable?" We have in this concept of biblical justice a theological tool with which Christians can probe empirically and theologically any human situation. In our commitment to participate in building a more just society, Christians have the right to ideological options. But God is no respecter of human systems. The concept of accountability frees us from the tyranny of labels and theisms, and enables us to go into the real workings, the causes and effects, the operating assumptions and values, of relationships and structures in places where we have been called as witnesses to a just God.

April 1985

16

In last month's letter, I argued for an understanding of justice as accountability. To be just is to be accountable. To do justice is to establish relationships of accountability. A just society is one in which every person is included in the structure of accountability. To deny accountability is to do injustice.

I would now like to draw an important implication in our witness to justice. To begin with, it may be useful to remind ourselves that Christian efforts in the area of justice are in fact efforts to imitate God's justice, to work towards an approximation of the biblical model. Our effort, and its results in whatever form, are not and cannot be the "real thing" in its fullness, but it should be real enough and full enough to be recognizable as God's. That is what we are after. This is not to be understood as an excuse for complacency (in fact, most of us have done precious little to be complacent about). This is a reason not to stop but to keep going. A reason against a holier-than-thou attitude, and a reason for working with all people of good will. Besides, it is necessary to know that there is such a thing as human limitation, even Christian limitation, if we are to have any credibility in our efforts to do justice — that when we talk justice, we know what we are talking about! And that when we act in justice, we have some idea what the consequences will be.

Now, I would like to put forth an idea which is absolutely axiomatic to my thesis, but which may prove to be polemic vis-a-vis a popular assumption about justice. I want to meet it head-on, not to be controversial but to add clarity to my thesis. The concept of the covenant, which forms the basis of this understanding of biblical justice, does not assume equality of power in the parties concerned, nor is its goal a balancing of power. Covenantal justice does not speak the language of power or of power-sharing. It speaks about each being accountable to the other. It assumes that all the parties are inextricably bound in togetherness. Covenantal justice assumes a relationship of fundamental oneness among the parties, that, whether we like it or not, we share one destiny, and that therefore we must work for each other's well-being and interests even in the interest of our own interests. On this assumption, accountability is the only way to think and to act which makes sense. Covenantal justice does not speak about parties being equal in power. It speaks of each party being accountable to the other.

In biblical times, when slavery remained unquestioned, Mosaic justice underlined the humanity and the dignity of slaves. Slaves remained persons, with their place in the family, and rights of inheritance (Gen. 24:2, 15:3). It was a case of justice understood not in terms of equality but in terms of accountability. Today, no interpretation of biblical justice could tolerate the existence of slavery. But this is so not because we have rejected Paul who did not repudiate slavery in his letter to Philemon, a Christian and a slave owner, but because we have been taught by Paul who insisted to Philemon that Onesimus, a slave, was in fact "a dear brother" and should be received as such. From being a slave under Roman law — a piece of property, possessing no rights, disposable at the owner's whim — to being "man and brother" there can be no greater transformation. Today, with hindsight, and centuries of inculturation, we can be critical of Paul's lack of modern knowledge in structural analysis. He failed to condemn the institution of slavery. But even with the same hindsight and the same centuries of inculturation, how many of us have grasped Paul's deeply theological analysis which sees the least, the totally powerless and the most despised, as "brothers" to whom we owe an account of ourselves? This is the substance which makes all forms of structural slavery ultimately untenable as a Christian proposition. That is why justice understood as accountability is not less, but more.

Justice as accountability is more also because it provides a new perspective with which complex situations can be seen in a new light, thus making possible new options for action.

I would like to quote from a recent meditation by Stuart Brown, a colleague of mine in the Council:

> Every region of our aching planet has its full share of suffering and injustice, but the Middle East, from Afghanistan to Libya, from Somalia to Armenia, presents the most intractable tangle of overlapping and intertwined threads of injustice and inhumanity. To say that peace is impossible without justice has become a futile commonplace. But how can we find peace? What is the justice we seek? Simple human demands for fair play in so complex a morass of conflicting claims and competing grievances have long since taxed human ingenuity beyond its capacity, while generations have suffered untold hardships waiting for a human justice which is unlikely, to say the least, to assuage their grief or restore the slightest vestige of the peace of which they have been so unjustly deprived....

It would be foolish and naive of me to suggest that the concept of justice as accountability can resolve these conflicts. But at least let me say to Stuart who will know what I mean: "Take this idea and see what you can do with it. Tell the various peoples with whom you work in the Middle East that, like it or not, Muslims of all schools, Zionists, Maronites, you are all inextricably bound together. You share one single historical destiny, for good or for bad. You have no choice but to be accountable to each other." Now, having tried to persuade you that it is more biblical and more fruitful to think of justice in terms of accountability, let me be more specific as to what accountability could mean for our mission involvement. The first and most obvious is that biblical justice demands that Christians and churches become accountable to the poor of the earth. People of no account. People who do not count at all. For God has made himself accountable to them, gave them the power of account-

ability, and listened to their story. That is the way I read Matthew's
narratives.

> Jesus went about all Galilee, teaching in their synagogues and preaching
> the gospel of the kingdom and healing every disease and every infirmity
> among the people. So his fame spread throughout all Syria, and they brought
> him all the sick, those afflicted with various diseases and pains, demoniacs,
> epileptics, and paralytics, and he healed them. And great crowds followed him
> from Galilee and the Decapolis and Jerusalem and Judea and from beyond the
> Jordan (4:23-25).

Jesus was spending most of his time with common people, in close
range with their experience and aspiration, touching their lives. Then,
"seeing the crowds, he went up on the mountain, and when he sat down
his disciples came to him. And he opened his mouth and taught them"
(5:1-2).

Whether the beatitudes were addressed to Jesus' disciples only, or to
all, is, in my opinion, immaterial. He was stating who, to him, are the
blessed. He was announcing who the people are to whom God has made
himself accountable. He would spell out his preference. Those he
considered blessed were not the people who shaped the dominant spiritual
values and attitudes of the day.

The priests and the Pharisees were not poor in spirit. They prayed:
"Thank God we are not like other people" (Luke 18:11). They did not
mourn. They laid heavy burdens on men's shoulders; but they themselves
would not move them with their finger (Matt. 23:4). Nor were they meek.
They did all their deeds to be seen by others. They made their phylacteries
broad and their fringes long. They loved the place of honour at feasts and
the best seats in the synagogues (Matt. 23:5-6). They tithed mint and dill
and cummin, but neglected the weightier matters of the law, justice, and
mercy and faith (Matt. 23:23). They did not practise mercy. They simply
passed by the wounded man (Luke 10:31-32). They were not pure in
heart, for they were like whitewashed tombs, outwardly beautiful but
unclean within (Matt. 23:27). Nor did they make peace or suffer persecution on account of their faith. On the contrary, they killed and scourged
and persecuted those whom God sent (Matt. 23:34).

Not all priests and Pharisees were like that of course. But Jesus did
make these blanket condemnations because, regardless of differences in
individual conduct and motivation, he was repudiating the religious
norms of the day which were based on the experience and perception of
the scribes and the Pharisees, and formulated to serve their needs. The

experience and perceptions of the common people were not taken into account. These were not material for theology. Religion was not accountable to the poor. Those who controlled religious articulations and practices did not consider themselves accountable to the people. In their view, God would speak to the priests and the Pharisees only. God was not accountable to the common people.

In the beatitudes, Jesus made his dissent and announced that God was accountable to the poor in spirit, to the poor, to those who mourn and thirst and hunger. They are the blessed in his kingdom. This is not to suggest that the beatitudes provide a factual description of the crowds around Jesus. They were a capricious lot. And Jesus charged them to follow him, with all that it implied. What the beatitudes do is affirm all those who are commonly regarded as people of no account. Jesus chose not to use the experience and category of the priests and Pharisees to formulate his manifesto. He opted instead for those of the poor, the sick, the afflicted, the outcast. "Blessed are the poor in spirit, the mourner, the meek..." To the common people, this spells acceptance, hope, dignity, challenge. God in Jesus Christ has made himself accountable to them.

In this reflection on biblical justice, I have made no reference to evangelism. What then is my justification for this reflection in these pages? It belongs rightfully here because — here I want to be as humble and open as I possibly can — I think much of our ministries which come under the labels of "justice", "empowerment", "development", "mission among the poor", have no evangelistic impact, in the sense of drawing people to face the claims of Jesus Christ on their lives. And I further think this is so because many of these ministries have failed to establish a relationship of accountability with the people with whom they work. And without a relationship of accountability, there is no room for mutual challenge and mutual growth. That is why we find the integration of justice with evangelism so difficult. The biblical concept of justice as accountability could help bring it about.

May 1985

17

You must be tired of the word "accountability" by now. My only excuse is that in this concept we may be able to discover a way of integrating service with proclamation, and social action with evangelism.

As a Christian way of acting in justice, I think of accountability in a very simple way. That is, whatever we are or do as Christians, we must be prepared to give an account of ourselves. Our being and our action must be accountable, capable of making sense. The emphasis is not so much on providing after-the-event answers in response to questions and challenges (although that is certainly part of it), in a permanent awareness that we are answerable for how we place ourselves, what we do and say, how we spend time and money, how we set our priorities. In this sense, I think our church structures and ways of organizing Christian work generally measure up, from the point of view of the membership. Churches are organized differently, but it is safe to say that the principle of accountability is present and that basically our church and mission are just, to their members and supporters, that is. No church leaders can long maintain their authority within the church unless their members perceive them to have done justice to what they consider important.

But biblical justice as accountability is first of all accountability to the poor, to those who are outside. And that means that if Christians are to be just, we have to be accountable to the poor and the marginalized. We have to be cultivating that permanent awareness that although the poor do not have membership with us and no votes in our business sessions, and they pay neither our salaries nor our bills, they are nevertheless our "constituencies". They are the people in front of whom the church must report itself and explain its action. In this sense, very few of our churches measure up, not even Christian programmes which come under the category of "justice", "development" or "empowerment". To be sure, much of our mission efforts aim to serve the poor. But we serve them as our "recipients" or "clients". Here, the church offers assistance, attempts to meet needs. The church does not give to the poor an account of itself and its involvement. Given the nature of the relationship, there is no need and no reason to. Neither is it often asked for. Occasionally, our relationship with the poor is described as "partnership" or one of "solidarity", and happily, there is sometimes a degree of reality to that. But even so, it is only accountability over a particular project, a particular amount of money, or a particular issue, unrelated to the total life and work of the church. Towards the poor, there is much good will and generosity, and at our best, even respect and recognition of their "subjecthood", but not much sense that the church is accountable to them.

To put this in a different way, the church has declared anathema on slavery and its modern equivalents. It has provided help for the liberation of slaves, occasionally at considerable cost to itself. But we have not affirmed the free slaves and their counterparts today as our brothers and sisters, on which very understanding the theological case against slavery rests. The apostle Paul did. He did not have any knowledge of structural analysis to repudiate the institution of slavery. But he could make a theological analysis which bound him and his Christian friend Philemon inextricably with Onesimus, a slave. And that is accountability to the poor, the acceptance that they are our brothers and sisters. Not necessarily in an emotional sort of way, but in a basic and unadorned, and I trust biblical, sense that really there is no choice. We cannot choose our brothers and sisters. Brothers and sisters do not always agree with one another. There is neither rule nor reason that we must enjoy each other's company. Each is a human person, good or bad, moral or immoral. Each has his or her own struggles and responsibilities. Each has his or her own life to live. But regardless, in the final analysis, when the need arises, when the worst happens and there is no one to turn to, we are stuck with our brothers and sisters, and they with us. And each could lay claim on the other on the basis of kinship. This does not always happen nowadays. But it happens often enough and is a sufficiently realistic model to guide the church in its involvement with the poor.

If the church accepts that the poor of the earth are our brothers and sisters in this only too common and obvious sense, then we begin to enter into a relationship of accountability. The church and the poor will have to start giving an account to each other as to why and how each conducts its life and action, to lay open existing limitations and restraints, to question each other, to make demands on each other — all on the basis that there is no real choice, that we are inextricably bound together as brothers and sisters. Perhaps I should add that the no-choice position applies only to the Christian church. Accountability to the poor is the only option, only in the context of the Christian faith and our faithfulness to it. From the perspective of the poor, most of whom are outside our churches, their accountability to the Christian church is not the only option and, in some cases as things now stand, not even an attractive option.

This puts the burden on the Christians. We have to take the first step in establishing a relationship of accountability with the poor. We have to make a unilateral declaration that we are committed to giving to the poor, not so much by funding their projects, or by advocating their causes in the corridors of power, but by giving an account of ourselves, the rationale and mechanics of the total life and work of the church, and to seeing if it makes any sense to them. In short, a unilateral declaration that the church is accountable to the poor. Then, there is a chance that the poor will reciprocate, that a covenant will come into being whereby mutual sharing, challenge and growth can take place. Let me share with you now a very limited and imperfect attempt by a Christian group to be accountable to the poor, and what happened as a result. I refer to my experience with the Christian Industrial Committee (CIC), an urban industrial mission group in Hong Kong, before I joined the WCC some three years ago.

We took the understanding of accountability literally. We tried to make ourselves answerable to working-class people. It meant that whatever we planned, whatever we did, the first consideration was always "how would the workers take it?" When faced with a decision, our primary concern was not "how do we explain it to church leaders?" It was "how do we explain it to the poor?" At the end of the day, it was the assessment by the poor which counted most with us. We heard all voices, often different voices. But it was the voice of the poor we heard first and last, and to which we gave most weight. There were many interesting theological issues and programme impulses which invited our attention, but if they were not pressed upon us by the poor, we did not feel a sense of urgency about them, important as they might be in themselves... It was simple accountability. The rest was logic.

So the CIC staff kept odd hours. Most would not show up at work before noon, in order to be around in the evening when workers came off their assembly line or finished their shift. The governing board had to meet at 8 p.m. otherwise worker board members would lose part of their pay check; and the annual general meeting was always on a Sunday, to the chagrin of pastors and bishops. On staff salary, we figured we could justify a scale roughly double that of workers and still keep our credibility with them; after all, most of us had university degrees, and they didn't. We made our case and we got away with it. We lobbied for — one sample among many — paid maternity leave legislation alongside women workers, against the fierce opposition of employer groups, including Christian employers. It was not a difficult decision at all. We had long decided and declared that we would walk with the poor rather than with the Christians, if it came to a choice. And of course we appreciated the YWCA and the league of women lawyers who joined hands with the women workers who spearheaded the successful lobbying effort. And when I was about to leave the post and a successor was needed, the committee opted for the most suitable person, although he knew no English, a distinct disadvantage in the worldwide organized ecumenical movement, but no big deal at all in the world of the poor.

The Mass Transit Workers Union is housed in the CIC office, the union having begun there. With approximately 80 percent of drivers unionized, it sought company recognition as a collective bargaining partner. It succeeded in its first industrial action. Within three months, the union inclined towards another action over the issue of break-shifts. Management was pressing down hard. The CIC advised against industrial action. The timing was all wrong. Public opinion would be hostile. It would be politically unwise to precipitate traffic chaos. But the membership voted in favour of a strike. With some misgiving, CIC threw in its lot. The strike was called and in three days it was beaten. Officials from other supporting unions were rightfully harsh on the young leadership. The failure had not only harmed the budding union, it had put a temporary brake on the growing labour movement. At the end of the last late-night strategy session, everybody left except a CIC staff person keeping vigil with the lost, exhausted and emotionally-spent union leaders who had no job to return to the next day.

Most dispute cases were far less dramatic. Workers showed up in the mission office; no appointment was necessary. Their grievance was analyzed, options outlined, and useful addresses and telephone numbers given. They were helped to learn to fill in forms, to present their case in front of the labour tribunal where happily no lawyer is allowed, and to face the employer across the table on their own. Very rarely did the staff attend the hearings (there was so much to do and so little time) unless, of course, the workers were so young or elderly that they needed help. The poor after all are not the recipients of our assistance, nor our clients. Nor are they simply to be regarded as victims. They are allies to whom Christians owe accountability in terms of who we are and what we do.

I remember also the occasion of a sharp challenge from two workers, who were very close to us. We had been advising groups of labourers in disputes with companies owned by capital from China. The two were unhappy that we dealt with the companies in the same way we dealt with others. In rather strong language, they tried to make a case for preferential treatment. We rejected their case, but not before we presented a thorough explanation based, among other arguments, on the Christian faith. That was the end of a close and fruitful working relationship with the two. But we had given accountability — and retained their respect.

I could go on. Christian accountability to the poor rules out Christian indifference and asserts that the liberation of the poor remains their own primary responsibility. CIC has volunteered itself into a covenant with labourers and workers in Hong Kong, and is committed to fulfilling its part of the bargain. But the poor alone could make that covenant work by accepting accountability and fulfilling their part of the bargain. If the poor are empowered, the victory is theirs. If they are not, it is they who suffer. It helped that CIC has taken the first step. And in this case, the poor have reciprocated, to the advantage of both. In mutual accountability, workers and CIC have achieved much in the city-wide conscientization of the poor, in the improvement of labour legislation, in creating new legal protection and rights, and in the public's recognition of labour's increasing political role. CIC in turn has benefitted. CIC's solidarity with the poor leads to the poor's solidarity with CIC. Without workers supporting it, CIC is nothing in the eyes of people. With workers, and in large numbers, on its side, CIC carries weight in the corridors of power and in the estimates of the established church. Today, workers are the largest financial supporters of the CIC budget — a simple evidence of accountability at work. Give and take. Giving and receiving. Within this covenantal relationship, CIC has been able to assume the moral authority and spiritual power to say to the poor, its ally and constituency: "We've done our part. Have you done yours? We have chosen to follow Jesus. Have you given any thought to that?" And the poor have responded, some in terms of professing Christ as Saviour and Lord.

Finally, I am only too aware that it is one thing for a group like CIC to hold itself accountable to the poor and another thing for a church to do so. After all, CIC was especially created to serve the poor. So I am not putting it forward as a model, only suggesting that its struggles, reflections, its rationale might be useful to the church. The basic lesson is relevant: if the church wishes to declare the good news that God is accountable to the poor, then it must be willing to be similarly accountable. The church must not only say to the hungry in Ethiopia: "Here's 200 tons of food relief." The church must justify to the hungry why it is 200 tons, and not 100 tons or 1,000 tons in the light of its professed theology, in the light of other commitments in its total budget, in the light of its Christian testimony in the social and political areas of life. And thus, give an account of the reason for our hope. This is what I mean by being accountable, by being just. And this is what I believe can practically bring the passion for justice and the passion for evangelism into fruitful action.

June 1985

Chapter 4

Dialogue with People of Other Faiths

18

For this particular issue, I have asked my colleague Wesley Ariarajah to write a personal letter to an ordinary Christian in Sri Lanka to help that person engage in evangelism among his/her Hindu neighbours. Wesley is on the staff of the WCC's Sub-unit on Dialogue with People of Living Faiths. I have asked him to do this because I would like to think that evangelism is a concern not only of the Commission on World Mission and Evangelism, but of all other WCC programmes as well, and that dialogue with other living faiths, in particular, is an integral part of Christian witness.

* * *

Dear Ranjith,

You asked me to give some advice on bearing witness to Christ among your Hindu neighbours. Hindus believe that anyone who has an experience of spiritual truth has the right to share it with others. They therefore do not object to authentic witness. It is important that this trust and openness to witness should be used not for manipulation of one religion by another, but for a genuine sharing of religious experience and the truth as we have come to perceive it. It is in this spirit that I put down some of my own thoughts on this matter.

I am pleased to know that your interest in witness arises from deep convictions about Christ which have actually fashioned your own life. Why do I make a special note of this? There are some Christians who would argue that evangelism is based on the "command" to preach the gospel. They would say that the truth of the gospel message is not dependent on the preacher and that the message can be effective on its own.

This is not the place to argue the theological validity or otherwise of such a position. But I am aware that Hindus will not separate the preacher and the message, the evangelist and the gospel, the truth and its manifestation. This arises from a long-established Indian tradition that only a person who has undergone a spiritual experience can have authority to impart it to others. "Can anyone recommend to others what has not been profoundly true to oneself?" they would ask, and add: "How can we believe what is said, unless we see its effects on the one who says it?"

This is why doctrinal claims about Christ, or belief statements on what God has done in Christ, leave Hindus unimpressed, even though they have a great respect for Christ as a spiritual leader. Anyone who wishes to witness to the Hindus should not ignore the long-established Indian tradition that the person and the message cannot be separated. This is a simple but profound perception among Hindus: if it is a good message, it must be both heard and seen! I know many Christians have problems with this attitude. They would want to separate the message from the messenger and to preserve the integrity of the message itself. But this is not a selective treatment that Hindus give to Christian preachers. In their own history they have always applied this principle to distinguish truth from error. This is how Hinduism functions as a living religion without a centralized authority to lay down the essentials and the limits of what they should believe. Instead of reacting too quickly to this attitude, you should reflect on it, relating it to our own Christian history. Perhaps we must also meditate on Christ's invitation to the disciples in Acts 1, where the emphasis is on "you shall *be* my witnesses".

For the same reason, witness to the Hindus can never be based on any prior absolute claims about Christ. Such claims hinder rather than help Christian witness. Let me give an example. A preacher proclaims to a Hindu: "Christ is the only way; there is no salvation except through him." However sincere and well-meaning the preacher may be, the Hindu will consider him or her both intolerant and arrogant. Why? Because they see in such a statement an implicit refusal to consider any other way. This they consider as intolerance. More seriously, such a statement or claim precludes and denies anything others may have to say on this subject even without giving a hearing to it. Nothing hurts the Hindu more. Hindus cannot even understand why Christians have to say such a thing. This does not mean that the Hindu denies the witness of the preacher. They would admit that this may be profoundly true for the preacher. Christ to him or her may have become the "only way". But they would argue that such a statement has no validity outside the preacher's own experience and conviction. It becomes true once again only when another person comes to the same conviction for oneself, and is able to experience and see Christ as the way. This may appear to be an artificial distinction to some Christians. But it has a very important bearing on witness to the Hindus. They believe that the hearer should *recognize* the truth and should not be forced to accept it.

If you ask me to single out the one factor that has been the greatest hindrance to genuine witness, I would say that it is such absolute claims some Christians make for Christ. The decisiveness of Christ must be a matter of experience and should never be a matter for preaching.

Again, some of the evangelists behave as though they are bringing God for the first time to the Hindus. The Hindus are amazed by the claim. To begin with, how can God be "taken" anywhere? The whole creation lives and moves in God. God's own witness has never been absent at any time or in any place. More importantly, Hindus have a spiritual tradition reaching back over four thousand years of seeking to understand the mystery of life and its relation to God. Within it there is every shade of theological opinion; a variety of philosophical reflection on God ranging from atheism to strict monotheism. Many modes of relating to God have been tested over centuries — meditation, good works, yoga, the way of devotion, the way of love. Much more importantly, there have been within the Hindu tradition great spiritual giants whose experience of God, spiritual depth, and total devotion to God's service can be neither denied nor ignored. To know Hinduism and the Hindus at their best is a humbling experience for any Christian. Here we are confronted with a living spiritual tradition tested and tried over centuries, within which there is undeniable experiencing of God's grace and love.

Faced with this reality, what can an evangelist do? Some simply deny that this spiritual tradition has any validity at all. They would say that their whole religious pursuit is a "human" attempt and that Hindus can never have the actual knowledge of God until they know God through Christ. Others choose simply to ignore the whole thing. They pretend that Hindus have had no spiritual history behind them, and behave as though the world was born only yesterday!

"What does this mean?" you may ask. "Are you not arguing that Hindus do not need the gospel? Are you not, by implication, saying that there is nothing 'new' that you can take to the Hindu as Christian witness?"

This is a valid question, but the real challenge to witness also lies in that question. Hindus already have some of the loftiest ideals any religion can offer. If you want to engage in witness to the Hindus, therefore, you should think very deeply about this and know why you want to witness to them. And, whatever you offer as witness should be credible in so far as it is seen to be true to your own experience, and should be seen by Hindus as answering specific questions they have about their life and destiny. That is why it is important to know them personally and to share our message in ways that make sense to them, and answer the questions they have. If we frame both the questions and the answers how can there be any effective witness? Please look up the many ways in which Christ dealt with people.

As I said at the beginning, there are no basic problems in offering witness to Hindus, because Hinduism is an open-ended religion able to consider, test and incorporate any spiritual experience that may prove to be beneficial to humankind. Precisely because of this openness, it will also reject any meaningless claims that are not backed by actual spiritual experience.

Apart from these points, which in a sense can also apply to any witness situation, there are some specific matters you should remember. This concerns the thought-patterns in which the Hindu operates.

In the Bible the human predicament of alienation from God is depicted within the framework of "sin, fall and alienation from God". Much of the way we understand the significance of Christ speaks out of this framework. A good example is the understanding of Jesus as the Christ — the Messiah. The concept and all that it means are well understood within Judaism and the church that was evolving out of it.

But Hindus understand the human predicament within an entirely different framework, using such concepts as Karma, rebirth, cycles of life-processes, etc. How do they perceive the human condition? In what way can the good news become incarnate within this tradition? These are points worth pondering. There are some who feel that all this is an unnecessary preoccupation. "All people are alienated from God; they are in sin; and what is needed is the direct presentation of the gospel," they would say. You should consider whether this is really so. The Hindu religion, culture and belief are so entrenched in the Indian heart and mind that it is difficult to imagine a Hindu operating outside them.

Let me mention just one more point. This relates to the presentation of the gospel and the expectation on how it should be received. Some evangelists think that the gospel message is a "package-deal". They would insist that Christ and all that Christians have come to believe about him (Saviour, Son of God, Redeemer, etc.) should be accepted by the hearers. Often this package includes baptism and church membership. In an earlier age, this also included a change of name, dress and culture! If you want to witness to Christ to a Hindu, you should first get over the "package" idea.

Hindus would accept Christ as a great teacher, guru, saint, etc., and one should never attempt to force one's own understanding on them. It is of interest that even Christ's disciples had various perceptions about who Christ was and they grew in their own understanding with the passage of time. What is wrong with such development in one's understanding? Let Christ be to them who he will be to them. Insistence on a package acceptance was what alienated Mahatma Gandhi from Christianity as a religion.

A word on our attitude to the act of witnessing itself. The most important lesson I have learned from the ministry of Christ is the great integrity with which he approached people. The Hindu is not an object for conversion. He or she is a fellow pilgrim with whom we share the decisive impact Christ has had on our own lives. Even as we do so, we should be prepared to listen to any witness he or she may have to offer to us. Their lives may be greatly enriched by our witness. Similarly, we may be enabled to see the unsearchable riches of God through their witness to us.

In such a witness situation a Hindu may recognize a challenge to discipleship to Christ which he or she may want to accept openly in freedom. On the other hand, the Hindu may see no reason why he or she has to make such an open commitment of discipleship to Christ.

Can you, in both circumstances, accept the Hindu as your brother or sister who stands, like you, within the unfathomable love and grace of God?

If you can, then you have received the spiritual maturity to be a witness of Christ to the Hindu.

Much love,

Wesley   *July 1982*

19

Wesley Ariarajah's letter to a Sri Lankan Christian on the subject of witness to Hindu neighbours has elicited a number of responses. The issue is crucial. Do we or do we not proclaim "Christ is the only way; there is no salvation except through him"? Wesley says "no". What do you think? But first let us listen to what our readers say.

From Parmananda R. Divarkar, SJ, India

I found myself very much in sympathy with Wesley's line of thought. Of course, he does not say all there is to be said on the subject, nor does he claim to. But he does open up a lot of questions that need to be examined; and which, moreover, are relevant not just when addressing Hindus.

One of my own reflections on this matter is that we need not only new "models" of evangelization but a new type of model. The traditional models envisaged communication in one direction; the point of departure remained firm and stable; and a change, indeed a conversion, was expected at the receiving end. Could we not think of "dialogal models" for accomplishing the evangelical task?

From L. Suohie Mhasi, Nagaland, India

The statement of Wesley in the form of a letter is very interesting. Once a Gandhian leader came to Kohima and we had fellowship with him. As I was sitting by him, he started conversing with me about religious matters. He said: "My mother is a wonderful religious woman. But she does not kneel when praying because that is what Christians do. There are some extreme Christians who say that man can be saved through Christ only and there is no other way. What is your view?" I replied: "It is what I believe." "There are millions and millions of people in other major religions in the world. What will be their fate then?" he asked. "According to the Bible, those who do not believe in Christ will perish," I replied. He was angry. My conviction is that whether one likes it or not, one cannot compromise the truth.

Once I shared the word of God with a Hindu young man in a hotel. Several times when I said something, he replied: "Yes, it is in our religious books too." At last I put a question to him. "Do you have the joy of salvation in your heart?" He replied: "No." "We Christians have the real joy of salvation in our hearts," I told him. However deep their search for the truth, their devotion, their philosophy, however old their religion, they do not have the peace and joy of forgiveness of sins and of having communion with the living God; and therefore, seeking peace they practise self-immolation. We must love them and must present Christ, the only living bread from God, to them.

From Israel M. Kabalimu, Bukoba, Tanzania

"Christ only is the Way" is a common conviction among many Christians in Africa. Since the witness of the preacher is based on his/her own reflection and experience, no one outside the preacher could deny it. Some of the revivalists I have talked to in our diocese stress that when a person testifies to the power of Christ, he does so in ecstasy. At such a moment a person becomes so full of the Holy Spirit that he may feel "born again" with Christ. However, this is not done to force the hearers to do the same but rather it is an open encouragement to share Christ's love and salvation among themselves.

If the Hindus do not find any reality in such a Christian witness, we cannot force them to accept it. The Holy Spirit, after a Christian witness, functions among the hearers and a few might become genuinely converted.

From W. Morgenstern, Dresden, German Democratic Republic

1. The basis of all Christian witness and all missionary and evangelistic activity is the fact that God acted decisively and comprehensively for all human beings in Jesus Christ: "God was in Christ reconciling the world unto himself" (2 Cor. 5:19) and "God so loved the world that he gave his only Son that all who believe in him should not perish but have eternal life" (John 3:16).

2. The real motive of Christian speech and action is rooted in personal experience of the love of God. Paul writes: "Having received mercy, we weary not..." (2 Cor. 4:1). And Peter tells those who would forbid him from witnessing to Christ: "We cannot keep silent about what we have seen and heard" (Acts 4:20).

3. Because it is God's will that all human beings should be saved and come to the knowledge of the truth (1 Tim. 2:4), the mission of the church can have no limits. The dialogue with people of other faiths and ideologies is a specific form of mission, calling for a special measure of sensitivity, humility and receptivity.

4. Christian witness can only be accepted when it is accompanied by the witness of life. In the encounter with people of other faiths, therefore, it is essential to respect both their integrity and their freedom.

5. Dialogue is possible only if the partners are ready to listen to each other and to take the other partner's conviction seriously. The absence of this readiness to listen on the part of the person witnessing to Christ, however imbued with a sense of mission, will always prove a fatal

handicap preventing him or her from successfully commending the good news to others.

6. In the dialogue with people of other faiths, the one witnessing to Christ always finds him- or herself in a tense situation. However friendly, humble, receptive and patient his or her approach to the dialogue partner may be, the point will inevitably be reached when he or she must testify to the Lord Jesus Christ, and indeed to "the crucified Christ, a stumbling block to the Jews, and foolishness to the Gentiles" (1 Cor. 1:23).

7. The gospel is a message which necessarily calls for a decision. This being so, the dialogue, too, will reach the decisive — i.e. the "critical" — point, sooner or later. The Christian who seeks to witness to his or her Lord will have to allow seriously for the possibility that his or her witness may also meet with resistance, rejection or even violence (Acts 9:20-23; 13:44-46; 17:22-23, etc.).

8. In dialogue, too, love and truth are inseparable. The ruthless fanatic for truth is just as incapable of dialogue with people of other faiths as the Christian who, out of a spurious love, keeps silent about the consequences of rejecting the truth. Christian mission is constantly exposed to both these dangers. But the special temptation to which dialogical mission seems to be most exposed is that of telling only half the truth, out of a mistaken tolerance or fear of the reactions of the partner in dialogue. But the whole truth is: "Whoever believes in the Son has eternal life, but whoever refuses to believe in the Son will never see life; the anger of God rests on him or her" (John 3:36).

From Moti Lal Pandit, New Delhi, India

The letter to Ranjith is thought-provoking. While going through the letter, certain important questions arose in my mind.

1. There are many ambiguous expressions and terms in the letter. It is very difficult to understand what is meant by *spiritual experience*. Spiritual experience of what? There must be some truth, a belief, a way of life to be experienced. An experience, whatever its nature and content, is always cognitive, and therefore operates within a particular frame of beliefs or ideas, predispositions and so on. It is, therefore, fallacious to speak of experience without any reference to the truth which I am to share or experience.

2. It has become a fashion to say that Hinduism values experience rather than doctrine. This is not, historically speaking, true. The study of classical Hinduism, even of contemporary neo-Hinduism, makes it quite clear that teachings, doctrines and beliefs of every Hindu denomination or

sect are based on the ideas of a particular prophet or saint. Each denomination has its own belief-system. Hinduism may not have homogeneous doctrines, yet certain beliefs are universal among all Hindu denominations: the concept of *samsara*, *karma*, dualism between mind and body, eternity of soul, etc. It is, therefore, wrong to say that Hinduism is basically oriented towards experience and not towards a belief-system.

3. No religion exists without the dimension of experience. The same is the case with Hinduism. The experience of one person, whether he be called a saint or a prophet, is concretized into what one may call doctrines and beliefs. Take the case of *Advaita Vedanta* of Sankara. Whatever Sankara wrote or said has been transformed into a particular school of beliefs and doctrines by his followers. These beliefs and doctrines are not accepted by those who follow Ramanuja or the Trika system of Kashmir. Take the contemporary examples of Ramakrishna or Ramana. Ramakrishna has been raised to the pedestal of a deity by his followers, and his teachings have become the doctrinal basis for his followers. The same is the case with Ramana. To say that Hindu denominations have no founders or prophets is, from a historical viewpoint, not correct.

4. The letter maintains that God can be experienced through different ways, such as bhakti yoga, karma yoga, jnana yoga, etc. This unfortunate classification is not found at all in traditional Hinduism. It is the creation of Vivekananda. If we, for example, study the classical texts on Yoga dispassionately, it becomes clear that the aim of Yoga as such is not to experience God; rather, it is to reach the state of isolation (*kaivalyam*). I shall not here go into a textual exegesis. However, we must remind ourselves that when making use of such terms, we must be aware of their meaning, and how they have been applied in the contexts in which they sprang. Carelessness can lead to confusion and chaos of thought.

5. In this context to say that Hinduism in tolerant is to misread history. This fallacious argument started with Vivekananda, and has now become a slogan with contemporary neo-Hindu writers and leaders. What is maintained to be tolerance turns out, when perceived carefully, to be intolerance.

6. The question is not whether we should preach Christ to Hindus or not. The question is, how to preach him. I agree with you that we cannot separate the message from the one who carries the message. But this does not mean that the truth-claim of Christ depends on the person who carries it. Truth must subsist in itself. If truth is dependent on something other than itself for its validity, it is no more truth. If Christ is God, he *must*

validate himself as God. This assertion — that Christ is God, and therefore redeemer of mankind — must vindicate itself. If human techniques can lead to the experience of God, then God is nothing but fiction, an illusion created by imagination. What is needed is not the negation of this truth (that Christ is God) by entering into a false pluralism (all roads lead to the same goal), but a re-interpretation in the context of historically-conditioned human experiences. The need for preaching Christ as redeemer exists as much now as it did when the incarnation took place. If this point is missed in our Christian life, then we have missed the central meaning of the incarnation, death and resurrection of Jesus Christ.

7. We cannot separate the witnessing of Christ to Hindus from the message of Christ. We cannot witness to Christ outside of his message. To bring a dichotomy between Christ and his message is to deprive the incarnation of its significance and meaning in the plan of God. I agree with what is said in the letter on the problem of methodology. There is no doubt that the church in third-world countries suffers from the sins of all historical aberrations which took place in the West. We have various denominations, we have different modes of worship and confessions, we have different structures in the church — all of them imported from the West. In this sense we can say that we do not have the authentic gospel, and therefore not the authentic Christ. Our Christ is a Christ of the Western denomination, of Western confessions, of Western cultures, etc. We have to rectify this situation. The Western garb of Christianity has put us in a defensive position. It has isolated us from the mainstream of our culture and history. But we have to be careful on this point, that is, this aberration does not absolve us from our task, which is to preach Christ authentically in the contexts in which we live.

8. Let us keep this in mind always: if we really believe in the uniqueness of Christ, we will have to make this belief a reality through our witness. Christ's uniqueness is a hindrance not only to Hindus, but to everyone. It is proving a hindrance even to the church.

From Johannes Aagaard, Denmark

I appreciate the letter to Ranjith and I shall express my gratitude for the letter by offering some critical questions and statements:

1. During my many visits to India I have been impressed by the pluriformity of Hinduism. This fact has put a full-stop to most of my *generalizations* about "Hinduism" and thus made life more difficult! I would like to make Wesley's life more difficult too, for I am not sure that his generalization of "Hinduism" holds water. In fact, it is my impression

that his "Hinduism" simply means that limited part of neo-Hinduism, which took off from Ramakrishna/Vivekananda and similar synthezisers.

2. I am somewhat worried because of the tendency in the letter to emphasize *knowledge* and not faith. Does this represent a terminological trend only? Or does it reveal a certain one-sidedness? The letter speaks of knowledge as a counterpart to experience, while the counterpart to faith is obedience. I would not exclude that dimension, but I do think that it is only biblical if and in so far as knowledge is part of faith and experience is part of obedience. I know well that this terminology is not at all as easy in relation to my Hindu friends, but it may still be necessary.

3. The letter underlines that "God" cannot be taken anywhere. But this fact does not exclude — I hope — that the good news and its affirmation of life and of God's love to mankind can and must be taken everywhere. *It has to be taken* to all of humankind, not as a package deal, of course, but still as something which has to be sent off and received.

Neither Nordic people nor Indian people have been able to find the truth by themselves. Nor has the Jewish people been able to. No one can experience or see Truth. It has to be revealed "from outside". We cannot escape that hard fact. Faith can only be shared when it has been accepted as a gift which is and remains in a way foreign to all of us.

4. The reason for this *foreignness* is not imperialism or colonialism or other-isms. The reason is our sin and our alienation from God. The concepts don't matter, but the fact does. The human condition is fundamentally determined by the fact that we do not know who we are ourselves, and definitely not who God is.

We not only do not understand our human condition, but we most probably are not able to understand it. We do not even put the right questions, not to mention speak about the answers to our dilemma. I see no fundamental difference between people and people in this respect. Danes hate to acknowledge this hard fact and so do all other people. We prefer our own religious projections — and although they differ from people to people, they are fundamentally the same: *we see in a mirror* and thereby we see ourselves. We are our own horizon and constitute our own limitations.

Jesus and his communication to humankind is different from all that. He is the way in a very specific way, specific because of his specific mission. This specificity is not part of the church's reality. The way of the church is *inclusive*: those who are not against the church are for it, but those who are not with Christ are against him (Luke 9:50 and 11:23). This *exclusive* claim is part of his love and in fact is the most inclusive mission one can imagine.

God's name is Christ, for Christ reveals the face of God, creates the love of God, gives the faith in God. God always spoke to humankind in Christ, and there is *no other way* from God to us than this revelation. But from that revelation there are *many ways* to humankind in all its religious diversity. All these ways can be used by the Holy Spirit who always speaks out of the wisdom of the Truth which Christ manifested.

I know well that this double dimension is not easy to express in an actual dialogue, but it is necessary, I hope, that we never forget this dialectic and attempt to communicate it. The church is itself more of humankind than of God, as are all religions in the world. The church is not the presence of God or Christ. It is at its best *a pointer to God*. It is very necessary never to forget this distance between us and God. This unites us with all of humankind. We are all in the same dilemma.

I fear that some of my friends may sneer: European theology. *I am* a European theologian, and I speak and write as such. If not I would be cheating. We have a lot of escapism in modern theology, which makes people behave as if they were someone else. Let us not join this farce which threatens to empty the theological task of its seriousness.

From Vinay Samuel, Bangalore, India

I appreciate the concern of this letter to be sensitive and to be aware of a number of pitfalls in Christian witness among Hindus. Most Christians whom I know would affirm the necessity of an integral relationship and proper congruity between the messenger and the message. But there is an important distinction between the Hindu and Christian world-views in the emphasis given to this relationship. The Hindu perspective is that the messenger must reach the status of a guru before he can instruct others about matters of faith. There is no dominant concept of bearing witness in Hinduism because the fundamental relationship within which religious communication takes place is that between a guru and a disciple. On the contrary, the Christian perspective is that an ordinary disciple can share matters of faith with others. A person does not have to reach a state of enlightenment that identifies him as a guru or master before one can share with others, nor in so doing does one make any claim to be a master.

Consequently, when Christians share with Hindus, they appear to be making an implicit claim to a status as a guru, which they do not demonstrate. So it is important that Christians do not bear their witness in a didactical manner, using categorical or absolutist terms. Rather, they must humbly share their convictions in a fashion that shows that they are disciples of the guru who enables his disciples to share. The issue is whether we can speak with conviction without being categorical. For our categorical statements give the impression of a claim that we have reached perfection.

I fully agree that in dialoguing with Hindus, we are dialoguing with members of a religious tradition which includes great spiritual giants. Only ignorance mixed with arrogance would dismiss all such as not of God, merely human or even evil. But the very open-endedness and plurality of Hinduism which make it easy for the Christian to begin a discussion with a Hindu at any point, make it impossible for him or her to reach a conclusion anywhere. In the popular understanding of religious pluralism, all expressions of religion have equal validity. Thus an atheist and a devout Bhakti follower have equally valid stances. The ethical and social implications of such a view are obvious to any observer of Hinduism. The oppressive dimensions of casteism are not merely rooted in economic or social realities, but are reinforced by the religious world-view. Any witness to the religious world-view of Hinduism must not neglect the religious sanctioning of casteism.

Therefore, while Hinduism has a concept that truth has many dimensions and takes a variety of religious forms, the only basis of truth is religious experience. The content of that experience can only be known and authenticated by the individual who experiences it. It cannot be evaluated by anyone else. This renders it almost impossible to formulate criteria for evaluating truth within any religious experience.

But people do form judgments within Hinduism. The religious experiences of the vast majority of Hindus who may be committed to the world-view of karma and reincarnation are set in the context of being victims of oppression. Within that situation they are forced to ask questions and make judgments for which their own religious system provides no objective validity. Christian witness and dialogue must therefore not be restricted to only one type of religious experience among literate and sophisticated Hindus. It must begin with the questions and judgments of these marginalized groups, especially the women and the poor. For it was with the questions of these groups that Jesus began to explain the good news, even to the rich. Not all human questions point to the realities and answers of the gospel. The quesions of the untroubled rich did not lead them to appreciate the answers of Jesus. It was those rich who experienced for themselves the questions of the marginalized, Zacchaeus the outcast and the prodigal son who experienced degradation, who found in Jesus the answer to their quest. When they found them-selves victims of oppression, they asked the right quesions and came to Jesus for the answers. That is part of what is meant by repentance.

A crucial area, therefore, for Christian witness to Hindus is to begin with the questions of the marginalized within Hinduism, the women and the poor, and to share the answers of Jesus which affirm the validity of their questions and of their judgments. The aim of Christian witness is not to enable the literate sophisticated Hindu to have a religious encounter with a mystical figure from another religious tradition. The gospel comes with questions. It enables the questions of the marginalized Hindus to be affirmed, and addressed by the gospel, and addresses those questions to the socially elite Hindu.

Again, because the Christian gospel is about breaking down barriers between God and the human person and between human beings, it addresses issues such as the barriers between rich and poor, caste and outcaste. So the Christian witness cannot be the witness of one, all on one's own, testifying to one's personal religious experience. It must be the witness of the life of a Christian community in which the new life of reconciliation is being expressed. A person's Christian witness must not be confined to claiming a privileged status for his or her own Christian religious experience as superior to other religious experiences. It must be to witness to the participation in the reality of the reconciliation which one's Christian community is experiencing, mediated to it and offered to all through Jesus Christ.

August 1982

20

Now let me share some of my own reflections on Wesley's letter. For me, it is probably the most lucid dialogue statement on witness. It defines the problem clearly. Before a Hindu, or others of another living faith, do we or do we not, as Christians, proclaim that Christ is the only way, and there is no salvation except through him?

The letter says "No". "If you ask me to single out the one factor that has been the greatest hindrance to genuine witness, I would say that it is such absolute claims some Christians make for Christ. The decisiveness of Christ must be a matter of experience and should never be a matter for preaching." Thus the field is open for debate. For this I am grateful.

Another event which makes me become alert is the passage in the WCC statement on "Mission and Evangelism: An Ecumenical Affirmation". In the section on "Witness among People of Living Faiths", the wording is "in him is our salvation", instead of "in him is salvation", let alone "in him only is salvation". The wording denotes the lowest common denominator in the thinking of the ecumenical movement. My hope is that the World Council of Churches will engage itself on this vital issue.

As an Asian, I have long been aware of the minority status of the Christian churches among neighbours of different faiths. We need the ministry of dialogue for mutual understanding, for cooperation, yes, for our own survival, and yes, for the enrichment of our own faith. I have also put much hope in dialogue because it challenges much of the missionary practices of the churches. In terms of world evangelization, the modern missionary movement and the evangelistic endeavour of the national churches that emerged out of it have not made a dent on countries and peoples which have long-established cultures and religions. India, Burma, Thailand, China and Japan provide ready examples. Our way of doing the job obviously has not worked. So I eagerly look for another way. Although fully aware of the fact that dialogue does not speak the language of evangelism, I was, and still am, prepared to see in it an ally or even a teacher, indirectly, in the church's evangelism task. Now, I've been put on alert. Do we or do we not proclaim that Christ is the only way?

Arrogance, let me assure you, has nothing to do with it. There's absolutely nothing in Christianity today that we can be arrogant about. Similarly, for that matter, in Islam and Hinduism. Conflicts, violence, totalitarianism, casteism. They provide the most compelling reasons in the world for people not to believe. That's why, for us Christians, there's all the more reason not to point to ourselves but to Christ. And the only asset Christians have in pointing others to Christ is found with the recognition and confession (1) of our failure to follow him, and (2) of his love which compels us to continue on this journey. This, in all fairness, is somewhat of a strange asset, but herein depends our credibility with all those who are on a journey too.

Back to the question of the finality of Christ. Probably, there is no one ecumenical answer to it, perhaps because of the nature of the ecumenical movement, or perhaps because of the nature of the question. But I am glad the problem has been defined. How shall we approach the issue? I believe we should debate it head-on at a practitioner's level, i.e., let practitioners of evangelism share their experiences and conceptualization of evangelism among people of other faiths, to see if proclaiming Christ as the only way does or does not work. That will give us a good start.

We could, of course, take a more theological approach. But I don't know if we can break new ground. Or we would have to go a long way back and say: "The question is all wrong. Let's bring in a new formulation." I am aware, for instance, that a few theologians in Asia have been attempting to understand Christianity afresh with a creation focus rather than the salvation focus. Potentially, this has the promise of easier sailing for Christology in the Asian context. We may be able to steer away from having to deal with the question of the finality of Christ with regard to other offers of salvation. But I am not sure. It is a monumental task. I am suspicious of academics making structures of words and calling them theology. And I suspect "What do you think of Christ?" will always remain a question and a challenge with us, as it did in the gospels.

My preferred approach to the whole concern of world mission and evangelism among people of other living faiths is — and I must be careful now and I ask you not to misunderstand me — the approach of solidarity, of participation in people's struggles for justice and dignity. During my 14 years of involvement in industrial mission in Asia, my every encounter with the poor was an encounter with people of another living faith, except when they happened to be Marxist-inclined. In most cases, we got through to each other. This is not to suggest that all non-Christian religious believers are poor. On a world scale, the overwhelming majority of them are. Neither do I suggest that the faith elements of the poor are not important to them. They are, and extremely so. As a matter of fact, I wish those of us who work with the poor for justice would have a much better appreciation of the religious in people. My experience has been simply that credibility, trust, openness and respect can be more naturally achieved if we, Christians and others, work together on our felt-needs, struggle together against forces which sin against us.

December 1982

21

How do Christians understand God's presence and work among people of other faiths? This is, of course, not a precise formulation. There are many different ways of putting it, depending on one's theological orientation and purpose.

I recognize the legitimacy and seriousness of the question itself. It bears strongly on how Christians communicate their faith. However, I am coming to the conclusion that to the Christian *obligation* to evangelize, it is basically irrelevant. Whatever our responses are to the question of God's presence and work in Hinduism, Islam, Buddhism and other religions, "Christians owe the message of God's salvation in Jesus Christ to every person and to every people" ("Ecumenical Affirmation: Mission and Evangelism", paragraph 41). The answers we choose will influence our attitudes towards persons of other living faiths, and even our own self-understanding, but it will not fundamentally affect our commitment to share the good news of Jesus Christ with them.

Let me take an obvious example, Jesus' encounter with Nicodemus, recorded in John 3:1-21. Surely, there can be little doubt, in the Jewish faith God is present. Yet, even then, to Nicodemus, a Pharisee, Jesus declared that "unless a person is born again, he cannot see the kingdom of God". To this "teacher of Israel", Jesus in the same breath issued an invitation to "believe in God's one and only Son". If, from the Christian perspective, the need for conversion, for faith in Jesus Christ, applies to persons of the Jewish faith, in which Christians see God as already clearly present and at work, surely the same, if not much more, applies to persons of other living faiths. This conviction does not give Christians the right to make judgments on the destiny of others. It makes urgent our obligation to share our faith.

It is therefore clear to me that a strong affirmation of the experience of people of another faith, indeed, even a strong recognition of the theological significance of that same faith, does not argue against the Christian imperative to evangelize. I for one find it difficult to hold that God is absent in other religions. The fullness of our Triune God — Creator, Redeemer, Comforter — makes such a view difficult. The same fullness also compels us to want to proclaim his name.

It does not follow, however, that since God is present and at work in living faiths, God is necessarily present and at work in the life and practice of a particular religion as we know it today. Or, for that matter, of a particular church, even a Christian church. That is something we cannot come at only by theologizing. Neither, in my opinion, should we. To seek to find out where God is at work in others is Christian humility and wisdom. To seek to find out where God is not at work is Christian arrogance and stupidity.

I feel Christians today, by and large, are still unprepared to take the faiths of their neighbours seriously. Perhaps, despite the physical proximity, unquestionably in Asia and Africa, and increasingly so in Europe and North America, few of us have yet the chance to encounter in a personal way godly men and women of, say, the Hindu faith, the Islamic faith, the Buddhist faith. At a recent consultation, Father M. Amalodoss, an Indian Jesuit, told us of the two years he spent learning Hindu music. On one occasion, he had the use of his teacher's personal notebook for his studies. There, on the margin of every page, he found the name of a Hindu god appearing over and over again. His teacher had scribbled them while making music. It takes a callous person not to take this man and his faith seriously.

At the same meeting, Dr Wayan Mastra, head of the Protestant Christian Church in Bali, Indonesia, and a noted evangelist, shared with us the story of his daughter who had been drowned, and how he spoke with her through a medium. It was an experience he deeply cherished, and he offered it as a matter of course. But for me, it was not something to be taken for granted. In fact, I find it impossible to engage in such an act. And I told him why. But in our differing fashions, we are together in taking the faiths of our neighbours seriously. To us, the world of faiths is no mere arena of ideas. The world of faiths is the world of spirits. Dialogue among people of living faiths is an encounter of one spirit world with another spirit world. It is a serious venture. The spirit world is real. There are benevolent spirits which free and comfort. There are malevolent spirits which bind and hurt. The encounter could be dangerous or it could be joyful. In every step of the encounter, we need to exercise the gift of spiritual discernment.

In Wayan Mastra's case, on that occasion, he discerned the workings of a benevolent spirit in the living faith of his people in Bali. He boldly entered into an encounter and, from out of it, he was able to proclaim that Christ is the greater spirit who sets men and women free. And the people responded.

In my case, I have too much respect for the world of spirits, and too little confidence in my own spiritual fibre, to dare venture into such uncharted territory lightly. And so I tell the story of Jesus, who is human and known, and continues to be open to being known, and tell people that when we come to know him we come truly to know God.

Probably, culture plays a not unimportant part here. I do not live in Hindu rural-Bali. I have been living in secular urban-Hong Kong and now in secular urban-Geneva. And an important tenet in my Confucian upbringing reminds me always to "respect the gods and keep them at a distance". The teaching is meant to be both humorous and serious.

Whatever our theological assessment is of another living faith, our neighbour's faith must be taken seriously, which means it must be taken as it is. As it is, we will inevitably discover that any dialogue between that faith and ours can no longer be conducted only on the level of ideas and concepts. It will have to be an encounter of spirit with spirit(s). Such an encounter should not be entered into without reverence, neither can it be entered into with a neutral stance. Here, the total claims of Jesus on our own lives become our only source of discernment and our only protection, and the same claims of Jesus on our neighbour's life our only message.

The nature of the Christian faith, indeed the nature of living faiths, renders the occasion of their encounter a missionary encounter. Yet, I think there must be time and space too where the faiths voluntarily give up their missionary intention on each other in order for their adherents to listen conscientiously to each other, to enjoy each other as human persons, and to work together as members of the commonweal. This is especially necessary for missionary faiths such as Islam and Christianity in the kind of world we live in today. I am thinking for instance of consultations among articulate teachers of these faiths or leaders of their respective churches and organizations. On such occasions, to attempt to convert would be anti-witness. I am also thinking of residents' groups in mixed religious neighbourhoods, gatherings to discuss community affairs, or to have fun together on special occasions. Here, Christian witness will stress not distinctions but togetherness. In such settings, Christians witness to their faith, and others to theirs also. And this suffices.

But, as I suggested, these are times especially set aside, spaces especially created, where we willingly forego our missionary design. The daily encounter of faith with faith is a daily encounter of one spirit world with another, each laying a claim for human allegiance. The encounter is therefore a missionary encounter in which the decision to convert, i.e. to change allegiance, is invited.

The act of invitation, in my opinion, is what distinguishes "evangelism" from "witnessing to our faith" as many of us use the term today. Too often, we talk about "witnessing to our faith", period. Without thinking about "to whom". We take part in a public worship service, and in so doing, we are surely witnessing to our faith. We reaffirm the creed. We carry a peace symbol. We sign a public statement based on a biblical perspective. Some of us suffer for our faith. Some work selflessly for the cause of the poor in the name of Christ. Through all these, we indeed witness to our faith. And they are precious acts in the eyes of our God. But unless we are witnessing (to our faith) to somebody, somebody with a name and a face and a location, our witnessing will not be effective evangelism. This is not to say that such "witnessing to our faith" cannot be evangelistic. I believe it can, and it is. I believe any act which points to Christ is by definition evangelistic (provided of course that there is somebody for that act to point Christ to). The point is that in ordinary circumstances, "witnessing to our faith" is not likely to generate a change of allegiance to Jesus Christ on the part of our neighbours unless Christians witness (our faith) to them. This suggests that for witnessing to be effective evangelism, the act of invitation must be incorporated. That in addition to communicating "this is the God we believe in", we also find some ways to indicate to our neighbours "would you also serve him as your God?" That after saying "this is where we stand as Christians", we say to our neighbours "would you consider joining us in this journey?"

There are of course persons whose spirituality is so strong and transparent that its sheer charisma is sufficient to draw others to a point of decision. And there are circumstances, mostly of a nature bordering on martyrdom, where the silent suffering of Christians is capable of winning the allegiance of others to Christ. But for most of us, in our day-by-day, ordinary and very imperfect living, we do need, given the lack of clarity in our life and witness, to issue simple invitations to our neighbours to consider the claims of Jesus Christ on their lives, whether they be Jews, Muslims, Buddhists or the indifferent.

It is not enough that Christians tell what the kingdom of God is like. It is not even enough that we strive to be a concrete sign of that kingdom. Christians need to invite people to come in, to come to the table, to partake of the bread and the wine, to be involved in the King's business. Even as Jesus invited. If we don't, people may stay out, unsure of our intention, and confused as to the terms of entrance.

Looking back, if I had not been invited, I would not have come in, however good the food, however warm the fellowship. And neither would a generally-issued invitation have sufficed. For after all, I was invited to change my allegiance, to put at risk, at the very least, an essential part of me which made up my very identity as a human person. I lay justifiable claim to a specific, clear, personal invitation from Jesus Christ, or whoever purports to speak in his name. Our neighbours too can lay a similar claim.

I think one of the most serious weaknesses in mission and evangelism in many of our churches today is our reluctance to invite others to faith in

Jesus Christ. It could be an understandable response to massive abuse of evangelism yesterday and even today. It could be a response of integrity against practices of proselytism and manipulation based on economic and political power and motivated by cultural chauvinism. But if our reluctance to invite stems from an unpreparedness to accept others into our fellowship, or even an indifference, then we ourselves are in desperate need of another invitation.

July 1984

22

I think it is time for another reflection on Christian witness among people of other living faiths. This time, I wish to be as concise as I can. Hence the numbering.

1. There is no question in my mind that the ministry of dialogue is important for the Christian church and its witness. I have no doubt that the church must find means of educating its people towards greater respect for Hindus, Muslims and Buddhists, and greater appreciation of their religious convictions and practices. I have encountered far too many Christians, churches and missionary groups, who continue to bear false witness against their neighbours of other living faiths. Simple human decency, let alone Christian ethics, requires that we attempt to get rid of cultural bigotry, racial discrimination and class prejudice in ourselves and in our communities.

2. Today, there is a widespread consensus in Christian circles on the need for respect and appreciation for and openness to people of other living faiths. This, in short, is the substance of the operating guidelines on the subject from the World Council of Churches and the Vatican Secretariat for Non-Christians. Both documents * deal with dialogue primarily as a matter of attitudes. On this level, there is no controversy. And it is on the level of attitudes that the present ecumenical consensus officially rests.

With this attitude of respect, openness and appreciation, Christians are urged to relate to our neighbours of other living faiths. In some cases, Christians need to do so to ensure survival of the church or of the community. Often, cooperation is necessary to bring about a greater

---

* *Guidelines on Dialogue*, WCC, 1979. *The Attitude of the Church towards the Followers of Other Religions*, Secretariat for Non-Christians, Vatican, 1984.

degree of peace and justice for all. Through an interfaith encounter, whether in the business of daily living or in the intellectual exercise of sharing faith tenets, one also arrives at a greater clarity of theological understanding and spiritual assurance. And then, of course, there are the testimonies of Christians who tell of the need for openness and appreciation without which one can hardly get within listening range, much less share the story of Jesus Christ. The reasons differ. But they all call for respect, openness and appreciation. Today, Christians by and large agree on a positive attitude towards people of other living faiths. This, I am happy to say, represents an important step forward.

3. Given this consensus on attitude, what should follow is of course implementation. That Christian people learn to be respectful, open and appreciative of our neighbours of other living faiths. Apart from that, the next step is the intellectual exercise of theologizing. Attitudes have roots. The attitude of respect, openness and appreciation towards Buddhists, Hindus and Muslims springs from beliefs. What is the Christian understanding of our own faith, and of the faiths of others, which provides a basis for respect, openness and appreciation? The ecumenical movement, as distinct from individual theologians, is now taking up this intellectual task. It is a logical next step after reaching the consensus on attitude. Corporately we are seeking to break new ground, but as yet there is no theological consensus on the subject, and no attempt to forge it, within the ecumenical movement. Theologizing is an exciting intellectual exercise, but it is also a deeeply serious matter that has to do with truth, especially when undertaken corporately by a council of churches. This exercise will have pastoral bearings on the faith and faithfulness of believers in our local congregations. (At this point, I am envious of the division of labour between the official teaching function and the speculative theologizing function within the Roman Catholic Church.)

4. In the search for theological support for the attitude of respect, openness and appreciation towards people of other living faiths, the most poignant question has taken the form: "What is the (Christian) theological significance of another living faith?" Offhand, the formulation sounds blatantly imperialistic, imposing our own Christian values, categories and thought-patterns on another faith which claims to be different and has an identity of its own. I still think so and have little enthusiasm for it. In addition, I doubt if anyone can really work with a formulation like that. However, I can understand the inevitability of the question. As Christians, we live in the world. We relate to people. We enter into dialogue with our Muslim, Hindu and Buddhist neighbours. We cannot but touch

the question, or be touched by it. We cannot avoid it. As it is, we had better deal with it consciously rather than otherwise, the danger of imperialism and the futility of problematic formulation notwithstanding.

My approach to the question is (a) accede to the possibility and viability of a high theological view of other living faiths, and (b) suggest that a high view does not mean that Christians give up the imperative to evangelize among Muslims, Buddhists and Hindus. The WCC "Ecumenical Affirmation on Mission and Evangelism" states in no uncertain terms that "Christians owe the message of God's salvation in Jesus Christ to every person and to every people".

I do not find it difficult, as a Christian, to affirm the experience of people of another faith, or even to recognize the theological significance of that same faith. I find it more difficult to hold that God is absent in other religions. The fullness of our Triune God — Creator, Redeemer, Comforter — makes such a view difficult. This same fullness also impels us to proclaim God's name.

5. In our theological exploration in the context of religious pluralism, a theological methodology has emerged which I regard to be very important. Simply put, it is the idea that since Christians believe in a Triune God, theological emphasis on God the Father and God the Spirit should become more pronounced than before. There is no denying that the formulation of Christian theology has always been more Christ-centred than Father-centred or Spirit-centred. In our dialogue with people of other living faiths, perhaps a God-centred or a Spirit-centred approach may prove to be more fruitful. I find myself intellectually excited by this methodology.

But as of now, I am unsure. I am unsure because what do we, and what can we, know about God and the Holy Spirit except through Jesus Christ? Of course, we can try to know more about God by learning about the creator(s) in the scriptures of other living faiths. And we can try to do the same with our knowledge of the Holy Spirit. But this would be, at best, speculative. The process could certainly yield new knowledge but not necessarily new knowledge of God. Until this new knowledge is judged by the revealed knowledge about Jesus Christ and is found consistent, we cannot be sure that we know any more about the Triune God.

It seems to me that as long as Christians are human beings, living in human history, on this planet earth, we are destined, or condemned, to knowing the fullness of God only by knowing Jesus Christ. It might be different, and this is clearly speculative, for rocks and trees and insects and animals. Or with lives and beings on other and unfallen planets. Being unfallen, they may not need redemption. They may be gifted with other ways of knowing God. But we, my fellow Christians and fellow human beings, are stuck with Jesus Christ; and Christian theology has to be, fortunately or unfortunately, Christ-centred.

6. Let me now go on to a concern about dialogue and evangelism. Some theologians have difficulties with Christians making certain biblical "exclusive" assertions in a religiously pluralistic society. To make the claim that Jesus is the only Saviour in the face of a Muslim or a Hindu is tantamount to a declaration of war. I know situations where this could happen, and has happened. Much, of course, depends on the circumstances. There are wise and stupid ways of communicating the message "Jesus is the only Saviour". With an attitude of respect, openness and appreciation, a Christian who is already involved with others in community can certainly find ways of communication without becoming a counter-witness. The key is not so much theology as maturity. There is no necessary reason to associate the exclusive claims of Jesus Christ with Christian arrogance. Every Christian assertion is a confession of faith. When I say to my neighbours, "Jesus is Lord ", I am saying "I believe Jesus is Lord". When I declare, "There is no other name", I am expressing the conviction of a believer. I cannot say anything about God without the preface "I believe". The prefacing has nothing to do with my particular theology or philosophy. This is simply how language works. When I communicate the exclusive claims of Jesus Christ on human persons and on the world, I am confessing my faith. I am doing no more than what my neighbours of other living faiths have told me about their religious convictions and their faith.

In the final analysis, a Christian confessing faith is a Christian confessing his or her inability to make others believe, admitting that the evidence is conclusive only to those who already believe. In my confession of faith, my statements are not a proof but a conviction of which I give the God I believe in the credit. As it is, confessing faith does not put the other person on the defensive, but allows that person the freedom to assess the evidence and make his or her own application. *

So when I say, "Jesus is the only Saviour ", I am in fact saying, "I believe Jesus is the only Saviour ". My task is not to prove that Jesus Christ is indeed the only Saviour. That I can never do. My task is to show

---

* I wish to acknowledge my indebtedness to Richard Stoll Armstrong on this point. See chapter 2, *Service Evangelism*, Westminster Press, Louisville, KY, 1979.

that I believe he is. By making this confession, however, I am not saying something similar to what a little girl says when she claims that her father is the best daddy in the world. Mine is not a piece of personal opinion at a given moment. "Jesus is the only Saviour" is indeed my confession of faith. But it is also the confession of the church all over the world, throughout the centuries. And, what is more, it is a confession based on the scriptures. This may not mean much to my neighbours of other faiths, but surely it means a great deal to me and to my fellow Christians. The Christian confession of faith does not take away from the confessions of other faiths. Nor should it be muted in the pantheon of other spirits and deities. Christian proclamation is by nature confessional. The attitude of respect, openness and appreciation towards people of other faith forces us to realize our inability to establish a rational proof or to legislate belief. Out of this sense of weakness, Christians confess.

7. In ecumenical circles today, the conflict between dialogue and evangelism has nothing to do with dialogue as such and evangelism as such. It has everything to do with belief. It has everything to do with whether or not Christians should want others to become Christian. Dialogue calls for honesty and openness towards one another. If a Christian is committed to dialogue, he or she is committed to sharing what he or she believes in. So if we are convinced that it is a good thing for others to be Christian, then the requirement of dialogue compels us to evangelize. If, on the other hand, a Christian does not believe that Christians should want to see others become Christian, then it follows that the requirement of dialogue would compel that Christians do not evangelize.

This question whether Christians should or should not want others to become Christian is, of course, a very very important one. But it is not technically a dialogue question. For if you are in dialogue, you have to be honest with your dialogue partner, and that means you have to communicate to them what you truly believe in, whatever it is. Else, there can be little dialogue.

So if in dialoguing with my Buddhist, Hindu and Muslim neighbours, I wish to tell them the story of Jesus, I do so not because dialogue equals evangelism. Neither do I do so because my neighbours want to follow Jesus. They may or may not, today or a few years away or never. I do so because I believe in the story and in its importance, and that I must share with my dialogue partners what I treasure most.

At this point, prayer, sensitivity, commonsense, readiness takes over. If you are a mature person, you will know what to communicate to your neighbour of other faiths, and when and how. You will also know when to shut up. You will know what to do and say, not simply to express yourself, but also to communicate, to build trust and to safeguard each other's integrity. Mediated through a mature person or a mature church, a theology which normally calls for aggressive evangelism may well lead to a quiet, relaxed witness, and a theology normally emphatic on sacramental presence may well find the need to shout from the mountain-top. Religious and social contexts, our neighbours' state of mind, the degree of their readiness (and ours as well), and the maturity of mutual ties are among the determining factors.

Christians cannot claim that all nations and peoples will be converted to Jesus Christ. We can pray. We can hope. But we cannot lay claim as a right. It is the exclusive domain of the Holy Spirit. What we can claim is our call to proclaim. This is a vocation that has already been passed on to us, all of us.

8. Let me now make a plea for an important element in evangelism which the ecumenical movement has been rediscovering — intentionally inviting others to faith in Jesus Christ. I would like to make a special plea that Christians be ready for that specifically with regard to our neighbours of other living faiths.

Conversion to Christ is costly under any circumstances. It is particularly so with people of other faiths. We should never forget that for a person of another living faith, to become a Christian is to put at risk an essential part of that person which makes up his or her very identity. There are also familial, social and political costs which are real enough. So the Christian response to the call to evangelize among Buddhists, Muslims and Hindus must be one of a profound dialogue in which lives are shared, and close personal, family and community ties forged.

Given the cost involved, and the risk and challenge to their very identity, our neighbours of other living faiths can lay justifiable claim to a specific, clear and personal invitation from Jesus Christ, or from whoever speaks in his name. No general Christian witness will suffice. Nor a general invitation. The invitation has to be specific. It is not enough that Christians show what the kingdom of God is like. Out of profound respect for the other person's faith, with a trembling hope which is totally alien to religious imperialism, Christians invite their neighbours by name to faith in Jesus Christ.

9. Finally, a tentative thought on evangelism among people of living faiths from a macro-global perspective. Let us boldly think in terms of evangelization among the millions of Buddhists, Muslims and Hindus in

their natural territorial and cultural habitats, as distinct from among migrants to the West. It seems to me that the most crucial question is one that has to do with the doctrine of the church. Namely, whether and how we have the kind of Christian community which will do justice to our neighbours and to their faith, and to the vision of profound life-dialogue through which the gospel is articulated and shared. Let me just describe one way of naming the problem from a Protestant perspective.

By and large, the Protestant understands the church in terms of denominations. And it has, I think, served the church fairly well in most parts of the world. Leaving aside theological considerations for the moment, the denominational understanding of the church has proved its functional advantage. It is capable of sustaining itself. Its organized structure has released energy and influence far beyond what its numbers warrant. But it has not worked at all in the vast stretches of land masses where Buddhists, Hindus and Muslims and their cultures dominate. I cannot imagine a Baptist congregation, or any Protestant denominational local structure as we know it today, even at its best, fitting into the environs of, say, the Muslim Middle East or Buddhist-Taoist rural China, or Hindu rural India, as a credible, inviting and sustainable witness. A totally new understanding and structure of the Christian community is called for.

I do not refer to things commonly associated with congregational renewal such as improving Sunday services, giving new energy to prayer meetings, mission outreach and so on. I refer to fundamentals which shape the life, the form and the message of the church. I am thinking, for instance, of a full-time salaried clergy, of Christians gathering on Sundays, of church membership, of missionary and pastoral activism. Let me explain, and here I must confess I am simply speculating, drawing bits and pieces from my mission reading. I wonder whether, for the evangelization of these lands, instead of having trained pastors and evangelists to develop and manage congregations of believers and to reach out, we should not have congregations of people committed to prayer, to scholarship and to healing, who will draw Muslims, Buddhists and Hindus into their midst. Or perhaps, instead of a salaried pastor which presupposes an organization that generates regular income and therefore must have the machinery of money supervision etc., we should not have a religious teacher whose support comes from the services he or she renders. And, perhaps, instead of having a clearly defined church membership, with the clear expectation of attendance in Sunday services, we should not develop a much less organizational definition of Christian identity, relying more on personal and familial identities and cultural practices. Perhaps, instead of us drawing a circle and saying whoever is inside is a Christian and whoever outside is not a Christian, we should not draw an arrow, indicating that there are people who are moving towards Christ and others who are moving away from Christ. I could go on. I am aware that I am speculating. I am aware that I may be treading on thin theological ice. I ask for your indulgence because I am simply stimulating thinking by thinking out loud. Think we must, towards a new understanding and an appropriate structure of the Christian community as evangelizing communities in the ancient lands of the great peoples who profess the Buddhist, Hindu and Islamic faiths.

January 1988

Chapter 5
Trends in World Evangelization

23

I'd like to report to you, from where I am, on what has been happening in evangelism worldwide, and what hasn't happened. I'd like to identify five global trends and tell you why they excite and occasionally worry me.

1. Faith healing

Quantitatively, the number one means of evangelism today is probably faith healing. I am fairly convinced that, globally speaking, more people have come to a felt personal faith through this means than through other ways. This is not to say that people are healed by prayer or exorcism and then they are converted. Healing in the physical sense may or may not occur, but the whole process of Christians providing a healing ministry has proved to be extremely effective in awakening personal faith.

It is happening all over the world. Its local expressions vary radically. It happens among illiterate peasants and outcasts in the midst of rural deprivation. It occurs among professional and business people in affluent suburbs. Faith healing can take the most elemental forms of pentecostalism such as snake-handling. It can also assume the sophisticated pedagogy of the gospel of health and wealth. Faith healing is practised by pentecostals, charismatics and also Baptists, Presbyterians, Lutherans and Episcopalians. Faith healing is offered through the TV. It is offered in open-air mass rallies. And in the quiet of homes and hospital wards, or in great cathedral churches. Nowadays practitioners are not confined to people who claim the gift, but include those who do not have the gift but are keen to be part of the healing of persons and families.

Faith healing or spiritual healing is part and parcel of the traditional healing fundamental to the life and mission of the fast-growing African Independent churches. It is also offered through healing services by new charismatic groups and churches which draw thousands of people in villages and cities. The occasions are marked with the whole crowd responsively chanting, indeed shouting, "Jesus" — "Power", "Jesus" — "Power". One comes across similar scenes in India, Indonesia, Latin America and the southern parts of the US.

In China, the Christian community has grown very fast. There is no doubt that the growth has come mainly from the countryside, and largely through healing and exorcism. There have been gatherings of thousands of people, but the norm is the many small daily encounters in homes and worship services. Lay evangelists and itinerant preachers spread the word and place their hands on the sick and the disturbed. The gospel is understood largely in terms of liberation from evil spirits which afflict the body and the soul. People in rural China expect this of Christianity, and when they see certain signs in that direction, they respond. For people who have had no contact with organized church life for some twenty years, no Bible, no Christian literature and very little teaching, living isolated in the midst of suffering, poverty and hardship, their most solid catechism must be the vivid memory of Jesus walking the earth, driving out the demons and healing the sick.

In the major cities of Europe — Hamburg, Stockholm, London — where most regular Sunday services of the historic churches are poorly attended, special healing sessions in the same churches, whether attached to ongoing services or held as regular monthly events, draw hundreds and thousands, including many who seldom grace a pew. In the United States, Lutheran and Episcopalian clergy have begun to turn to that part of their prayer books they had hitherto seldom used: the pages on spiritual healing and exorcism. The cathedral church in Washington DC now offers on request prayers for healing and the laying on of hands. There is a need.

Enough of the description. What do we make of the phenomenon? I think the Holy Spirit has been, and is, at work. And through the ministry of faith healing, many have come to a personal faith in Jesus Christ. But I have reservations and I shall state them in many more words. But all my anxieties about the faith-healing phenomenon do not add up to negate this positive assessment.

I worry about the faith-healing phenomenon because I have seen Christian healers becoming corrupt and manipulative. I have seen credible Christians becoming counter-witnesses after attaining some level of human success in their healing ministry. I think of a very fine evangelist in India who added the component of healing to his public witness. His ministry immediately expanded. Many poor people look up to him and support his work. And some wealthy people too. Now he goes around in a luxury car. Every day he spends time interceding for people who have written in for his spiritual intervention, always with a small donation enclosed. He does this by praying over a computer print-out with thousands of names on it, and laying his hands on the terminal. A number of letters would come in, gratefully testifying to illnesses healed, with larger sums of money enclosed. He faithfully publicizes his healing successes and his computer print-out inevitably grows longer.

I also have in mind a clergyman from Ireland and three old pastors serving a number of Christian communities in Szechuen, south-western China, where many minority tribal people live. The background here is different, but the stories are the same. Not one of the four claimed to be endowed with the spiritual gift of healing. All four wanted to be available to the Spirit. People around them felt the need for healing and urged upon them the leadership role. Soon they found themselves engaged in the laying on of hands. Their desire for prayer and for spiritual depth and power grew. It was all as it should be. But within a brief period all four found themselves deciding to give up their involvement in healing. The people were puzzled and unhappy, unable to understand the reasoning behind the decision: "It is extremely difficult to be such a direct and immediate channel of God's blessing. There were times when I wasn't sure if I was a mere channel or playing God."

Another of my worries is that the conversion experience of many does not seem to last. Through the ministry of faith healing many come to confess Jesus, and join a Christian community. But many drop out. Mission researchers record the gains, seldom the losses. The numerical growth of Christianity in Africa and rural China falls into such a category. The growth remains substantial but much less dramatic than is often supposed. That is why the churches there equate evangelism with Christian education. They have little problem getting people into the church. The problem is keeping them there.

There are fundamentally two ways through which people come into the faith. One is through contact with scripture — Bible reading, preaching, Christian literature, etc. The other is through contact with the church —Christian family, parish life, liturgy, etc. The first normally involves more deliberateness. The second is a sort of osmosis. By and large, the two ways have produced the Christians who have peopled the church throughout the ages until today. What we have in the faith-healing phenomenon is, I believe, a third and historically new way. This way does not in any sense preclude the traditional ways. At its best, this new way can and does contain strong elements of scripture and church life. But it doesn't have to. People can and do come into the faith through faith-healing experience without recourse to scripture and church.

My third problem has to do with the recognition of the simple fact that faith healing is not a Christian monopoly. Other faiths, other religions, also heal. There is the Spirit and there are the spirits. Christ is not the only name people call upon for healing. And to say "Jesus", in any language, is not necessarily to call on the Name. It can be a mantra. It can be magic. One of the dangers of the phenomenon of mass conversion in rural China, for instance, is superstition and syncretism, with all kinds of spiritual consequences. This, perhaps, is my fundamental anxiety about the phenomenon of faith healing. Not out of scepticism about things of the spirit. But precisely because I know that the spirit world is real and powerful, and therefore must be handled with the utmost care.

2. Home Bible study and prayer groups

Next to faith healing come home prayer meetings and small Bible groups as the other most effective setting for evangelism. This too is a worldwide phenomenon. One can go into practically any city, any town, any village, any slum (except in a few countries in the world where there is little or no indigenous Christian community) any day of the week and find a group of people gathering at a home and conscientiously trying to figure out how to live out their faith in their context. Lay-led and lay-directed, it is meant as a way for Christians to help one another. But almost inevitably, it begins to include others who are not Christians. The honesty and the seriousness of the group and the informality of the setting are emphatically inviting. In Australia I attended a meeting on conversion growth. There congregations that have grown in number through adult baptism, rather than achieved natural growth through the baptism of children or through transferred membership, had come together. All their stories pointed to the evangelistic role of home Bible study and prayer groups.

I find this an exciting phenomenon. There were serious tensions between the traditional church and the home meetings to begin with, and some ecclesiastical problems. But today, by and large, in most parts of the world, such difficulties have more or less sorted themselves out.

3. Crisis with evangelism among young people

There is a real crisis today. The church separately and as a whole has lost the young people. Not only in Western Europe. Also in North America, although the loss is less obvious. And no less in rural and urban Asia, Africa, Latin America, the Caribbean and Oceania. Not only mainline Protestant churches but also conservative, evangelical denominations. Not only institutional churches, but also para-church organizations dedicated solely to mission and evangelism among the young. And I am referring not only to young people who are heavily marginalized: the long-term unemployed, the drug addicts, the school drop-outs, the casual labourers, the homeless — those whom you find loitering around train stations and market squares. Those who have a 14-, 16- or 21-year old body but whose soul is easily 40 years old. I am surely referring to them, but I am also talking about young people in schools and universities, well-adjusted people who lead a "normal life". I am talking too about young people from respectable Christian homes.

The crisis is that while churches and para-church organizations, especially the latter, have put a lot of effort into reaching the young, while there have been all kinds of youth mission and evangelism events and extremely well thought-out youth programmes on every level, and young people do come and participate, sometimes enthusiastically and in large numbers, we — at least those of us in the churches who are personally involved in youth work — don't know what we are doing. And the young people don't seem to know either. We face a worldwide situation where young people are willing to listen to the gospel, where many are taking part in Christian activities, responding positively to Jesus' invitation, and then the next day or the next week the same young people behave as if nothing has happened to them. There is interest and concern. And then it is all gone. And no one, including the young themselves, knows why. A lot of sociological data is available on the young and their attitude towards religion in general and Christianity in particular. Based on these data, numerous books have been published on programming youth activities. But no one seems to be able to get the soul of the young to sing.

I have no real answer. I can only describe the scene. With the heavily marginalized youth — the drop-outs, the drug addicts, the unemployed — I don't think anything of an institutional approach will make any difference. These young people have been so severely wounded that nothing but a full-scale, long-term missionary movement will do. I mean the church sending out their best, young or old, it doesn't matter, who feel the call to be brothers, sisters, fathers and mothers to them. The church letting loose these missionaries, with no job descriptions, no deadlines, only plenty of goodwill and a readiness to listen. Then, maybe, in the midst of sharing and acceptance, some ways may be found.

With the evangelizing of young people who lead more "well-adjusted" and "normal" lives, maybe less drastic and less dramatic approaches are available. I don't know. I'd like to hear from you — the young people, those who enjoy being with the young, you who make music and write songs...

We have a crisis. The church does a lot of things with young people. But we don't know what we are doing when we are doing it. And I am not comforted by thoughts such as: "Don't be so anxious. By the time they are 30, when they start their family, they will come back with their babies. Or when they are 60 when they feel lonely. They always do." I am not comforted by such wisdom because my concern for evangelism among the young is not a concern to fill church pews, but a concern that people experience the joy of knowing God and belonging to a Christian community and of making a contribution to the kingdom, in the days of their youth.

March 1989

24

I had expected strong reactions to my letter identifying contemporary trends in evangelism. Instead, many of the letters I have received are affirmative. Some gently point me in other directions. I'd like to respond, in order to make fuller this picture of what is happening today in evangelism worldwide.

On evangelical movements

What about the organized evangelical movements since the early 1970s? Are they not a significant factor in evangelism worldwide? Quite a few raised that question. This is a tough question for a WCC staff person, especially one, like me, who is considered family in some evangelical circles, and alien in others. So, with as much objectivity as I can command, I would agree that, yes, the contemporary organized evangelical movements represent some of the most influential factors in world Christianity today. We don't need future church historians to tell us that. But whether evangelical movements are equally significant in world evangelism, in calling people to faith in Jesus Christ worldwide, I am far less sure. What I am sure of is that evangelicals and their organizations have done a great deal more than any other Christian people in the promotion of evangelism. But being significant in promoting evangelism is not the same as being significant in doing it.

Sadly, evangelicals don't know any better than ecumenicals do about evangelism in a secular culture. Sadly, we in the worldwide churches of whatever persuasion have very little idea how to share the gospel convincingly with secular men and women, whether in Europe, North America or the third world. Churches do not know how to deal evangelistically with people who can manage their lives reasonably well without Jesus Christ. You and I must know many people, including ourselves once upon a time, who fit this bill. And here we are talking about billions of people, "unreached" or more accurately "unmoved". This is a most crucial area where none can claim to have done significant work. The other major area in world evangelism where all have come short is, as I indicated in my previous letter, youth. Here evangelical Christians have tried a lot harder than ecumenical Christians have. But the struggle has remained extremely uphill, and the going is getting tougher. And no significant breakthrough is in sight.

Many evangelical Christians are of course involved in what I regard as being the most significant global evangelistic phenomenon of our time — faith healing and small prayer and Bible study groups. I've been happy to recognize it. But to attribute such global phenomenon to any single movement would be a mistake.

On young people

A little more reflection on my observation that the world church has failed miserably with evangelism among young people is in order here. Of the readers' responses, more focused on this subject than on others. There was no big disagreement, only the puzzled observation: "Yes, my church has failed and knows it. But we thought other churches in other lands are doing well with youth. You surprise us with your picture of global gloom. Are you sure?"

I am afraid that it is true that those of us who work among the young in mission and evangelism don't really know what we are doing when we are doing it.

In Asia and Africa, during the decade beginning in the early and mid sixties, most urban churches had strong youth movements. Baptist, Methodist, Presbyterian, Christian and Missionary Alliance denominations could show youth fellowships and Sunday schools working with hundreds in many of their urban congregations. And the strength was not only in terms of numbers but also in leadership and Christian commitment. Today, this is no longer the case.

In the USA, despite the popular religiosity of identifying social success with believing in Jesus, or perhaps because of it, the same thing is happening to the youth fellowships in congregations. Only large and affluent congregations of a thousand members and over, which can offer almost non-stop youth activities provided for by a team of well-trained youth ministers, can withstand the erosive tide. But such an arrangement, while meaningful to the particular congregations, cannot be meaningful in a wider context or in the longer run.

What seems to be happening worldwide is that Mammon presents an irresistible temptation to young people, with a lot of help from the adult world. And no one can serve two masters. What seems to be happening is that Western ways of doing things are fast becoming a global norm, the universalization of the values of "Wall Street". Undoubtedly materialism is nothing new. But the nakedness, the force, the speed, and the pervasiveness of contemporary materialism seem to be qualitatively new. It is legitimized, propagated, glamourized by governments and corporations and, yes, even by Christian churches. These values are now being taken for granted. And young people cannot escape. It is in the very air they breathe. But materialism is supposed to be chiefly an adult disease. And Christians are supposed to have seen different days. We are supposed to have breathed a different air. And if we are Christians, we are supposed to be linked to One who has broken into, and out of, human history.

On good news to the poor

I was challenged by several friends as to why I did not include the missionary priority of good news to the poor as a significant global factor in world evangelization. Latin American bishops have put this emphasis on the Roman Catholic map. And CWME did likewise with Protestants and Orthodox in 1981 at the world mission conference in Melbourne.

Looking back, I must say a lot has happened. The agenda of good news to the poor has exerted tremendous impact on churches worldwide, on their theologies and mission policies. It is a significant factor in the struggle of the world's poor for justice and liberation. But I find myself unready as yet to say that this mission emphasis has proved itself sufficiently significant in calling the world's poor to faith in Jesus Christ. I see the poor responding to the gospel in many different ways or a combination of ways — faith healing, prayer and Bible study groups, involvement in the struggle for justice and liberation. There are some encouraging signs that the church's preferential option for the poor is being responded to by the poor exercising a preferential option for the church. I believe liberation theologies are significant for evangelism among the world's poor. How significant they are remains to be seen.

The mission agenda of good news to the poor is understood by the Melbourne conference in two ways — what is the gospel which indeed can be perceived as good news by the poor, and how may Christians share the gospel with them? As potently evangelistic as any agenda can be. The reason it has yet to live up to its full possibility, in my opinion, is that it has not been adequately enough theologically developed — and practically enough. I think we have stopped at this point: in the suffering of the poor, Christians see the suffering of Christ; in their faces we see the face of Jesus. This is indeed a profound Christian thought. But let us be honest about it. While this idea may be helpful to the Christian, how is it helpful to the poor? And what does this profound idea tell us if the poor need also to believe in Jesus Christ?

But this agenda has high potential. In so far as the working out of the agenda increases the credibility of the gospel in the eyes of the poor, it contributes to world evangelism. In so far as it fails to invite the poor to come to a saving and transforming knowledge of Jesus Christ, it deprives the poor of the good news. We have here a lot more work to do.

May 1989

25

This summer, I was invited to participate in the global mission event of the Lutheran Church in America. One thousand six hundred pastors and lay people gathered at Luther College, Decorah, Iowa, for an intensive learning process around world mission. The heart of the event was the free university with a daily offering of 110 courses on every conceivable aspect of "mission in North America and overseas". On me fell the lot of "evangelism: a global perspective", "the WCC", and "the church in China". There were of course plenary sessions too. I gave the keynote address on the first day, responded to a series of testimonies from the mission field, and had my first experience of an American "TV talkshow" — billed as a conversation with Dr George Anderson, president of Luther College.

All in all, it is an experience I am not likely to forget. So let me record here a substantial part of the exchanges during those plenary sessions. Many of the ideas have been expressed in the pages of the monthly letter and at other ecumenical meetings. I repeat them here because on this occasion, I tried to communicate them live to the church's grassroots in North America.

* * *

Herewith a slightly edited version of my address on "The Church in Mission" given on the first evening.

I am very grateful to be part of this important occasion. I want to share with you my understanding of a crucial development in world mission today, a development which has and will continue to have a tremendous impact on the churches and on the world. When we talk about Christian mission we are really talking about God's mission. And this development I'm trying to describe to you contains rather disturbing elements, disturbing to a lot of us who love the church we are part of. Yet this development contains much hope. I suppose it is only natural that God acting in history both disturbs and brings hope. When we study the parable of the Good Samaritan in Luke 10, most of us, probably all of us, identify ourselves right away with the priest and the Levite. Religious people, who saw the wounded man lying on the road to Jericho, passed by on the other side. As we come to this text in the scriptures, we realize right away that here is a mirror in which we cannot but see ourselves. The priest and the Levite forcefully and yet rather easily remind us of the many occasions when we too passed by on the other side of the road. So we identify ourselves with them. And this identification judges us and challenges us and compels us to do a better job, to be more caring, to be ready to act in mercy to whoever is in need.

I believe this text — and similar texts in the Bible — constitute one of the most powerful motivating forces in global mission today. It has resulted in tens of thousands of Christians reaching out to all corners of the world to heal the wounded, to feed the hungry, to educate the young, to denounce injustice and to proclaim the gospel of salvation in Jesus Christ. And yet, have we ever paused to wonder why, as we study the parable of the Good Samaritan, we very rarely identify ourselves with the person who was hurt? Why is it we do not see ourselves in the wounded traveller? The person who was waylaid by the thieves, stripped and exposed? Who was beaten up and left half-dead? Why do we naturally identify ourselves with the priest and the Levite, the unwounded? One wonders what would happen to Christian mission in our homeland and overseas if Christian people were to see themselves as the wounded instead of the priest and the Levite who are the unwounded.

My friends, this is exactly what has happened in the last decade or so, in world mission thinking. There have emerged in the world church thousands upon thousands of Christian people, particularly in Latin America, Asia and Africa, who, when they read the parable of the Good Samaritan, read it differently from the way we do. They see themselves as the wounded man. They do not see themselves in the priest and the Levite. They identify themselves with the person who was hurt and was suffering because they themselves are hurt and because they themselves suffer. And this phenomenon, this emergence of Christian people in the church who read the Bible in this way, who do not see things or understand things from the point of view of relative comfort and relative security but from the point of view of the hurt, the wounded, the marginalized — this emerging phenomenon has a profound bearing on the way the churches understand and practise world mission today.

As Christians proclaim Christ all over the world, we have to ask the questions: "Who are we?" "How do we see ourselves?" How do we understand the reality in our own lives as we proclaim Christ today in North America and overseas? I affirm Christian mission borne out of a sense of gratitude to God for the good life he has given us. I want to salute a mission undertaken by privileged people to help the underprivileged. But there is a world of difference between this kind of mission-understanding and a mission understanding borne of shared hurt, of sympathy, of fellow-feeling, a mission to the wounded because we too are the wounded and we know what being wounded is like. This, in my opinion, is the mission challenge to North American churches. Are you ready to engage in mission not on the strength of your affluence but on the strength of your poverty; not on account of your privileged position, but on account of your shared hurt with the rest of humanity? I think the need for world mission and evangelism today calls upon the churches to re-examine the way we read the Bible, the way we engage in mission. It calls upon us to try to see things from the perspective of the wounded traveller rather than the perspective of the priest and the Levite.

Let me now share with you a more or less historical framework, a reading of world mission history which has been a challenge and an encouragement to me and to many others who are committed to the global mission of our Lord Jesus Christ. There have been periods in church history when the church suddenly grew tremendously and in the process experienced profound changes. I think we are on the verge of another such period. Let me put it this way. As a result of the council of Jerusalem reported in Acts 15, the door of the church was thrown open to the Gentiles. From then on, a Gentile person could be a believer without going through the laws of Moses. As a result, the church grew, in number and in understanding. Christianity ceased to be only a Jewish cult. It took upon the dimensions of a world faith. But to do that, the power of Jewish Christians over the church had to be broken, and Gentile believers allowed their full participation, not only in terms of participation in the life and government of the church but, more importantly, with their particular Gentile perspective on theology given due place and respect.

With the modern missionary movement of the nineteenth and early twentieth centuries, and despite its connection with imperialism and colonialism, autonomous churches eventually came into being in every land. The door of the church was thrown open to Asians, Africans and many others. The church grew in number and in understanding. As a result, Christianity ceased to be merely the white man's religion. It has become truly a universal faith. But to be truly that, the power of white Christians over the world church has to be broken, and believers from other races and other cultures allowed their full participation in the body of Christ.

Some of us feel, even now, that the door of the church is not yet open enough to people of other races and other cultures. European contextualization of theology is still regarded as normative. The perimeter of "legitimate" theologizing and church involvement is still largely determined by white cultural values and categories. Some of us feel that the inability, or the reluctance, of the Christian church to appropriate the diversity of cultural insights, and the abundant gifts of all peoples, is a hindrance to world evangelism efforts. Much remains to be done. Nevertheless, we must rejoice that the basic step has been taken, the direction set. We must rejoice that the Christian church, as a result of the great missionary movement of which the Lutheran church is a part, is now a church of all peoples from different races and cultures.

Who will come into the church next? Who will be coming into the church in large numbers, and becoming part of it, making the church even more universal, and closer to the biblical image of the world's nations bringing their gifts to the throne of the Lamb? From what I have learned of the world mission situation, I think there is good evidence to believe that the people who will next come flowing into the Christian church are the world's poor, the poor of the earth.

During the last decade or so, we have seen an increasing influx of these people into the churches in Latin America, in Africa and, to a lesser extent but still in large numbers, in Asia. In the West, churches among the recent immigrant populations have been the fastest-growing. The trend continues today. Worldwide, masses of the poor are turning to faith in Jesus Christ. It follows then that for this process to continue, to mature and to bear fruit, the power that middle-class Christians have over the church has to be broken. In the first world, but no less urgently in the third world. For while many third-world churches consist mostly of poor people in their congregations, the theological understanding and mission agenda of these same churches often reflect the middle-class perspective of their leadership, with very little participation at that level from the poor. Unless middle-class dominance of the world church is broken, the masses of the poor who are outside would not want to come in.

Here I must add a couple of footnotes. When I use the term "middle class", I do not use it in any derogatory manner. For the purpose of this discussion, the term connotes no negative meaning. There is nothing wrong in being middle-class. The problem begins when the middle class, which constitutes only a part of the total sociological make-up of the world church, claims and exercises total power over the church and deprives all others of the openness to participate. In that situation everybody suffers, especially the church's understanding of the gospel and hence its credibility as evangelist.

The other footnote has to do with the argument that for world evangelization to succeed, the power presently dominating the church has to be destroyed. "To break" is not the same as "to repudiate". The council of Jerusalem did not repudiate the early Jewish Christians. It recognized the limited applicability of their convictions and their practices. Neither did the coming into being of national autonomous churches in the third world repudiate the white missionary churches. The new churches simply claim the protagonist role in the mission drama among their own peoples in their own lands. So too, the breaking of the power that middle-class Christians hold over the church is no necessary repudiation of the middle class. It is a necessary move for the sake of world mission, for the sake that many more may come to know Jesus.

It seems to me that world evangelization requires the evangelization of the poor who make up the bulk of the human population and who are at present outside the church. It also seems to me that the renewal of the churches requires the full participation of the masses of the poor whose experience has until recently been largely excluded from the churches' theology and mission agenda. But the poor, given the nakedness of their situation, have a lot to tell us about God, about the Bible, about the church and its mission. I am not romanticizing about the poor. The voice of the poor is not the voice of God, but theirs is a voice that God hears, a cry that God listens to. The poor are the recipients of the good news as well as its messenger.

What is the message the poor have for us today? I think, going back to the parable of the Good Samaritan, it is that you and I too are the wounded traveller. That with all our affluence, our relative comfort and security, we too are the hurt. And here the poor are right. Beneath your sociological reality is the deeper theological and human reality of being bound, and being hurt. I am aware that this is a very dangerous message for global mission. I am aware that this message may drive us to self-pity. It may tempt us to self-righteous unconcern and provincialism. On the other hand, it may provide a new and powerful surge for mission once more as we find within our own lives, as we find within the history of our church and our people, the experience of hurt which binds us to our neighbours and to the suffering people all over the world.

Finally, I have been wondering why I should come to peaceful and prosperous Iowa to suggest to good Lutheran folk like you that you consider thinking of yourselves as a wounded person rather than as the unwounded wholesome priest and Levite. Well, as I have suggested, woundedness is your reality too, as it is mine. And we must accept it, bring it up to our God and let him deal with it in our mission engagement. Secondly, I believe the scriptures ask us to have the perspective of the wounded man. It was a lawyer, a teacher, a professional person, who asked Jesus: "Who is my neighbour?" Jesus' response is that it is the wrong question. He provides an alternative question: "Who is neighbour to the man who fell among the thieves?" In other words, Jesus asks the lawyer to adopt the perspective of the wounded man. To understand and to act as the hurt and the marginalized would. The same is required of us today. Lastly, I think the task of world mission requires this particular perspective on the part of North American churches today. We proclaim and share Christ in North America and overseas as we laugh with those who laugh and cry with those who weep. The perspective of the wounded man would enable us to do that. That is Christ's way for mission. In Christian mission, only those who have been wounded and are not ashamed of it can bring healing to others in our community and to the world.

At the following evening plenary, five persons shared their experience in mission through stories or vignettes on pastoral work in a fishing village in Chile, inner-city care in the USA, ministry to the blind in Japan, legal assistance to Spanish Americans, and Christian witness in Cuba. And then it was my turn to make a public response.

When we speak about world mission, we are in fact speaking about the ministries of Dale, of Earlean, of Andrew, of Devi, of Elmer [who gave the testimonies] and many thousands of Christians like them everywhere in their home towns and in their mission field. Theirs is the story of global mission. Most of the stories we just heard are happy stories. Stories which tell of experiences which have generated what we regard to be results. I trust I'm not taking anything from them by also suggesting that behind one success story probably there are ten failures. For every happy ending, I'm sure Dale, Earlean, Andrew, Devi and Elmer must have experienced many unhappy endings, gone through sleepless nights, and offered prayers from the depths of frustration. And that is also the story of world mission. So the task remains enormous. The stories our friends shared with us are signs of hope to urge us to go on. Let us try not to be too sorry for the people they have described. This young chap in Chile who died, this woman who lost her job and was forced out — let us not be too sorry for them. You see, the life of the poor is the life of misery, but let us not forget that in every slum, there is laughter. Even in the most desperate situations, people sing and people dance and they make love. There's always hope. Poor people do not simply crawl into corners of resignation. They are also proud people. So I hope that these stories will not only make us feel sorry for them. That's not what they are asking us to do. Andrew told us of this man with polio. There is wholeness in his broken body. I think these stories are attempts to remind us that there is wholeness in human brokenness. At the same time, there is brokenness in our apparent wholeness.

My second point has to do with the human reality that these stories try to convey to us. Again, allow me to borrow Earlean's observation. People not knowing where to go. Like sheep without a shepherd. And this idea comes across very strongly in all five testimonies. Sheep without a shepherd is the classical image of human reality in the Gospels. And we often summarize this image by saying people are sinners. Hearing these stories, I'm not so sure that this word is the proper description of the human situation in which human beings are like sheep without a shepherd. When we talk about you and me as sinners, we are saying that you and I violate the laws of God. And this is a reality that we all have come to understand. This is the reality which has driven us to God in repentance. And yet when we hear these stories, the people that my brothers and sisters serve, these are people who are sheep without a shepherd. Of course they are sinners. Of course these people sin and they know it. But it seems to me there is another reality in their lives. It might be more appropriate to describe these people, who are like sheep without a shepherd, as the sinned-against. That is, we are not only violators of God's laws. We, and particularly the people that my brothers and sisters just described, are also the violated. If people are sinners and if they are also the sinned-against, that has a lot to say about the evangelistic message, about the content of the good news. If human reality is sinned-againstness, then obviously the good news is to say: stand up and struggle against the forces of sin; and the Christian responsibility, the evangelistic calling for the church, is therefore to stand on their side.

My third point is a challenge. We have heard these stories and we have just sung a beautiful hymn, "I Love to Tell the Story". What is the connection between these five stories and the story of Jesus? I do not think evangelism is simply telling Jesus' story, period. Evangelism is telling the story of Jesus in relation to Andrew's story, to Dale's story, to Earlean's story, to Devi's story, to Elmer's story. To evangelize is to relate the human story with the biblical story. To relate the human story with the story of Jesus. And when the poor and when those who are not in the church, who are not interested in the faith, see themselves in the world of Jesus, then Jesus becomes a live option for them. Jesus becomes real. They then have to make a decision. That to me is evangelism and may I challenge you to look into your Bibles and to find a Jesus story which would connect with one of those five stories. A Jesus story which would enable you to tell the persons whose experience you've heard that what they care about the Bible also cares about.

And finally, I think I want to register a complaint. I want to ask why it is that there is no vignette, no story from rural and suburban America. Why is it that we do not hear one story from all you "missionaries" sitting here who operate daily in the important mission field of rural and suburban USA? I long to hear your story. Because what happens in the USA, in your church, whether it be in the inner-city among new migrants, or in a nice neighbourhood in the suburbs, is important to global mission. It is important to the ecumenical movement. I want to hear that story and I want to complain that that story has not been included in this panel. Thank you.

I must say happily I got a round of spontaneous applause mid-way into my last point.

On the last evening, Dr Anderson sat me on a bar stool, in front of a camera crew, and we had a one-to-one conversation with 1,600 people eavesdropping. Together we explored a number of important world mission issues. I give here a couple of exchanges to supplement what has gone before:

Anderson: One of the concepts that you have mentioned here is the idea of sinned-againstness. Can you say something more about that term?

Fung: I find this term useful for mission thinking. If we define the human situation in economic and political terms, then of course the answer must also be found in the realm of economics and politics which, we know as Christians, do not suffice. It's not enough. It does not touch the basic reality that we are in as human beings. And so I feel that we should use theological language. That's how I come to the use of the term sinned-against. It includes economic and political exploitations, but it is also very much spiritual exploitation. Let me give an example. If you are deprived of a job and you have a family of five — well, you are deprived economically, but you are not simply deprived economically. Your whole human dignity is at stake. You can't provide for your spouse; you can't provide for your children. You get up every morning and you don't want to face your family. You become a worm. That is sinned-againstness. That is economic exploitation but it's a lot more than that. And if we understand our reality as sinned-againstness, then of course the way out is to seek a solution in the forgiveness of sin. Soon we will realize that while a person is sinned against by various forces, that same person will soon realize also that he or she is also a sinner. Let me be very specific. In Hong Kong, workers get poor pay. So I say that they are the sinned-against — not only that they get low pay but because they have little say in the running of their lives. But of course while they are sinned-against they also beat their wives. They also trample on other people — on other poor people. Now how do you communicate the gospel to them? You do not go to them and say you are a sinner. The answer is, of course I am a sinner, but so what? You go to them and say, look into your own reality. You are the sinned-against, but my brother, you also sin against other people. You also sin against God. That's how I find that expression useful.

Anderson: That's a dimension, then, that would also have relationship to us. That is, those who are not classed as the world's poor. If we are in some sense also victims as well as sinners.

Fung: That's right. If we define our reality in terms of sinned-againstness rather than only as economic and political exploitation, then it's much easier for us the fortunate, the well-to-do, to find out how we too are bound and how we too are hurt, in a different way of course. Fundamentally we share the same human condition as the rest of humanity — you are no exception — I'm no exception. We are much better off than a lot of people in the world, but our basic reality remains the same.

Anderson: So that's a kind of human experience — both being sinned-against and also being sinner. Well, now, how about all of us here? We talked a good deal about the poor but some of us here are saying, when you say that the new team is coming on field there are going to be some new stars. That makes us has-beens in a sense. That puts us on the bench. How do you see the middle class? Is it kind of a lost race now or is it a group of oppressors? What do you have to say about the middle class?

Fung: When I talk about the middle class I am also talking about myself. Well, I think it is true that the missionary impulse is now coming from the non-white Christian world — the desire, the enthusiasm to proclaim the gospel. Of course the USA is a mission field. You are missionaries here. That is your responsibility and this is the job that you can best do. Not me or others from Africa or from Latin America. You are the best persons who can do the job here. Just as I can do a better job in Hong Kong than you can. Now where does that leave the missionary movement? The missionary movement of Christian people crossing boundaries — cultural or national boundaries — to proclaim the gospel in a new land, in a new context, remains valid. But let me be perfectly honest. Take the third world. Take Asia. If we are talking about the basic ministry of the church — if we are talking about the present agenda of the churches in the third world, worshipping, teaching, evangelizing, visiting the sick, all these churches in the third world can manage on their own without Western missionaries, without Western money. But this present agenda is not enough. The whole world has not been reached with the gospel. The bulk of the human population, the poor, even in your land, have not heard the gospel. In the third world, while we have some experience of doing that, we are still not very good at it. Some of us are not even willing to do it and this is something that the Lutheran church is not very good at either. So here we have an important missionary agenda to reach out to the world's largest grouping of people who are outside the church and, because neither of us on our own can do a good job, this gives us a reason to work together. I know that I am trying to say something very beautiful in a negative manner, but unless we encourage each other and say we need a new missionary agenda... I'm not asking that the US churches work out the agenda of the third-world churches — no, and I'm not saying that third-world churches should work out your agenda. I'm saying that we must come up with a new common agenda. Something that we have not been faithful to and yet is mandated by God — mainly, the proclaiming of the gospel to every person and particularly to the poor. So I think we have a big opportunity here. We all have some experience of doing it but not much. It is an area where we can really work together.

Anderson: What would you say as you look at us either from the perspective of Hong Kong or from the perspective of people who are, let's say, the core of the world — the third-world people? How do you analyze our situation in terms of what gospel we need to hear? That is, what's our spiritual weakness from your point of view?

Fung: I hesitate to do that, but let me just share a story or two from personal experience. In my last trip to the United States, I went to Youngstown, Ohio. I had a chance to talk with an unemployed steel worker. He must be in his mid- or late-forties. He had run out of his unemployment benefits. He was standing in the welfare line. There were a few others in the line, a few elderly persons, a young mother, I think two or three black people. I had been told that a steel worker is among the highest paid industrial workers in this country. Now he is in the welfare line and, as we talked, I was surprised that he was still speaking in terms of "we" and looking at the others in the line as "they". I think the pastoral message and also the evangelistic message for this man is that "he too is the sinned-against". He couldn't see himself this way even now. The other story — I took a bus, a Greyhound coach, coming here to Decorah from Cedar Rapids. There was a young boy, thirteen, tall and lanky. The driver would not let him play his music because he didn't have an earphone. By some kind of federal regulation, you cannot play music in a public vehicle and that suited me fine, until I realized he became very uneasy. It was a three-hour ride. Apparently he did not know what to do with himself without his music, and so he came to sit beside me and asked me what music I liked and so on, and I couldn't distinguish a "Western" from a "country". He had a whole stack of music cassettes with him. And so he tuned the volume to the lowest and soon we were listening to his music — he trying to teach me, you know — and again that suited me fine. He was on his way to spend a few days with his mother who was separated from his father. We got to know each other, and he treated me to a coke and some chocolate. What was the good news to this young man? He was so terribly lonely. I'm not romanticizing here. I'm sure even a teenager like him might very well be manipulating his divorced parents all the time, trying to get the most from them and so on. I have a very sceptical mind, but my heart went out to him. To me, his basic reality remains sinned-againstness, and I came up with the idea as I prayed and meditated that probably what Jesus said to his disciples would make sense to this young man. Pick up your own cross and follow me — an offer of community, and a rejection of self-pity. You take up your own cross. You are thirteen but you can do something for others. You follow Jesus together with us. He leads the way. Could your church make this offer of companionship, community, and challenge that's really worthy of one's life commitment?

October 1984

26

What use is it to bring Christians from the third world to the churches of the first world for a brief period to help with mission? John Poulton tackles this question with candour in a speech we reproduce below.* He is speaking from a British perspective, to a British audience, with a concern for evangelism in Britain.

Let me attempt to explain why I think it is timely. Within the WCC, third-world churches have been able to influence appreciably mission policies and funding priorities of first-world churches. But until we can share each other's stories on a congregational level in such a way that each comes to know God better and communicates the good news more authentically in one's own setting, we have yet a long long way to go in our sharing and our search for unity remains very incomplete.

* * *

* A talk by Canon John Poulton to the British Council of Churches, Conference for World Mission Home Committee, 8 October 1982.

I shall not beat about the bush but speak frankly to my theme. Evangelism in Britain or elsewhere in secularized Europe is not easy and we possess few clues to it. When people claim to see the way through we need to probe carefully what they are actually talking about. Usually you find at the heart of it a magnetic personality with his or her following, not really a lasting or applicable clue as to method or message. Alternatively you find you are looking at a specific application of local insights and resources to a well-researched need.

Two background facts need, I think, to be accepted before we can go further.

a) The institutional church is tearing itself apart at the seams. It cannot afford itself. It is not attracting the people of this country. It has no clear message. It rests on its history but is fearful of tomorrow. Its leadership faithfully reflects its condition. Where they are concerned, we deserve what we have got.

b) There really is a theological problem which for the most part Christians are avoiding. The scene is muddied because those who preserve a conservative approach are likely to pick up followers at this time of turmoil, leaving others either frustrated or with a guilty conscience because they cannot proclaim the gospel in quite the same way. The theological problem is that which the Vancouver assembly theme addresses. Did God so love the *world* or is his concern merely with his people, the church? Does his love focus in ecclesiam or in mundum? Too often we are New Testament Christians reflecting the old Israel's sin of domesticating God to our own purposes. Hitherto our churches have behaved as if they were the centre of all meaning, and evangelism was the recruiting of more outsiders into this crucial centre of life.

This brings me to our theme. What help might experience of, and in, the world church give to us in our evangelistic task in Britain? I bracket that with the question: What use, honestly, are Partners-in-Mission-style exercises which bring in Christians from elsewhere ostensibly to criticize or assist in our mission? I suggest that in so far as these are perhaps unintentionally but nonetheless surely designed to bolster up existing structures and patterns of mission, they are predestined to abort. They tend to be designed not to deal with the deep-down problems of our inabilities to communicate.

I am tempted to liken this to the Anglican experience of non-stipendiary ministry which, setting out to place ordained leadership within the professions, trades, etc. in our society, in fact produces mass priests to hedge-hop with the sacrament on Sundays. It is implicit in much of the old-fashioned training methods used and the content of the training that this will happen. Nevertheless, the leaders go on speaking as if the auxiliary pastoral ministry was making real inroads into various work-oriented sectors of society.

Let me give another illustration of this unfortunate principle at work. During the last holidays a faith-sharing team from Uganda was in Norfolk at the invitation of the bishop and the Diocesan Overseas Committee at his behest. At no stage was the church consulted as to what was needed here. The unspoken assumption was: "East Africa is a church in revival. These people come from East Africa; we can therefore expect revival here."

Yet scripture suggests that you first sit where others sit, study their language, learn their thought patterns, and then speak as God gives you to speak. (Indeed have not the missionary societies spent hundreds of thousands of pounds on missionary training down the years exactly designed to fulfill these conditions?) Today in the despair of future shock in international mission we fail to take our own prescribed medicine. We think we discern a need (multifaith dialogue in back-street Bradford, shall we say, or stewardship in Dorset...), and we do what the churches are always doing in making home appointments — we look to see who is available. Because today this can as well be an Indian or an Australian Aborigine as an English person, we globalize our traditional laziness in refusing to do our research properly. We more or less match possible need with possibly relevant resource and hope for the best. Sometimes it works and we feel justified in the way we planned things. It is of course more expensive to import somebody, but if the experiment fails we write it off to culture shock or "lack of understanding during so short a visit".

I must be even more blunt and say we shall usually not even admit or want to know whether it failed anyhow. In terms of evangelism and mission, we are so steeped in "leaving the results to God" that we deliberately avoid setting measurable objectives in almost all we do as church people. That way we can never be said to fail and can spend time praising the Lord for what are probably only side-effects for which we were in fact not specially in business. We have all said after an evangelistic effort: "We did not get close to many outsiders but our fellowship grew marvellously." Or maybe after some overseas visitor has returned: "Not much has happened here but we certainly have a much better view of Papua New Guinea, and are sending him a motor-bike."

Let me illustrate further from the church growth movement as it has been imported here by the Bible Society and a few others who have spent their sabbaticals in or near Pasadena. Donald McGavran, after an early career in primary evangelistic mission fields, devoted the second half of his career to writing up patterns of growth he had rightly discerned there. He and his disciples wished these onto other areas of world mission like the secularized post-Christian West and insisted that if they did not work there it was the local Christians who were at fault, not God and not the church growth hypotheses.

We have really not done our homework on evangelism in secularized society, nor do we seem to have the will to begin to do so. One hypothesis which could be deduced from church growth principles and from even our limited experience would hold that alongside an evangelistic and pastoral strategy based on the local congregation, should go a deliberate use of resources of leadership and money in sectors of life which are work- or function- or age-group-oriented ("fellowships of common interest", they have been called). This is an area we can probably get most help over from Europe or North America or Australia rather than the third world. Some of the WCC world mission studies are still relevant in this regard.

What we plead for is realism and honest assessment of need in the use of overseas personnel and insight, rather than the implementing of an abstract idea ("let's have overseas people in to help us"). Looked at close up, this is a plea for similar stewardship of *all* resources, including those locally generated.

Let me end by a local illustration. A diocese decides it will "go in for partnership in mission" by asking its overseas council to devise a plan and budget for one or two people from abroad to come here for a year. They do this in a vague response to partnership in mission, to things they have heard said in recent years in missionary circles, and in response to a certain feeling of ennui and despair over moving things forward in their area. (In part then this expresses a "Messianic hope".) At a first meeting people are told (a) of existing links with Uganda and Papua New Guinea, and of people from those parts likely to be in the UK in 1983 and 1984, (b) of the availability at once of South American Missionary Society people who cannot get back to Argentina, and (c) of possible financial help from certain sources (including the missionary societies) if a scheme has their blessing. In the discussion certain decisions are made:

a) It is the researched needs of the diocese which must be met, not someone else's view of what will be wise or possibly by way of an interchange.

b) Since one of the particular local facts of life is usually the need of church leaders to be open to thinking new thoughts arising from such an interchange, the visitor had better be someone of standing in the church they come from. This can maybe be expressed by making it an exchange, sending one of our leaders out somewhere for the same period, being careful however not to impose him on others irrelevantly to their need.

c) In the given circumstances of a particular diocese or district the real need may be for a North American, Australian or European partner. Many church people are not yet up to believing a third-world visitor could possibly help them. This we do not condone but realism demands it be said or an interchange can be an exercise in paternalism and ignoring of would-be advice and spiritual insight.

d) A married couple could well be worth more than two singles from another country.

Finally, in a first effort at facing the question, where do we need help in our evangelism here, they say:
— spirituality and commitment
— marriage enrichment and wives groups
— shared leadership encouragement and training

Yet all this is dynamite since it would undoubtedly bring to the surface all sorts of explosive questions about present patterns of ministry, Christian education and traditional attitudes. All too often a diocese (or similar church grouping) may accept a Ugandan faith-sharing team or a visiting Church of South India bishop precisely not to have to face its needs in advance or to live with the questions it will raise afterwards. I believe the missionary societies should be alive to this and not connive at it. One essential action, therefore, is the development of a proper assessment and appraisal system together for all overseas partnership visits. Upon the results of this can grow an authoritative contribution by the missionary agencies to the home churches' awareness of their true needs and basic priorities in mission and evangelism today.

March 1984

27

Some time ago, we had rare guests. Bishop K.H. Ting and Mr Han Wenzao of the China Christian Council visited Geneva for five days. The bishop preached at the regular Monday service of the Ecumenical Centre, and then went from reception to meeting to meetings. K.H. Ting was last in Geneva thirty-two years ago, serving on the staff of the World Student Christian Federation. In 1951, two years after the founding of the People's Republic, he and his wife chose to return to China. At a general staff meeting where Ting addressed us and fielded questions, Philip Potter reminded the audience that the bishop had gone through "a great deal of suffering and pain" during those three decades. Ting's is a testimony, Potter said, that "at the end of the day, God reigns".

One of the first things Ting said in public was that "we are no longer angry with 'Korea'". This was a reference to a WCC statement highly critical of China's involvement in the Korean war in the early fifties. Protesting, Dr T.C. Chao, one of the founding presidents of the WCC, resigned his position. This, together with the disappearance of denominational structures in the church, effectively rendered the participation of the churches in China in the WCC inoperative. Ting told us that this episode is over and done with.

The other message from Ting was that we, i.e. Christians and churches outside, should be much more relaxed in our relationship with the churches in China.

Many of you have heard of the growth of the churches in China. The attached paper represents an attempt on my part to understand and interpret it. I wrote this several months ago for a gathering of church people involved in China studies, and it is now slightly updated.

* * *

Evangelism in China

Since 1979 when the communist government in China normalized its religious policies, after ten years of near-total disruption during the Cultural Revolution, the Christian church has re-emerged in the shape of over 1,500 congregations in cities and towns, and house churches many many times over in the rural areas. The re-emerged church, to everyone's surprise, is found to be much bigger than before. No overall statistics of any kind are available. The leadership in the China Christian Council estimates a number of between two and three million Protestants and three million Catholics, compared with 700,000 and two million respectively before the founding of the People's Republic in 1949. These figures, given to visitors or foreign hosts, are probably conservative. The Chinese leadership has studiously avoided any hints of triumphalism in reporting about the church in China. I suspect, however, their figures are closer to the truth than the inflated figure of 15 to 20 million (Protestants) put out by some outside "experts". Among a population of 1,000 million, the number of Christians is small. The fact remains, nevertheless, that since 1979 there has been a marked swelling of the churches; and the growth, while nothing like an explosion, can be said to be truly unprecedented in the history of the Chinese church in terms of the number of conversions and the persistency of their occurrence. The process continues.

How do we understand this phenomenon? What are the reasons for the achievements in evangelism and growth?

Addressing these questions, Bishop K.H. Ting said recently: "Given a God whose supreme attribute is love, given the love for men and women as fellow children of God, and given a line of communication, evangelization happens in places where Chinese Christians live and work. We do not give much urging or stress on the 'Great Commission' as given in Matthew 28." Commenting further on the "line of communication", the Bishop reflected: "We do not think the success depends to a large extent on the identification of ourselves with the people in the experiment."*

I would like to reflect on the recent growth of the churches in China with a view to learning from their experience. Bishop Ting's reference to "identification", in my opinion, provides a key to an understanding of how evangelism is done in China today. It has a lot to do with the church getting close to the people. The following testimony from a Christian woman shows what this means in concrete. She had been working as a pastoral worker in a church.

> My only contact with those outside the church was as objects of evangelization. It seemed I always assumed a higher status. With the Cultural Revolution, I worked in a factory for eight years. This was a completely new life for me. It took more than ten of us cooperating in the workshop to complete the day's duties. I was just an ordinary worker in the collective. We worked together. We exercised, rested, studied and laughed together, and became true friends. There was a childless solitary old worker who contracted cancer. Some workers and myself requested that the factory authorities not only pay for his hospitalization, but also arrange special care for him so that he could die in peace. When one of our female colleagues was badly hurt in an auto accident, I went voluntarily to the hospital to help look after her; now she has recovered. At the factory I never kept my faith a secret. I feel that factory life helped me grasp more deeply why, at Jesus' birth, the angels announced

---

* "The Church in China", a lecture given by Bishop K.H. Ting on 14 October 1982, sponsored by the Great Britain-China Centre and the China Study Project, British Council of Churches.

the good news to shepherds tending their flock. Jesus' exhortation to "preach the gospel to the poor" has a deep significance for us. At the same time, I discovered that the workers understood me and because of this began to come into contact with the reality of Christian faith. When the churches were reopened, some people said to me: "Is it all right if we go to the church with you?" Of course they were welcomed. Similar experiences are common among Chinese Christians. *

By regarding "those outside the church... as objects of evangelism", she was referring to the emphasis, common among Chinese congregations of the time, on "mutual opposition between belief and unbelief", and the automatic assumption of moral inferiority of the unbelievers. Such an attitude resulted, among other things, in Christians "isolating themselves in the tiny world of the church".

The communist victory of 1949 opened up possibilities for change. The departure of foreign missionaries and foreign resources, the elimination of privileges, the charge of non-patriotism and the invitation to participate in national reconstruction, drove the church in China to soul-searching and confession. When the Cultural Revolution burst upon the scene, religion was regarded as one of the four old things and condemned. Christians suffered, amidst the suffering of almost everyone else, including communist cadres. But all along, the commitment to a church of self-support, self-administration and self-propagation provided glimpses of meaning and purpose. Of course, neither poverty, nor persecution, nor the three-self principle, by itself, could "tear down the wall dividing the Christians from non-believers". These conditions, however, certainly made it easier for Christians to "go among the broad masses of the people and merge with them".

In other words, Christians in China find themselves in a position where non-believers are no longer "objects of evangelization". They are simply neighbours and fellow-workers and peasants with whom normal human relationship is possible, including of course exchanging one's deepest convictions, religious or otherwise. Here religion is no determining factor. Christian witness, to use the language of China, lies in Christians "merging with the broad masses", not in stressing distinctions.

Within this very ordinary reality of daily relationships, Christians have occasions and means to proclaim Christ. The "controlled situations" for evangelism that churches in many other countries have — church

---

* From a talk on "Christian Witness in New China" by Tsao Seng-chieh, given at the CCA consultation with church leaders from China, March 1981.

schools, hospitals, orphanages, open-air rallies, youth centres, etc. — are now non-existent. Hospital visitation and weekday Bible classes on church premises are possibilities. But the most commonly available and most easily exercised means is the very act of going to church, or to a Christian home gathering. Credibility garnered by daily togetherness with people enables the Christians to say to their neighbours: "For this one hour, we must go and worship our God." To such corporate prayer and worship non-believers, the young in particular, are drawn. Here, through Bible reading, the contents of the gospel are explained, and through fellowship and singing, Jesus Christ becomes a live option. Yet even in this hour of "separation unto the Lord", Christians are not unmindful of the presence of the non-believers among them. Arrangement is made so that the latter can be physically indistinct from the body of believers during the service. For instance, in many congregations the eucharist does not take place in the regular worship. There is a separate occasion when only baptized Christians are notified. No offering is taken during the service. A collection box is placed outside the door instead. Christians are concerned to involve non-believers in worship without embarrassing them. In this spirit, all over China, Christians proclaim the gospel through the act of corporate worship.

Why do non-believers come to Christian worship? Some because they are genuinely interested. Some out of curiosity. Whatever the motive, the basic attraction of Christian worship is that it is different from whatever they have in daily life in China. In a highly uniform society, totally authoritarian, the only regular corporate life experience different from what the state can provide and yet easily accessible to people is the Christian church. More specifically, the weekly gathering of Christians for fellowship and worship. So people come. They do not come for the intellectual depth of the sermons. The sermons are generally long and moralistic, given by people deprived of biblical tools and burdened with memories. Chinese preachers would be the first to admit their own inadequacy. Liturgically, the services are neither colourful nor dramatic like, for example, those of the Orthodox tradition, which have proved so enduring in Eastern Europe. The structure does not invite corporate participation of those in the pew. There is no group reading or prayer response because there is as yet no common worship book, and only in very rare cases do congregations have printed orders of service. Neither is this a case where suffering and despair make people feel more in need of God. Before 1949, Chinese people were struggling for a survival which bordered on despair during some thirty years of widespread famine, civil war and national humiliation. Yet the churches at that time failed to grow at all.

Today, the church in China has a much stronger evangelistic impact. Its fall from a self-made religious pedestal, its closeness with ordinary people, indeed, becoming part of the "broad masses", is basic to its transformation. But while this points to the breadth and width of what Bishop K.H. Ting calls "the line of communication", and its tremendous potential advantages for evangelism in China, it does not identify the element which, more than other factors, draws non-believers to Christian corporate worship. Closeness to people is essential to evangelism, but it is not the cutting edge. Many rural congregations in China's countryside have all along been part of the village life. But closeness to people does not always result in congregational growth. In my opinion, the reason non-believers come to church contains an element of protest — not protest of an articulate, organized political nature against specific govern- ment policies, but a protest of the heart against an uncaring bureaucracy whose mighty decrees often come on people's lives unexplained and unexplainable. It is a protest of the spirit against the acceptance that people live by bread alone which, paradoxically, is not so much a Chinese communist dogma as a day-to-day reality which so corrupts human relationships. People come to church with an element of protest, trying to be a part, maybe only for an hour or two, of that which, not by design or outward action, but by its very existence, delivers a defiant message that "life must be more". What is more, the protest which people perceive in the church's very existence is a protest of the humble, the powerless. In the Christians gathered for corporate worship, non-believers see them- selves — poor and powerless. But they also see something else — hope. Here the heart is not dead. Here the spirit finds rest. Here the powerless acquire strength. Christian identification with people leads to people's identification with Christians and, with it, the faith which challenges and the strength which sustains.

Bishop Ting wrote recently:

> How strongly many Chinese Christians feared at the time of the liberation in 1949 that we were losing so many things dear to us, only to find later they were mostly just excess baggage! But it was during the Cultural Revolution, which turned out to be quite anti-cultural and not much of a revolution either, that the Chinese people suffered so much and we Christians suffered so much with them. We felt the gospel to be something precious, but the Red Guards and the so-called rebels thought of it as nothing but poisonous weed. We had no means of communicating it or of answering the attacks in the big-character

poster. Not a single church remained open. There was left no government organ to protect us from lawlessness. We had no rebel group of our own to support us, nor any bandwagon to ride on. It would be fortunate if we could just worship in a small group in a home. We were very weak indeed, a little flock. By all human reckoning Christianity, perhaps for the fourth time in Chinese history, was again breathing its last breath.

What we were blind to was that, although we were weak and dying, life was in the offing. When winter is half spent, can spring be far away? as some poet asks. Strength is found in weakness, as life in dying. As Paul put it, what you sow does not come to life unless it dies. What is sown is perishable, what is raised is unperishable; it is sown in dishonour, it is raised in glory; it is sown in weakness, it is raised in power. After having lost much, we find there are more Christians in China than ever before, and more dedicated too. Every church having been closed, we find that for three years now one or two churches are being opened or reopened every two or three days, and with much greater enthusiasm and vigour. And because we have been a part of the suffering fate of the Chinese people, we today are no longer so dissociated from them, but are in much better conversational relations with them than in the past... Thus, we seem to understand Paul when he said: "We are afflicted in every way, but not crushed; perplexed, but not driven to despair; persecuted, but not forsaken; struck down, but not destroyed; always carrying in the body the death of Jesus, so that the life of Jesus may also be manifested in our bodies", and all this by the grace of God. A grain of wheat remains a grain if it does not get into the soil and die there; but if it does, it will bear many seeds. This is reassuring and seems to have been proven.*

Perhaps no better picture demonstrates the power of powerlessness than that of a communion service in China. I was privileged to be present on several such occasions — two with several hundred and others with just a handful at homes. Mostly old people, in their sixties and seventies, dressed in dark blue and brown quilt jackets, sitting huddled, passing gingerly to each other the bread and the cup with trembling hands. Among them, a majority have not had communion for twenty years. They have been waiting. The premises have finally been handed back to the church, their pastors recalled from factories and farms. And now the Lord's supper was before them. And I saw their joy. And I wonder what earthly power can do this to people. They are the least, the totally powerless. Yet in their weakness is their strength. I believe it is in this sense that the power of the cross becomes manifest in the church in China. The seed buried in the soil dies, then rises and bears much fruit. The salt of the earth, invisible, and no less the light of the world, for all to

---

* Bishop K.H. Ting's address in Lambeth Palace Chapel, 1 October 1982.

see. This movement of the Christian church towards the people and powerlessness describes and explains evangelism in China today.

In the final analysis, I believe, it is here we find the crux of the matter, the secret to an understanding of evangelism: the power which draws people to Christ is the power of powerlessness. Such power alone is the power of the cross, the power of the Crucified and Risen Lord.

This understanding also spells out the dangers to evangelism in China. They are two: the church assuming the power of the powerful, or the church resigning itself to the powerlessness of the powerless. When the protest of the humble becomes the protest of the strong, or when there is no protest at all, then the church ceases to attract evangelistically.

First, the danger of the church succumbing to the temptation of assuming the power of the powerful. There is not only the possibility of political repression, should the state perceive Christianity once again as a threat. More fundamentally, the protest of the strong cannot any more manifest the power of powerlessness that alone approximates the power of the cross. By power, I do not refer to power in relation to the ruling authorities but power in relation to the people. Should the people perceive the church as a power, in contrast to their own powerlessness, identification will not happen. Or, very probably, it will produce a wrong kind of togetherness in order to exploit and manipulate whatever power they perceive the church to have. It takes great discernment and wisdom to keep the church moving without moving into a power in itself in the eyes of the people, and of the state. There is one factor that could push the church in China into such a position — power from outside of China. Foreign Christian groups and organizations, convinced of their obligation to evangelize China, insist on overt and/or underground activities within China. If their intention is to further the cause of the gospel in China, their action defeats the purpose. Attempts at Bible smuggling, to take an extreme but real enough case, can only associate the Christian church with black marketeers and adventurers and, to the extent that the attempt involves ex-servicemen of another country and resorts to para-military tactics, foreign aggression. Gospel radio broadcasts encourage people to write in, with offers of free colourful literature to be sent from abroad. This associates Christianity with foreign affluence and foreign power. In most cases, gospel radio broadcasting does not encourage listeners to participate in Christian meetings available to them locally, but instead offers a kind of fellowship by foreign correspondence, and makes subtle, sometimes not so subtle, insinuations against Christians worshipping in public places. Such attitudes and devices undercut the local churches and their evangelistic impact, and induce alienation of the listener from the people.

These intrusions may look innocuous to those who live in pluralistic societies, with daily exposures to outside forces. But not so to the people in China which has just recently opened its door to the West. The drive for modernization depends very much on foreign, particularly Western, partnership. These changes easily create among the people an uncritical admiration for things Western. Under these circumstances, Bible smuggling, gospel radio broadcasts controlled by an alien understanding, or activities of a similar nature, can cause much harm to the Christian church which continues to have to prove itself to be truly Chinese and to be recognized as such by the ruling powers as well as by the people.

The danger of the church in China becoming a power in itself distinct from the people does not come from foreign interference alone. There are also internal elements at work, some innate to the growth process, others distortions. The following situations illustrate some of these elements, and the way they are handled. Whether we agree or not, they show a consistent recognition that whatever the immediate advantages, the faithfulness of the church and its evangelistic effectiveness in the long run rests on being part of the people, and studiously remaining so.

"What do we do with the Sunday collection?" became a major question confronting a congregation immediately public services began to be held. Not that the Christians did not have plenty of use for the RMB$124.37 left in the collection box after the two morning services. Money was needed for repair of the premises. The piano needed a major overhaul. There were a thousand and one other needs.* The problem is long-term. What does a weekly availability of RMB$124.37, equivalent to a person's two-month salary and to be used for one corporate purpose — what does it do to the church in the eyes of the community, bearing in mind that in China, apart from the state, there is no other corporate entity which collects money regularly and exercises it collectively? The consensus in this instance is a pastoral reminder that the use of church money must be a witness to Christian humility before God and before people.

During the last three years, there was extensive flooding in central and southwest China, causing serious damages to crops and homes. In

---

* Today, in general, the money offerings of congregations in China go to repair and maintenance of the premises and the daily operation of the church, plus, sometimes, support of selected people to attend seminary or short-term (2-3 months) pastoral training courses. Church workers' salaries and pension payment have to come from income generated by church properties. This often imposes a heavy financial burden on the church.

neighbouring areas where municipal authorities mobilized people to help with labour and relief, the congregations responded with enthusiasm, and acted as local churches. A newspaper reported on the amount of money, clothing and food coupons contributed by one congregation. Where municipal or other levels of authority did not take the initiative, however, there has been no report of involvement by Christians as a church. Such an attitude, applied more broadly, might serve as an explanation as to why the China Christian Council turned down an ecumenical request to channel through it international relief funds for emergency use in China, and as to the readiness of Chinese secular bodies to accept such funds. It is apparent that the present leadership of the church in China is keenly aware of the need not to emphasize a Christian corporate distinctiveness other than what is inherent in the faith. Similar concern is shown in the effort to reclaim church premises for their original use. Given the present policy of religious normalization that gives legitimacy to these claims, the church has been cautious in pressing its demands. The attitude of the local authorities has to be assessed, and alternative housing found and compensation given for present occupants many of whom have been living there for years. In every case, the well-being of the people affected and that of the community is a serious factor in the church's consideration. As it is, the speed of recovering church property to house new congregations has been uneven and, in some instances, a source of tension among Christians. Some urge full speed ahead, giving only secondary consideration to the feelings of the people. Others opt for caution, trying to bring all the parties along, minimizing disruption and preserving good will. It is never an easy task for those in leadership positions: how to meet the needs of Christians long deprived of the experience of public worship, and the needs of the people for housing, how to press officials of the local religious affairs bureau* to do their job, and yet not be seen as part and parcel of a government bureaucracy which, in the China of today, is not universally admired.

In a few extreme cases in recent years, Christian groups, having had a taste of religious freedom, and stimulated by a strong desire to spread the gospel, sought physical confrontation with the neighbourhood mosques and publicly denounced the Islamic faith. Such action is reminiscent of

---

* The religious affairs bureau is a part of the ministry of state, in charge of implementing China's religious policies. In the case of repossessing church property, it is the government apparatus that the church works with.

the old days when Christian evangelists routinely engaged in open-air evangelism right in front of Buddhist temples. There are instances, too, of intra-Christian confrontation. In an incident in 1982, a group of followers of Witness Lee, of the Little Flock tradition, physically disrupted a special evangelistic service on theological grounds. The peasant Christians put up a fight. The police were called in and the intruders evicted. The meeting was called off. The local newspaper commented: "Red Guard Tactics by Christian Believers!" These are admittedly exceptional cases. But they illustrate the danger inherent in the process of church growth in China today, the danger of the church no longer being content with demonstrating the power of the powerless but trying to exert the power of the powerful. Despite its obviously minority position, religious fanaticism does carry the power of the powerful, with aggressive attitudes and combative behaviour. Fully aware of the new-gained right to religious freedom, absolutely convinced that they have truth on their side, hardened by years of suffering and persecution, a small community of Christians may become so intolerant and resort to the power of self-righteousness.

Similar tension, much broader in scope and more serious in import, has to do with the provision of Bibles. Here the tension is between the church leadership who naturally takes a long-term view, generally inclining to a more conservative approach, and grassroot Christians who have thirsted for Bibles and Christian literature for years and want them immediately, no matter what and where they come from. The leadership is keenly aware of the fact that every single copy of the Chinese Bible hitherto printed in the mainland has been subsidized by Western funds. They feel nervous about the probability of the Bible becoming the most visible book in villages and towns, next to official communist publications, that is. This, in a land where disgruntled parents can even now make a big fuss about the conversion of their sons and daughters to the Christian faith, and where Christianity remains a ready excuse for almost any political faction to start a power struggle, especially if the Bibles are found to have been printed in Hong Kong, Manila, Los Angeles or Amsterdam. Hence the leadership's fierce rejection of large-scale Bible provision from outside. These considerations may or may not be apparent to the Christian individuals at the grassroots level. Even if they are apparent, one may excuse the Christians for not taking them as seriously as they should. Who dares stand in the way of a Christian thirsting for the word of God? Thus, much grassroot pressure has been put on the leadership for large-scale Bible printing inside China, making it the topmost priority on the agenda of the China Christian Council. In 1982, over one million copies were made available. They are, together with the lot printed in 1980, the first Chinese Bibles entirely produced and funded with Chinese resources. The supply of Bibles still lags behind demand by both Christians and non-Christians. But it is catching up fast, and compared with Bible printing in Eastern Europe it is going at a truly extraordinary speed.

It is never easy to suggest solutions. It is downright presumptuous to try to do so from the outside. The job is best left to the Christians in China as they seek to share and examine one another's perspectives and assessments of where and how the church ought to move. In the important task of getting the Bible to Christians and others, a happy means has been found which takes into account the immediate needs of Christians as well the long-term interests of the Christian church. There is a clear recognition that the key lies in watchful vigilance, that the church, in all that it is and does, does not alienate itself from the people, that the Christian church as it grows remains part and parcel of the "broad masses". Such awareness, it seems to me, is the most pervasive reason for optimism for the future of the church in China.

The temptation for the church to turn away from demonstrating the power of the powerless and to exert the power of the powerful is strong. The other danger is that the church becomes complacent in its powerlessness, resigns itself to it, and loses the element of protest in its life. That will mean the loss of hope as well. There is no more reason for people to identify with the church and all that it stands for. At this point, Christian worship becomes escapism, and no longer the means of evangelism that transforms lives. A state of powerlessness, without power, does not evangelize. It alienates powerless people who long for power for the nurture of their heart and the sustenance of their spirit. In concrete terms, this refers particularly to church-state relationship. It refers to whether the powerlessness of the Christian church is a reality of dependency on the state, or a different reality which finds its dependency on God. A church dependent on the state reflects either the powerlessness of the powerless, or the power of the powerful. Neither places the church among the people. Neither evangelizes.

The leadership of the church in China is fiercely jealous of its commitment to keeping the church close to the people, resisting all the forces, ouside and inside, that intentionally or unintentionally attempt to steer it off course. Both the testament of the scriptures and the experience of the Chinese people prompt them towards a journey which rejects the power of the powerful and the powerlessness of the powerless, opting for one which embraces the power of powerlessness. So far, I believe they have succeeded to a very large extent. And many, for the first time, have joined in the journey.

I still remember the sermon preached by Pastor Shen Yi Feng of the Shanghai Community church, at the Chinese Christians' first international meeting in Montreal in 1982. He was reflecting on the priestly function of the church. As a priest, he pointed out, the church mediates between people and God. From the perspective of people, the church represents God. Therefore it is essential that the church seek and manifest God's will. God's will for eternity. And God's will for now. From God's perspective, on the other hand, the church represents the people. Therefore, the church must be with the people, stand with them, touch their pulse and share their dreams. It is never easy to determine when to be silent and when to shout out loud, when to build and when to destroy, when to mourn and when to dance, when to be strong and when to be weak. But if the church is indeed close to the people, living among them and sharing their dreams, then there is a better chance. The people's state of mind is in constant flux. The borderline between what is possible and what is not keeps changing. There are nuances to the people's understanding of their own sense of powerlessness, and their readiness to act. The process of identification and discernment does not stop. The church in China is embarking precisely on this kind of journey: inviting people, embodying and transforming their aspirations.

I look forward to the day when the church speaks and, powerless as it is, tells not only the stories of Christians, but speaks no less the voice and the hopes of the Chinese people. That would be power indeed, the power of powerlessness, the power of the crucified and risen Christ.

January 1984

Chapter 6

Debate with Donald McGavran

28

This is an invitation to you to participate in a global reflection on world evangelization.

The article that follows came to us from Dr Donald McGavran, Dean Emeritus of the School of World Mission, Fuller Theological Seminary in California. McGavran is, of course, known to many of us as the pioneer, exponent and advocate of what has come to be known as the church growth movement which has considerable impact on the Protestant churches in North America as well as in parts of Western Europe and the third world.

At stake are important missiological issues of a theoretical nature, such as the concept of the "unreached peoples" and the assumptions underlying the preference for the independent mission society over the "church". I am interested in Dr McGavran's "Giant Step in Christian mission" because the proposal is concrete, and therefore capable of stimulating concrete responses. World mission is not carried out in a WCC office in Geneva, or in Fuller's Pasadena campus. It is done locally, at a particular place in a particular time, involving particular persons. So I invite you to respond, from where you are, conceptually and concretely, with clarity and passion, and soon.

Our plan is this: your written responses will be carried in the next few issues of the monthly letter on evangelism. Then McGavran and I will each write a summary statement. And then what? The prayer that our "fanaticism" may be "tempered"? Rather, that it may be "nurtured" by truth as we learn from each other for the sake of the kingdom.

* * *

A Giant Step in Christian mission

(Ralph D. Winter, general director of the US Center for World Mission, observes: "This is a stirring proposal which I believe we must consider immediately and take seriously. It is written by an elderly man who by many is considered the foremost mission strategist in the world today. It is in effect a timely 'renewal manifesto' for this moment of history. All other renewal efforts must be built on the act of faith involved in putting other nations before our own salvation. Indeed, failing such a test of faith is probably the principal reason for God's judgment upon a Christian tradition.")

Christian mission, world evangelization, must take a new and significant step if God's will is to be done. We rejoice in past achievements — hundreds of missionary societies, thousands of young denominations (churches), the church firmly established in almost every nation-state, the Bible or parts of it available in more than 2,000 languages, new missionary societies arising in the non-Western lands, more than a billion souls who consider themselves Christian, and on and on. We praise God for all the great victories of the cross.

But we also note that world evangelization is very far from completing the task the eternal God commanded (Rom. 16:25f.). Three billion (soon to be four billion) have yet to believe in Jesus Christ or to hear of him. More specifically, half of the world's population is almost totally isolated from the gospel in "Unreached Peoples". Young churches (now in every land!) are often small and weak, engaged primarily in nurturing and managing themselves. In many segments of society and in some whole lands less than one in a hundred is Christian. Often it is one in a thousand. If the church is there, it has very little power. Often 95 percent of all church members are tribesmen or come from oppressed and depressed classes of society. Thousands of whole peoples (ethne or segments of society) believe intensely that "if any of us" becomes Christian, he leaves "us" and joins "them".

Some missiologists place the number of Unreached Peoples at 17,000. This is a surprisingly small number in view of the great potential of evangelical resources. But it is still huge, and is quite out of proportion to our present level of mobilization. (What shall we say to the fact that American evangelicals may spend more on pet food than on missions?)

The Center for World Mission in Pasadena, Fuller's School of World Mission, World Vision's MARC and other organizations have done valiant work in calling on Christians to reach the Unreached Peoples (plural). A new conscience on the huge undone task of world mission is already in the process of being aroused. This is good. But now in 1985 unless a giant new step forward is taken, all this may turn out to be mere words! Thousands of ambassadors and millions of dollars must very soon be devoted to the *tens of thousands of unreached segments of mankind*. It is not enough to call attention to the three billion who have yet to believe. Existing missionary societies — or *new missionary societies* — must very soon place well trained, well-equipped, lifetime task forces in *the thousands of remaining unreached peoples*. Today this can be both parallel to, and in partnership with, other churches and other societies, new and old, all around the globe. It is a huge but feasible task.

The Frontier Fellowship, now with 36 organizations collaborating, has launched a campaign to raise up a million American Christians who will use the *Global Prayer Digest*, pray and give loose change daily for the evangelization of one or more of the Unreached People groups (ethne or segments of society.) This is a good first step. *I am now proposing a Giant additional Step — that in every congregation in North America practising Christians organize themselves into frontier missionary societies, men's missionary societies, women's missionary societies, youth missionary societies.*

Let the Holy Spirit lead groups of earnest Christians to meet regularly to study one or more of the very numerous unreached pieces of the mosaic of mankind, and to give and pray to the end that within each group to be reached a beachhead of saving faith might be established. Let all monies raised by these local groups be given solely to frontier mission enterprises — through existing missionary organizations which promise to spend the money exclusively on new evangelistic efforts among unreached ethne, or through new organizations specifically founded to evangelize the Unreached People groups — those that are clearly out *beyond* the actual reach of any congregation or denomination or mission agency in any of the six continents.

All such new local missionary societies will focus on the unfinished task of world evangelization! These new, local societies will pray for the effective evangelization of specific unreached segments of society. They will give their sons and daughters to be lifetime missionaries to the millions dying in the greatest famine of the word of God ever to be seen. These new fellowships will send millions of dollars to establish effective, well-organized evangelizing forces to feed the lost and spiritually starving multitudes.

The word "unreached" must not lead us astray. An "unreached" ethnos or segment of society is not one in which individuals who are

Christ's followers are perceived by their fellows to have "*left their own people and traitorously gone off to join another people*". Putting it positively, a people is to be considered reached when its members who become Christians are perceived by their fellows as "still our people who are pointing the way to what they believe would be a good path for us all to follow". In Guatemala in 1985, when one asks a person: "Are you an evangelical?" he frequently hears the answer: "Not yet". This is proof that many segments of society in that nation are now effectively "reached" — i.e., they believe that while linguistically or ethnically they will remain themselves (Indians or mestizos), they probably ought to become obedient followers of the Lord Jesus Christ. Guatemala is a nation in which God is bringing great church growth. The evangelical churches there are working and praying that by 1990 half the entire population will be Bible-believing, Bible-obeying Christians.

Unless here in America literally *thousands* of new frontier missionary societies are founded, in thousands of local churches in most churches (denominations), the "Unreached Peoples" will not be reached. Let us boldly face that unpleasant fact. Existing promotional schemes are naturally tied to existing mission structures. These are sometimes philanthropic, sometimes educational, sometimes evangelistic. They are most frequently controlled by already established churches/denominations in Asia, Africa, Latin America or Europe. They do not intend to "reach the unreached". They intend to help younger churches.

Certainly some mission resources ought to be sent to help young churches. This is obvious. But all mission resources ought not to be dedicated to that end. Most mission resources — ambassadors and money — should now be spent working directly or indirectly to multiply sound churches among the two and a half billion lost men and women *who are presently locked out of and locked away from any personal witness within their group*.

Thus, here in America, in order to do our fair share of this global task, we must soon found thousands of new groups of Christians dedicated to multiplying congregations of biblical Christians in every unreached ethnos in the world. Unless this Giant Step is taken, all those earnest Christians scattered out across this country who would want to work for, pray for and give to the evangelization of the unreached will remain essentially unhopeful, if not hopeless, and will simply continue to give modestly to existing mission efforts.

We must act on our belief that there are at least one million individuals who would pray for and give to frontier missions, and we must encourage them to organize themselves into local missionary societies single-mindedly devoted to finding, fostering and founding new outreach to unchurched segments of humanity. The task is urgent and enormous. Today in early 1985 more than three billion are still closed off in unreached groups. They have yet to believe in Christ. They are lost sheep. The Great Shepherd wants them found.

As thousands of such local missionary societies are formed, each one will want to make sure that its God-given purpose is carried out. Each must not stop giving to existing efforts, yet must be allowed to add strength to those efforts designed exclusively to reach the unreached, to disciple a heretofore undiscipled people group. The Frontier Fellowship has followed the lead of Asian Christians who set aside a handful of rice at each meal specifically for missions. Their daily "loose change" giving, with this specific purpose, does not threaten any existing budget. Yet, one group with a goal of 10,000 participating estimates the loose change offerings brought in monthly will amount to $1 million per year of new money. Amounts in the hundreds of thousands of dollars are already coming in. One million people daily dedicating loose change will generate $100 million per year specifically for new frontiers!

In a given local congregation, the members of such a band of ardent frontier-minded men and women will gather daily in their families around this challenge, weekly at church with this vision highlighted wherever possible, and monthly in their own special meeting for study, prayer, praise and giving, all focused on some part of the unevangelized thousands of millions. The members of the band must be acutely conscious that they are doing a task for each unreached group which to date no one has ever done. It is a new task. The Holy Spirit is sending them, as He sent Philip to Samaria and Paul to Rome, as true pioneers.

These groups must number in the thousands even in 1985, but as the vision spreads there will be tens of thousands of them. Some denominations (churches) will themselves recognize, welcome and organize such groups. They will see that this is the best way to regain true missionary purpose. Other denominations will grudgingly recognize frontier groups, saying in effect: "Yours is not a good idea, but if you insist, we will see that your gifts go exclusively to evangelize the unreached." Still other denominational headquarters, we fear, may say bluntly: "Give through our unified budget. We will use the money as we see fit. We know the situations so much better than you do. God bless you."

Some local groups will hear of some new missionary venture to some unreached segment of society, evaluate how effective it is, and give to it through some denominational, interdenominational or faith mission which is clearly maintaining frontier mission among Unreached Peoples. Please recall the careful definition of the word "unreached" given a few paragraphs earlier.

In the spreading of this new realistic vision of devoting ourselves heart and soul to evangelizing the multitudinous peoples of earth, we shall see an enormous surge of Christian activity. The time is ripe. God is now pointing his finger at the most responsive world believing Christians have ever contemplated.

The DAWN movement is fast spreading. It believes that many regions and, in at least twenty cases, whole nations can now be discipled. That is the meaning of the acronym DAWN — Discipling A Whole Nation.

Africa south of the Sahara will soon be as Christian as North America. The Holy Spirit leads us to ripe harvest fields. He also calls us to many which have yet to be sown. The great day of Christian mission (in which Christians of all six continents will spend themselves) is dawning. We can at least set a good example for other concentrations of believers to follow.

Even in the lands where the gospel has long been present, the true power of the gospel is not wanting. After 67 years of suffering, the church in the Soviet Union is probably spiritually and perhaps even numerically stronger than ever. Certainly in China, despite 34 years of suffering, the Christian movement is unimaginably larger and stronger.

Now is the time to move forward. Let us "furiously" organize frontier missionary societies in every congregation of every denomination in North America. And other nations will follow.

An aroused Christian conscience on the world level is all it will take for the peoples and nations that are already "blessed" to fulfill the biblical mandate "to be a blessing to all the peoples of the earth" (Gen. 12:2,3).

August 1985

29

RESPONSES TO McGAVRAN

From S. Arles, India: theological teacher

I respond as an ecumenical, evangelical, third-world Christian concerned for genuine evangelization of our world. The adjectives I use are justifiable by the fact that I am a member of the "ecumenical" Church of

South India; teaching at the interdenominational and "evangelical" South India Biblical Seminary; and am Indian by nationality.

Basically I agree with and commend Dr McGavran for his simple and straightforward proposal. Of particular value are his calls to:

1) *Freedom in structuring our missionary concern*: This has been the cry of the younger churches of the third world. The "mushrooming of the indigenous missions in India" and the "proliferation of Independent churches in Africa" are but a few outbursts of this cry.

2) *"Life-time missionaries"*: Genuine missionary involvement must be incarnational, leading up to the cross. Mission as "from here to there", with a perpetual "detached involvement", is something less than the ideal.

3) *"Furiously" organize for frontier missions*: Devoid of this sort of a passionate activism, the church shall fall prey to redundant churchianity and cobwebby theologies.

4) *"Giant Step in Christian mission"*: This is in keeping with "American style". Going big would never be a luxury in world mission, as long as there are those millions needing to be reached! While affirming the value of these calls, I should sound the following three notes of caution:

First, should such furious organizing for frontier missions employ only Americans to go as missionaries? McGavran affirms: "American evangelicals may spend more on pet food than on missions." We could further ask: What about the air travel and hotel bills, "homeland staff", promotional literature, latest models of office equipment and all the extravaganza that accompany missions? Do not large percentages of the funds get short-circuited within the USA? As far as India is concerned, funds spent to send one American missionary to work with the unreached could sufficiently employ anywhere between three highly-placed leaders to twenty ordinary Indian workers at the present salary structures.

The questions are: Are American Christians capable of shaking off their cultural conditioning, in order to live a simpler life, incarnating into the actual context of the people they wish to "reach"? Can our strategizing give primacy to the employing of third-world Christians, indigenous missions and workers, as they are culturally closer to the unreached people — thus affirming that we mean it when we say "we are one family around the world"?

Secondly, "a shallow gospel" would not be "good news". If many committed Christians leave America to reach the unreached, but always keep referring to "back home in the USA" — fly home every three or four years with more pictures, curios and pep-talks — retire while yet strong and let younger recruits repeat "experimental missions all over again", what effect would it leave on people? The need in mission is to establish "good news" in such a way that the captives are set free; the blind are led to see; and the poor are offered the good news in tangibly understandable terms.

A limited understanding of the gospel leads to a stunted church which loses sight of its prophetic call and accepts all kinds of evils and injustices as beyond its missionary concern. Do South African black people feel free under a regime which is financially supported by investments of the US and other rich governments? If the strategy of the Giant Step stops short of an all-out concern and prophetic action to improve the lot of the Unreached People (who also happen to be the hungry, poor, exploited and oppressed of the world), and if it fails to face squarely the issues of socio-economic justice for all, what use would it be to take such a giant step? Herein, both the "content of the gospel" and the expected "results on a people" when they get reached should be clearly defined.

Thirdly, McGavran notes, "often 95 percent of all church members are tribesmen or come from oppressed and depressed classes of society" and the young churches are "often small and weak" with "very little power". This should naturally raise the question: if the church which has tasted the liberating good news is powerless, underdeveloped and un-attractive, why would non-Christians wish to become Christian?

Primarily the younger churches ought to nurture and manage them-selves, if they are to qualify to engage in credible evangelism. Until and unless they speak a better testimony to the power of the gospel to liberate and to better their lot, the proposed "exclusively new evangelistic work" may prove of no avail.

When a land-owning Takur is personally acquainted with the plight of the third generation Harijan Christians as "landless labourers in perpetual misery", it is hard to expect that he would become convinced of the gospel by an "American missionary" who comes to preach to him.

Let me conclude my response with a few suggestions. If the proposal for a Giant Step is heeded and if US Christians form numerous mission societies, then:

1. American personnel should be kept in low profile in the evangeliza-tion of the non-Western world.
2. Third-world Christians of simple life-style should be employed to reach the unreached.

3. US Christians should engage in evangelizing US and other Western Unreached People — they still would have ample to do.

4. Third-world Christians should be trained within their cultural setting and helped to preserve their simplicity and culture uncorrupted.

5. There should be a sincere effort to avoid the tendency to bring third-world Christians to the US or West, mesmerizing them with the glamours of technocratic computerism, gluttonous sophistication and theological nostalgia; deculturizing and turning them into agents of a Western denomination or agency, rather than "agents of the gospel alone".

6. US Christians who feel the call of God to serve in cross-cultural missions should be sent to do their theological studies and mission-ary training courses in third-world theological institutions, in order that they begin theologically to find a rationale and practically to find models for incarnational identity with the people they try to reach.

7. What sort of church would be expected to emerge among the Unreached Peoples, when the Giant Step is taken? Would they be following in the denominational footprints of the missionary? Free-dom should be ensured for the new churches to emerge as God would lead them.

I recognize that the proposal is made to US Christians, with the hope that others would follow the model. I should hope so.

From Robert D. Lupton, USA: Presbyterian lay evangelist who divides his time between his congregation and a family counselling service in inner-city Atlanta

I have an uneasiness within as I read Dr McGavran's article. Part of me wants to leap aboard his challenge and get excited about a new surge towards world evangelization. After all, I am an evangelical, Bible-believing Christian, committed to personal regeneration through Jesus Christ. But something down inside restrains me. Perhaps my hesitation has to do with my gifts being more suited for nurture and social action than for evangelism. Even so, I should certainly share Dr McGavran's excitement about a new evangelism movement, shouldn't I?

I suppose it is where the challenge originates that bothers me. I refer not to McGavran personally, but to the affluent Western evangelical church of which both he and I are a part. I have found it hard to get excited about the church growth movement in the United States since it seems to me largely a means of replicating an apostate church. We have baptized the values of our culture and so thoroughly incorporated them into our Christianity that we can hardly differentiate between the kingdom of God and the American dream. The radical teachings of the one we call Lord have been neutralized into religious rhetoric and have little impact on our relationships or life-style. Somehow the thought of the Western church taking the leadership in spreading the kind of gospel we practise seems more like an obstruction to the kingdom than a giant step forward. Repentance for our haughtiness and greed, for our refusal to touch our naked, hungry, sick and imprisoned Lord seems to me to be a more authentic spiritual response.

To be really honest, I must admit that I am ashamed of the gospel — not ashamed of my Lord, but of the American version of the gospel that has become mis-shapen by the rationalizations of the powerful and contaminated by the values of the wealthy. The gospel of prosperity embarrasses me in the city among the poor with whom I serve. It becomes downright obscene when I consider it against the immense poverty and pain of the third world.

Perhaps God will use McGavran to start a great movement that will expose the evangelical church to a suffering world and thereby reintroduce us to the Lord from whom we have hidden our faces. This Giant Step in mission of which he speaks may result in the evangelization of us.

From J.A. McIntosh, Australia: principal, Federal Training College, Church Missionary Society of Australia

"Stirring" and "inspiring" are the first words that came into my mind. Let not scruples as to whether McGavran is precisely right in his definition of unreached ethne put us off. The groups he has in mind are at least *included* amongst *panta ta ethne* (all the nations) that Jesus had in mind (Matt. 28:18-20). And it is right to focus attention on such groups, so many of whom are open to the gospel. What excuse can we have for neglecting them?

I was immediately reminded of the Scottish *Memorial* (1746) and Jonathan Edwards' *Humble Attempt* (1747) "to promote… extraordinary *prayer for*… the advancement of Christ's kingdom on earth…" These motivated Carey and others to form those missionary societies which have done so much to spread the gospel beyond the confines of Western Christendom. So many of the churches in the two-thirds world were planted by those (mostly) independent societies that *focused* their prayers and gifts and selves on Unreached Peoples. Such societies include my own, the Church Missionary Society.

Let us not balk at the independent mission society concept. The great Roman Catholic missionary orders had a considerable degree of autonomy, but faithfully planted (Roman) churches. How much would have been done if left to the pope and diocesan bishops preoccupied with pastoral care and administration? Theologically speaking there can be no objection to motivated Christians in local congregations gathering to pray for a specific end and giving specifically for that. The Giant Additional Step of organizing autonomous frontier missionary societies is certainly unobjectionable if organized in connection with particular denominations, or independently for independent congregations, at the very least!

In any case, does not Christian liberty allow for such flexibility? Are not all believers priests? Is it appropriate for a group of Christians to send a burden to pray for, give to, and/or serve a particular frontier? Surely yes! Are para-church organizations in principle unbiblical and untheological? Surely not! McGavran's proposal does not threaten existing mission structures, but opens up the way for the necessary new ones. It will also stimulate existing ones to move into Unreached People groups as yet untouched by them.

The Scottish *Memorial* and Edwards' *Humble Attempt* were general and broad in their aim as suited the situation then. Two hundred and forty years later there is some manifestation of the Christian church in almost every country of the world. But anthropological and sociological insights have shown us other boundaries, just as tightly sealed as national ones. Specific cross-cultural efforts are required to cross them. McGavran's proposed Giant Step is appropriately specific. Yet it is also capable of great flexibility. It can be adapted to most ecclesiastical situations.

Edwards' *Humble Attempt* took 46 years before it bore fruit in Carey's departure for India. But today there are already those who have initiated the concept behind McGavran's Giant Step (1984) proposal. This we ought also to do without leaving undone what existing mission structures are already doing. The openings and the responsiveness are there. This is surely God's providential leading. Let us follow it!

From Ms C.H. Wu, People's Republic of China

I am impressed by Dr McGavran's missionary enthusiasm but have doubts about the "strategy" of the Giant Step.

1. The writer, in spite of his call for a "careful definition" of the word "unreached", has himself not given a careful, clear and consistent definition of the word, and this will cause confusion and conflict as Christians begin to reach lands, groups and "segments of society" they

consider to be still "unreached", that is, by them and by their brands of the gospel. The presence of the church in a land is to him no mark of reachedness. Thus, while granting the existence of younger churches "now in every land", he nevertheless asserts that the "Unreached Peoples" of the world have in them "half the world's population" and, in another part of the paper, even "more than three billion today in early 1985". The last caricature is specially unfortunate and disrespectful. Many younger churches are certainly not existing for themselves and are, in their weakness and powerlessness, reaching the unreached around them, and with much success too. The writer calls for the founding in America of "thousands of new groups of Christians dedicated to multiplying congregations of biblical Christians" in all these and other lands, and pouring in "$100 million per year specifically for new frontiers". What interchurch divisiveness, chaos and feud this would bring, perhaps largely in the name of being biblical! New Testament and church history alike teach us that by virtue of natural cultural identity Christians native to the land should have the primary responsibility for reaching the rest of their people.

2. I agree we have good reason to "rejoice" in past missionary achievements, but I am loathe to limit myself only to rejoicing and "praising God for all the great victories of the cross". I expected a missiologist reflecting on mission history at least to be conscious of its unconscious association with Western colonial expansion and to sound a note not of triumphalism but of humility and openness to criticism. Blindness or silence on this crucial point invites doubts as to whether the strategy advocated for the present is not going to repeat past mistakes.

3. The writer notes that in certain lands a convert to Christian faith is regarded by fellow-citizens as a person who has gone off to join another people. I assume he would then understand the Chinese Christians' self-reproach upon hearing the common saying in pre-liberation China: "One more Christian, one less Chinese", and be sympathetic with our aspiration to make the church in China Chinese so as to keep open the line of communication with our own people. What surprises me is that he says nothing to advocate the building up of a national selfhood for the churches of these lands, but rather the taking of a Giant Step in pouring in more missionary personnel and funds from abroad. Does he know or care that, as history has shown, such a step would win "rice Christians", crush local initiative, foster parasitism and actually alienate the Christians from their people and nation? The whole approach smacks of the overpowering domination of the strong of another century.

4. Not unexpectedly China has to come in before the end of the paper for some attack. It is a bit alarming that one of the foremost mission strategists in the world today can permit himself to be so indiscriminating as to say "thirty-four years of suffering" and act as if he knows nothing about the freedom Christians do enjoy in China. And does he care to know that the churches in China have been reaching the unreached in the last 35 years and are "larger and stronger" today not through the "loose change given daily" by rich Americans, but through the earnest prayers and the untiring work of evangelism by words and by deeds on the part of Chinese Christians in all our weakness and powerlessness, yet very much in the power of God?

September 1985

30

RESPONSES TO McGAVRAN — CONTINUED

From Guillermo Cook: Latin American Evangelical Centre for Pastoral Studies (CELEP)

The reality of the Unreached Peoples and of their need to both hear and existentially experience the transforming gospel of Jesus Christ is a fact that no Christian can overlook. That they should become again a priority of mission after long being overlooked should not be disputed. My problem — as I reflect upon this from the Latin American context of poverty and oppression in which I work — has to do rather with some of the presuppositions that underlie the "Giant Step" that is being proposed by my venerable and much-respected ex-professor.

The perception from which this challenge is being made to us comes from one, like me, who is "at the top", so to speak, and not from "the underside of history". In his very first paragraph, Dr McGavran takes for granted that the task of mission has been and, seemingly, will continue to be the task of mission societies, young churches and old denominations, i.e., the institutional churches — each of which, in their own context, holds the reins of power in its hands. He assumes, further, that the solution can be found primarily in the multiplication of the US local church-related mission societies. While he does take passing note of the phenomenon of "third-world" missions (he seems to be unaware of large non-Protestant "people's movements", such as the Catholic base communities), his main emphasis is upon the decisive role of the

Protestant church in the most powerful nation in the "first world" — apparently because of the abundance of its financial and human resources.

In line with this McGavran fails to perceive that the primary social juxtaposition today (without which the theological juxtaposition of "reached" and "unreached" cannot be fully understood) is that of power and powerlessness. In actual fact, a "weak" church, socio-politically speaking, can be a powerful communicator of the gospel, precisely because of its weakness. Powerful ecclesiastical institutions, wherever in the world they are found, are usually the least equipped to communicate the gospel across theological, cultural and ideological boundaries — particularly if they are perceived as tools of powerful socio-economic interests. More often than not, as church growth studies have shown, it has been precisely where the "first-world" missionary presence has been less pronounced (for any number of reasons) that tribal and oppressed peoples everywhere have turned to Jesus Christ in large numbers. This is precisely the inference that one should draw from the closing reference to church growth in China and the Soviet Union.

Leaving aside questions that might be asked concerning the implications of an evangelism which might be perceived as focusing too narrowly upon existing race, class and caste divisions, there remain ideological questions regarding our own evangelistic motivation. Should not concern for those who die without a knowledge of Jesus encompass a deep anguish for those "unreached" peoples who are killed by brutal regimes of the right and the left? What are the reasons for peoples' responses? Why do people in Guatemala respond "not yet" to the question "are you an evangelical"? If they indeed eventually would like to be, this is in part because Protestantism is now being perceived as the religion of prestige if not of power, by a growing number of middle-class people. But interestingly, the same question is at times addressed by units in the Guatemalan army to tribal people (both Catholic and Protestant) as a way of discovering their presumed political ideology — with torture and death in numerous cases as the end result. At the grassroots of Guatemalan society (where most of the nation's vaunted Protestant growth is taking place) centuries of passivity and subservience have given way to creative resistance, such is the transforming power of the gospel. This is seen by the powerful (both churches and state) as subversive. At least ten Protestant pastors (not to mention many more Catholic leaders) have given their lives for the gospel. The blood of the martyrs is, indeed, the seed of the church.

In the words of Jim Wallis (*The Call to Conversion*): "The greatest need in our time is not simply kerygma, the preaching of the gospel; nor diakonia, service on behalf of justice; nor charisma, the experience of the Spirit's gifts; nor propheteia, the challenging of the king. The greatest need of our time is for koinonia. The call simply to be the church, to love one another and to open our lives for the sake of the world." Lest this be dismissed as so much romantic nonsense (a "watered-down gospel"), we should understand that New Testament koinonia is neither the empty culture-related "fellowship" of so many in the "first world", nor the inbred sectarianism of a fundamentalist Christianity. It is a unity that flows around the supreme authority of Jesus Christ in concentric circles which begin with local fellowships of believers (including "frontier mission societies" of the right sort!). But this community also encompasses our sisters and brothers of many confessions around the world (united in their common powerlessness). It reaches out in a very special way to those who have never heard the good news (united by our common sinfulness), particularly the poor, oppressed and marginalized. To these, God may have, in fact, begun to speak long before the Christian messenger arrives with the living word. This kind of perspective could help us to see ourselves ("frontier missionaries") potentially as "part of the problem" as well as of the solution. It raises the question of why there are, in fact, so many peoples at this late date in history who have not heard the gospel. Without in any way discounting the urgent need to channel the good news to them, could not the wrong kind of "frontier mission societies" make the problem more acute?

From Louise Tappa and Mosi Kisare: senior staff members of the Nairobi-based All Africa Conference of Churches

We read Dr McGavran's "A Giant Step in Christian Mission" with much interest and totally agree with him that this is a crucial time for the church of Christ to rethink its mission. However, we wish to disagree strongly with a statement which may seem unimportant in the article but which is for us indicative of the overall spirit of Dr McGavran's proposal: "Africa South of the Sahara will soon be as Christian as North America". To this we would like to propose an emphatic no! Africa cannot be as Christian as North America. We do not believe that North America can be considered as the standard for Christianity. This, of course, raises a number of key questions: What is truly Christian? Who is to spread it? The article proposes that every congregation in North America set up a missionary society with the view of bringing Christ to the "unreached peoples". Who are these unreached peoples? Where can they be found? Not within North America, it would seem. They are to be found in Africa, Asia, Latin America, and Europe. The spirit of McGavran's article suggests that North America is the centre of Christianity. We are amazed at the ease with which he by-passes what he calls young churches. They are weak, he says, therefore the churches in North America should do their job for them.

The young churches' weakness lies in the fact that they are caught up in structures that are alien and alienating to their people; structures that came about as a result of missionary irresponsibility and arrogance not unlike what is now being proposed. This is indeed a timely discussion, for at a time when it is becoming more and more obvious that missionaries and mission societies are irrelevant to Africa, someone has the audacity to propose that more of these be sent and founded. The motivation for such a move probably lies somewhere else than in Christianity *per se*. With the expressions such as "biblical Christians", "Bible-believing and Bible-obeying Christians", McGavran makes it clear that it is not Christ and his good news to the poor that is to be proclaimed but rather a culture. A culture which is bolstered by a religious movement that has little to do with the crucified and risen Jesus Christ but uses the Bible to colonize the minds of the people all over the world. Reading the article, we are reminded of Bernard Dadie's saying: *état gendarme, état pirate*. What McGavran is proposing is nothing less than "piracy for souls". And there is no doubt that more than enough money will be raised for that enterprise. It may be easy to manipulate people to give money for a vaguely defined cause in a far-away continent. But we contend that this is an extremely dangerous means of assuaging the guilt of a powerful and materially endowed society. To want "to feed the lost and spiritually starving multitudes" sounds quite noble, especially if one might otherwise be accused of spending more on pet food or personal computers than on missions.

We suggest that the Unreached Peoples are fortunate to remain unreached (free from contamination) and that the proposed frontier missionary societies prove their worth by bringing about love in North America, which has become a society of lonely individuals, alienated from one another. Only people who have experienced love can extend it to others.

Rural Africa is currently being invaded through various means, including "development", by the so-called biblical Christians who, very obviously, aim at controlling the consciousness of other societies for the sake of the American god. The challenge to the African churches at this moment is to unveil the subtleties involved in this kind of understanding of mission. It is a greater challenge now than a century ago when Africa was similarly penetrated. It is becoming increasingly clear that the concept of delinking is the most useful cognitive facility for Africa to maintain her integrity. All evidence points to the fact that the absence of a moratorium on funds and personnel from abroad has robbed the African church of the power to perform its mission in the African context as well as to help our governments and peoples in finding solutions to economic, social and moral dependency. A move towards self-reliance would be the only potent means of coming to grips with being ourselves and remaining an effective part of the one universal church.

From Kim Yong-bock, Korea: Third World Church Leadership Centre, Presbyterian Theological Seminary, Seoul

We should realize the painful historical lessons of Western evangelization as a limiting factor in church growth and the indigenization of the Christian faith in the third world. Given the Korean experiences of evangelism and church growth, Dr McGavran's proposal seems to me very strange and naive, even dangerous. Please let me explain.

There has been a tendency in the international Christian community, particularly in the evangelical community, to explain church growth in simplistic and single-dimensional terms. The main thrust of the explanation is that evangelism means church growth. There are complex causes for church growth in Korea. I regard the following three as important factors, besides of course the work of the Spirit: (1) The socio-political context in which Christians actively sought to protect the poor and the powerless; Christians participated actively in the Korean independence struggle against the colonial rule of Japan. Through it Korean Christians gained historical credibility among their own people. (2) Korean society has been shaken up from the bottom during the past one hundred years. No single social brick was left unturned; no single social nexus was left uncut. Completely uprooted, the people were looking for a home, spiritual and otherwise. And the church provided a home for them. (3) The church was highly disciplined to evangelize the social groups to which the individual members belong. Their relatives and friends were led to the church. Evangelism of children through Sunday schools has been remarkably successful.

The suggestion that strengthening existing national denominations and mission structures would be a waste, and that American local mission societies should undertake world evangelization is a strange one. It ignores the historical lessons, and the present reality in which the colonial association of Western mission is one of the most formidable obstacles of evangelism in many, many nations. Training third-world Christians as missionaries to be sent as surrogates of Western missionaries after the model of traditional Western mission is no less problematic. Missionaries should be trained and sent by national churches, and this means a new definition, a new theory, and a new methodology of evangelization.

From Anthony Smit S.D.B.: a Roman Catholic consultant to the commission of CWME

Donald McGavran's determination and enthusiasm are contagious. Would that many Christians had his zest and shared his zeal in spreading the good news of Christ! The project lays a heavy stress on the dimension of time and space, on geographic and arithmetic data. I doubt whether this suffices for a deep insight that goes to the core of the problem of evangelization.

It is true that Christ and his word have their own intrinsic power. And it is unparallelled. But it is not enough just to look at the world map to discover where the unreached people are and set out to sow the word. History tells us that it does not work too well. Asia Minor and North Africa were Christianized rapidly and apostolically but today very little remains both of the seeds and the plants. Europe "remained" more or less Christian but happened to become divided. Latin America is statistically the most Christian continent but the seeds of superstition are as luxuriant as those of the word of God. Yet, who can prove that the evangelizers of the past, especially of the apostolic and patristic era, had less evangelical insight and zeal than those of today? They were children of their age, like we are of our days, and they did a great job, difficult to be matched by any others? Yet it had its failures and its fruits which did not last. Why? Because besides the problem of the sower there is also the problem of the receiver of the word of God. The parable of the sower (Matt. 13) seems to suggest that the majority of the listeners are not ready to accept the word, at least in a lasting way. The marvellous news of the parable is not that it is enough to sow the word for making whole peoples and nations followers of Christ, but that the minority who accept the word become extremely fruitful. If we want an improved missionary outreach the primary task should be to discover this minority among the countless nominal Christians of today and to form new minorities among the innumerable "anonymous Christians" of the unreached peoples, instead of mobilizing everybody to go everywhere to bring the nations to the Lord within a short time.

History still warns us that the great troubles started with the conversion of the masses. Masses of people who became Christians one day became renegades some other day. Christian maturity is not, or rarely, an instantaneous process. The Bible refers to it as a growth. Not even an outpouring of the Holy Spirit, however instantaneous it may be, can break that law. Such an outpouring can be a good starting point, but it is not the end of the road towards Christian maturity, and the way back is always open as long as we are free beings. We cannot force that growth artificially in individuals and even less in peoples. And that growth is never only a matter of sowing the word of God, rushing on to the next station, and reaching the end of the earth in our fixed scheduled time. Time is not ours, but God's, especially that of redemption. Paul felt the urgency keenly, but he also knew that to win over just one person to Christ was worth of all the afflictions he had to undergo. If we aim too heavily at calculable results, perhaps we get what we may want but future generations may not benefit.

Our evangelical efforts should give priority to depth of faith and consequently to extension. We must also wait until the harvest is ripe and avoid any method of artificial fecundation. We must above all learn from the example of the Lord that his mission, the one we have to carry on, is not necessarily rewarded with outward successes. God's power is so great that visible failure becomes irrelevant, as long as it is not provoked by our own guilt or carelessness. The evangelizer must "burn with zeal" as Paul did, but not impose his timetables on God. The battle for the kingdom may look much like a lost battle until the very last moment (Rev. 17) but when it becomes night the light appears: through the cross to the light (*per crucem ad lucem*).

From Bernard Thorogood, Britain: United Reformed Church

First, divergences and then convergence.

There is a strange ambivalence in this article by Donald McGavran about the church and its calling by God. Yes, he agrees that we have to support the church and he rejoices in the reality of the world church. But no, he does not really trust the local church in its obedience to the commission of the Lord. So he writes of a host of missionary societies which will undertake what is the primary task of the church itself. Of course it is true that the work of the Spirit in the church is not always perceived or received. Correction is needed; reform and renewal are our constant prayer. But to advocate societies seems to me yet another alibi for the whole body of Christians.

That leads me to a deeper question. The article points to an activist personality, a get-up-and-go style, an impatience with quiet Christians, a lasso thrown out to catch the lost. I recognize something of the perpetual energy of evangelicalism which has always been a judgment on smug Christians. What I miss is the pain of carrying a cross. To incarnate the word of hope, to be alongside those who suffer, to enter into the very lostness of the defeated, to translate the very categories of biblical thought so that they live in our electronic age — this is a ministry of grace which does not count success in numbers nor count progress in small change. I question whether the McGavran style measures up to the depth of the missionary task.

But it is easy to criticize. We are not doing so well ourselves. Our missionary impact in Western Europe (whether seen in terms of individual conversion or in terms of moving towards social justice or in terms of spiritual healing) is not a matter for great rejoicing. There are whole unevangelized areas of our social life. We are failing to speak convincingly of God to children. We allow people to wither at the bottom of the heap without raising much protest. So, yes, we do need to pray for a rebirth of the missionary commitment and devotion in every local church. It is not so much new channels of activity that we need as the passionate concern for others which enables us to forget our defensiveness and risk our tradition.

If McGavran is right and the churches will block such passionate concern because of their refusal to accept new life, then the Lord will pass them by. But it is not for any one of us to assume that it will be the case — as though we are spiritually superior to the church. Our part is to minister, pray and learn, so that the gift of the Holy Spirit may be poured into our lives.

From Petr Macek, Czechoslovakia: Baptist pastor

I have never given much thought to the strategy of evangelism, let alone the problems of a global strategy. My field is interpretation, and I struggle with the questions of meaning and coherence of the gospel and of the content of Christian belief. In my own ministry I concentrate on the event of proclamation. In this way I promote evangelism. But that is about it.

Although the majority of the population is now progressively de-Christianized and could even qualify as "unreached", the cultural context is so deeply indebted to the Christian past that except for some segments of a-historical and culture-renouncing evangelicals, all sharing of the gospel is bound to use the spiritual heritage in guiding the victims of the spiritually-void present back to the source of truth and regeneration. If you know a little bit of our history you can imagine how sensitive an area this is and how interpreting the past would still be divisive, and thus stand in the way of a devoted and effective cooperation.

But this reservation on my part does not mean that my heart does not burn for the unfinished task of worldwide evangelism.

From D.J. Bosch, J.N.J. Kritzinger, P.G.J. Meiring, W.A. Saayman, South Africa: Department of Missiology, University of South Africa, Pretoria

McGavran's proposal makes good sense *if* one accepts his definitions and concepts. However, it is exactly in the area of concepts and definitions (e.g. of *mission, Unreached Peoples, panta ta ethne, mission societies*, etc.) that we have serious problems with his call. We limit our response to two areas.

1. Unreached Peoples; peoples' approach: This concept is central to McGavran's understanding of the task before us: missionary societies have to be formed to evangelize unreached *ethne*. It is, however, a concept with serious problems attached to it, and the South African situation probably can serve as the best illustration of these problems. This concept has an undeniable ethnic underpinning (*panta ta ethne*), which reveals itself very clearly in McGavran's "rediscovery" of German missiologists such as Christian Keysser. Keysser is described by McGavran as a "genius", and his approach to mission is valued very highly as innovative and tremendously important (see McGavran's foreword to the English edition of Keysser's *A People Reborn*). German missiology in general, and Keysser in particular, with their concept of an "ethnic church" had great influence on the Dutch Reformed Church's policy of constituting racially separated churches in South Africa. In fact, it can be argued that they provided a great deal of the theological justification for this policy. For this reason Keysser, Gutmann and others have been studied extensively by South African scholars. Unfortunately, the result of their studies has mostly been published in Afrikaans, so that it is inaccessible to English-speaking theologians. These studies have shown, though, that the "people's church" approach contains some very serious theological weaknesses. To quote just one of these studies: Krige, who made a detailed and thorough analysis of Keysser's approach, concludes that Keysser's emphasis on tribal and cultural bonds is unjustified and unjustifiable, because in this way ethnology acquires a positive theological attribution which creates the dangerous possibility to include ethnic (*völkische*) elements as revelatory principles (next to scriptures) in church formation. This is unacceptable, because the gospel must always be a crisis in the life and culture of a people; the Christian must always be called forth by the gospel from old life relations to enter into a new community. The ultimate question therefore is not the one about the indigenous (McGavran: people's) church, but the one about the reality of the universal church of Jesus Christ. Although it cannot be said that Keysser intended creating racially exclusive churches, the tragic reality is that his approach eventually provided the theological justification for racially separated churches, e.g. in South Africa. As South African missiologists we are therefore not convinced that the "Unreached Peoples approach" is a practical tool to speed up the evangelization of the world; this same argument was used in 1857 when the white DRC in South Africa took its momentous decision to introduce racial separation into the church.

More recent studies by South African missiologists have also raised serious questions about this approach. Saayman highlighted the danger that a seemingly admirable evangelistic practice can become a heretical ideology in a world where racism is still too prevalent. Bosch, in a study of the structure of mission according to Matthew 28:16-20, concludes: "There is undoubtedly validity in the church growth movement's honouring of the 'homogeneous unit principle' as a communications guideline. We may, however, not take a communications principle and make it an ecclesiological norm by reasoning that (1) homogeneous churches grow more rapidly than others, (2) all churches should grow more rapidly, (3) therefore all churches should be culturally and socially homogeneous.... Class prejudices and man's alienation from man only become more deeply ingrained into the human heart where ethnicity is regarded as an intrinsic feature of the church." The South African context has confirmed this analysis over and over again. Until the *theological* questions about the people's approach have been taken seriously, we cannot be enthusiastic about a scheme such as McGavran proposes.

2. *The understanding of mission:* In an assessment of McGavran's theology of mission, we firstly question his use of *military* terminology. He uses expressions like "victories of the cross", "mobilization", "ambassadors", "task forces", "campaign", "beachheads", "frontiers", "evangelizing forces", "bands of ardent frontier-minded" people, etc.

These words reveal a view of mission which suggests that Christians are "at war" and need to mobilize all their resources to try and "conquer" the world. It is clear that this campaign is not seen as a "conventional war", but more as a kind of "guerilla war" in which small "task forces" establish "beachheads of saving faith" in "enemy territory", which are then gradually to grow into whole "liberated areas" of "Bible-believing and Bible-obeying Christians".

It is true that this "antagonistic" motif is found in the Bible, but the way in which it is used and applied by McGavran is questionable to us. Since he uses "Christian mission" as a synonym for "world evangelization", it is clear that the only "frontier" on which Christians really ought to "wage war" is that of sin and unbelief. In this way the holistic Christian mission is reduced to the task of "discipling". The many other frontiers like poverty, hunger, oppression, injustice, illiteracy, etc. on which Christians should also "attack" and "overcome" the forces of evil and delusion are either ignored or regarded as less important. This theological reduction of the scope of mission seems to us to be a major weakness of McGavran's proposal. In a situation like ours in South Africa we are acutely aware of the fact that the very credibility of Christian mission depends on whether one fights only on the frontier of unbelief or on all the frontiers at the same time. To use the terminology of Fung, we cannot preach conversion to people as sinners unless we declare and live our solidarity with them as the sinned-against.

If these military terms are to be used at all, they should therefore be used in the overall perspective of the coming of the kingdom of God (the new world of justice and peace) and not merely in the perspective of the planting of churches. Let us by all means take a Giant Step forward and "furiously organize" Christian "task forces", but let them then be in the forefront of the struggle on *all* the frontiers between the kingdom of God and the kingdom of evil.

The above point leads to a second (and related) issue. Since Christian mission is seen primarily as "reaching the three billion unreached", and since these three billion people live mostly in the third world, it gives rise to an understanding of mission which does not really take place in *six* continents. The "people groups" in the first world which will be reached in this Giant Step will primarily be immigrant minorities. But how "reached" is the USA or Europe? Will this Giant Step not perpetuate the pernicious idea of one-way traffic mission from the North to South? Furthermore, does the strong emphasis on *money* in this proposal not aggravate this? McGavran hopes that nations will take a similar giant step when they see the USA setting the example, but which other countries will be able to raise "millions of dollars" so easily? Is not McGavran's own admission that the suffering churches in the Soviet Union and China have grown stronger "spiritually and perhaps even numerically" an indication that money and social power are not the most important resources of Christian mission? Should the "bands of ardent frontier-minded" people in the USA not first of all allow these weak and suffering churches to guide and instruct them, rather than "rush in" and repeat all the mistakes of the past? If *partnership* in worldwide evangelization means anything, then surely it means that the *resources* of mission are more than merely "ambassadors and money" and that the use of the resources be subjected to the wisdom of Christians who have previously been "on the receiving end". This may prevent a repetition of the many mistakes of the past. $ending churches and mi$$ion $ocieties need to learn to be accountable to the poor and weak communities of faith in the third world. Authenticity is more important in mission than efficiency. The enthusiasm and motivation contained in McGavran's call is admirable, but it must be subjected to a real partnership with third world Christians if it is not to fall into the traps of the past.

From Harold Lindsell, USA: editor-emeritus, Christianity Today

I find myself in agreement with his recommendation and conceive of the possibility that this is what is needed to complete the work of world evangelization.

If what McGavran pleads for is to come to pass, the WCC can help to make it a reality by stating forthrightly that all men are lost and there is only one way to heaven — by faith in Christ. Christianity is the one true religion and all other religions are false. Anything short of this nullifies what McGavran is asking for.

On the other hand, we know that the gospel of Jesus Christ will be preached to all the world for a witness and then the end will come. God has entrusted the task of doing this to the church. And right now the church is called upon to meet the challenge and finish the job. I am impressed by the power of radio and have reason to think there are fifty millions converts in mainland China due to radio broadcasting of the gospel. Churches are being started and the ministry is being trained by radio. If Christians would lay hold of McGavran's scheme and use radio, television, and other means to do the work of evangelization it is more than possible that the job can be completed within a reasonably short time.

Prayer and the infilling of the Holy Spirit are needed if this suggestion is to mature and work. And the WCC has before it an opportunity far beyond anything it has been faced with before. It can do much to make McGavran's proposal come to fruition and for this I pray.

Bishop Leslie Boseto, Solomon Islands: United Church

I also have a vision of world mission and evangelism, but not from Geneva or Rome or London or New York or even Fuller's, Pasadena! It must be blowing from the Pacific, and especially from the Melanesians' humane society, not from the kind of "missionary societies" that Dr McGavran has been proposing.

But our visions must be tested by God's will. McGavran's proposal asks "that in every congregation in North America practising Christians organize themselves into frontier missionary societies, men's missionary societies, women's missionary societies, youth missionary societies". This, for him, is the will of God. For me the will of God for Christian mission is different. What McGavran has proposed appears to me to be out of date, paternalistic, colonial and expensive.

Out of date because young churches which McGavran dismisses as "small and weak" are no longer interested in being called "good boy" by big fathers in the USA or Europe or Australia. It is time for us to relate to churches, not missionary societies. Paternalistic because it is dictated by one-way traffic missionary attitudes. We know, but you do not know. We know what is best. Colonial because the implications of setting up more missionary societies will mean perpetuating divisions within a given national community. Too expensive because the cost of administration of these societies will be enormous. It will only provide employment and comfortable offices for the oppressors!

Who are the "Unreached Peoples" today? Are they unreached because missionaries have not yet reached them? Is God the Creator, Owner and Giver of all things waiting for the creation of more missionary societies in North America before he will move? I am sure God does not wait for more missionary societies but more Christ-like missionaries!

The problem today for world mission and evangelism is not so much the problem of the "unreached" but that of people who are deaf because of pride, self-righteousness and lack of sensitivity. The centre of the problem is not the second son who said "no" but the first son who said "yes" (Matt. 21:28-32). God will judge the so-called Bible-believing and Bible-obeying Christians more severely than the unreached (1 Pet. 4:17-19).

We in the Pacific had experienced the essential nature of mission before the arrival of Western missionaries. Its nature is love. Because of that love, there was already a communal, human society. What the gospel taught and preached did was to change our attitude so that we learned to share our love with wider circles of people. Because of this we call this love "divine love". This divine love reveals the law of the kingdom (James 2:8) within the experience of what God had already given our ancestors, namely communal love which cares, shares and recognizes. It does not compete, does not exploit, and does not oppress and alienate.

October 1985

31

RESPONSES TO McGAVRAN — CONTINUED

From Nelson H. Charles, Sierra Leone: president of conference, Methodist Church

It may be true that three billion have yet to believe on Jesus or to hear of him. But how does this matter? How are they different, those who say they believe on Jesus from those who do not yet believe and have not heard of him? Consider the Western democracies — they are called Christian. How do they interact with third-world countries, some of which are manifestly non-Christian? Belief and hearing are not concrete enough. Evangelism as a concrete reality must not only be seen and heard but also experienced. What bedevils evangelism the world over is the growing gap between verbal affirmation and practical life. The number of those who pay lip-service to the tenets of the Christian faith is increasing. Those who by dubious means have become materially well-off are among them. They call themselves, and are accepted as, Christians. What is evangelism here?

In the villages which border Freetown on three sides, the people have had a profound change in their life-style in the years after the second world war. In the twenties, neighbourliness was very important and received greater attention than neighbourhood. They lived the community life of the early Christians in Acts 2. That is evangelism in word and deed — verbal and concrete action. Those village folk loved and served one another. They shared their goods and thanked the Lord, the giver of all good things. All were at once good Samaritans and wounded victims.

But now it is different. The village folk are not the same. A good many have died and their life-style with them. There is no evidence of belief any more. They sing and chant and recite the creeds. They no longer share their possessions or their faith. And evangelism? Well, the newcomers to the villages have it. They belong to the new independent churches. They walk the streets praising their Lord and Master. At night they praise the Lord by candle light. They share their faith and their joy. They were once the "unreached".

So we have new groups commonly called independent churches. Sometimes each group is dominated by a single tribe. Once established a group/ independent church draws its membership from all and sundry regardless of tribe. These independent churches continue to be known by tribal names, for example, Limba Pentecostal, Lokko Pentecostal, Mende, Timme, etc. Evangelism thrives under the aegis of those independent groups.

Evangelism is not the preserve of any group. Every time worship is in the open, evangelization occurs. All that is needed, especially in urban situations, in third-world countries is that existing churches throw off their defence mentality and reach out to the masses of simple folk. They will follow the gospel if they hear it preached and witness it happen.

Recently the Methodist Church in Sierra Leone organized a youth convention. The venue was Kenema, some 190 miles from Freetown. A large number of young people gathered on the campus of the secondary school at Kenema. They came from different parts of the country. They sang, they read the Bible, they preached, they danced. All the Kenema folk felt their presence. Long after the eight-day event they were the talk of the town. These were messengers who turned out to be evangelists. More conventions? Not really, more messengers.

The position of evangelism in Sierra Leone is fluid. The old-established churches are secure within their magnificent buildings on which they spend much time and resources. They need a jolt to get out of those "secure" confines and meet the people — all kinds of people, animists, heathens and followers of other faiths. There is a great need for the stoning of Stephen to be re-enacted so that it can be said of us today as it was said in the first century: "The believers who were scattered went everywhere, preaching the message" (Acts 8:4).

From Roger E. Hedlund, India: Church Growth Research Centre, Madras

Let me begin with a small disagreement. First, I do not believe that North America will lead the way. The centre of Christian gravity has shifted from North to South and from West to East. Second, the bulk of the world's population is in Asia where the two largest blocs (China and India) at the present time are not easily accessible to mission societies or churches from the West. Initiative there should come increasingly from local Christians.

As new companies of the committed create new structures for mission, I hope they will take time to learn from history. The proposed Giant Additional Step need not be without reference to all that has gone before. It is possible to profit from the experiences of others and to avoid repeating their mistakes. Asian mission societies, instead of copying the patterns and mistakes of the West, need new directions, effective strategies, and appropriate methods. Not the Americans but the Asians must lead the way in countries like India. Leadership should be well-informed, but it ought also dare to be non-traditional.

We have to get beyond the geographical concept of mission. I have a reservation about the DAWN concept. It is theologically incorrect to postulate "nations" as geographical entities. Countries such as India comprise numerous peoples. The evangelization of each of these diverse "nations" is a biblical and theological imperative.

McGavran's main objective is to see that the unreached are reached. The genius of the idea is that it does not bypass the church. The proposal is an attempt to revitalize existing churches by focusing the attention of local congregations on peoples outside the church. This is crucially relevant in Asia where the masses follow various religions and ideologies that are not Christian.

From Ms Adelheid Constabel, West Germany: retired pastor, Frankfurt

My first reaction to the proposal for a Giant Step was that I should cancel my subscription to the *Monthly Letter on Evangelism*. Then I decided to explain why. The matter is important enough.

I was horrified when I read the article. There does not seem to be the faintest memory left of the dark chapters of the history of Christian mission where the "victories won by the cross" brought harm to the peoples.

I consider it a tremendous presumption to think that we in our Christian churches have salvation at hand and only need to transport it with the help of the dollar to places where it is not known yet, as if it were only a matter of strategy. This "strategy" has nothing to do with the missionary methods of the early Christians. In his commissioning speech,

Jesus tells his disciples not to take money with them (Mark 6:8). They are to bring the message of the kingdom of God as people without possessions. Their effectiveness in the time of the early Christians does not come from an earthly power potential, but from endured powerlessness. That laid the foundation for the strength of the faith that defeat can turn into victory. Out of this experience it was possible to convince others that there is an inner strength and a saving power transcending all powerlessness which can overcome the dark realities in our world.

A strategy which grows out of a feeling of one's own superiority and power may be able to mobilize an ideological campaign, but it renders absurd the cross as the metaphor of victory. This plan may be based on good intentions. I do not want to deny that. It is probably not aware of the visions of grandeur that have produced it. But it must allow the question as to who it actually intends to serve.

I will be very interested now to see the next issues in order to learn what kind of echo the monthly letter has elicited from others.

From R. Stanley Good, Fiji Islands: New Testament lecturer, Pacific Theological College

I found the August letter interesting and pinned it on the college notice board with an invitation to students and staff alike to respond. Only one reaction reached me — verbally, from a third-year student of mature years who has a special interest in evangelism. It was so cynical I felt I could not pass it on. To be blunt, he took the whole thing to be a "con trick", just another clever American method for raising more money. So all I am left with is my own few thoughts and I pass them on for what they are worth.

The approach *is* American, but there are some things Americans are very good at — this could be one of them! Here we do not think globally! The wider world makes its presence felt increasingly in the South Pacific in every way. What is our contribution to world mission? What practical steps are needed now in this area? So far as theological education is concerned (and it is part of world evangelism or it is nothing at all) we are going international by developing a higher master's degree, to begin in January 1987. A vital part of this is the development of a Theological Bookshop Distribution and Resource Centre, to disseminate theological literature throughout the 5000-mile island chain. There is no specifically theological bookshop, as yet. Book prices are prohibitive and we must add mailing costs to that. But we want inter-island travel of theological specialists to be financed, so that from Tahiti to the Carolines we make sure the effort of theological schools is one with that of Pacific Theological College at the centre. We need the personnel with the specialist gifts to implement all this. We either go forward together or not at all. Ideally, we need an inter-island theological training ship, with library and audio visual facilities on board. Can any strategy help us implement this?

From J. Emmette Weir, Bahamas: pastor, Nassau

One of the most profound contributions to the question of world mission today from our region is that made by Terrence Julien of Trinidad, in his article "Christian Cultural Mission and Environment", which appears in the book *Out of the Depths*, (Trinidad, 1974). In it Julien puts forward the thesis that just as the early church had to face the problem of Judaizing so we face the challenge of "Westernization"; precisely as in the early church there were those who insisted that those who wished to become Christians must first become Jews, so today there are those who insist that in order to become Christians you must first become Westerners. This is putting it rather crudely but it gets to the bare bones of the article.

Surely the churches of Southern Africa and Western Africa, of Latin America and Korea need to be considered in setting out a programme designed to proclaim the gospel to the three billion who are not professing Christians. What is needed now is a missionary thrust not from the West to the rest of the world, but from the church in the whole world to the whole world.

From Dario B. Alampay, Philippines: pastor, United Church of Christ, Manila

What we and the unreached people here in the Philippines need more than anything else is not millions of dollars. What we need is freedom and justice that emanate from the gospel of God's kingdom. Only the powers that be in our government will be happy to hear about the millions of dollars that the churches in North America will raise.

May I ask, how many ministers and priests and dedicated Christian lay people have been murdered and imprisoned in solitary isolation in America for the sake of the gospel of the kingdom of God? Here in the Philippines they are unnumbered. God is here. He has not abandoned us yet. If, despite what we affirm about God's presence here in our midst, still nothing happens, then not all the millions of dollars can save us from the hell we find ourselves in. This, I believe, holds true in other lands where there is even a sprinkling of God's people.

Whatever the odds, the church of Jesus Christ must step out as never before in the deepening gloom and gathering darkness of the world to stage a concert, as it were, and sing the ever-new song of the gospel of the kingdom of God in Jesus Christ, the Risen, Reigning Lord.

From Denton Lotz: director of evangelism and education, Baptist World Alliance

Dr McGavran has always been a very creative thinker and a goad to missiologists to rethink their priorities and goals.

It seems to me that McGavran's idea needs to be tempered with the reality of the political world in which we are living. Bishop Neill once commented to me that the problem in many younger churches was that we have created a "missionary dependency attitude" in which nationals are led to believe that only missionaries can really evangelize. This, of course, is a false assumption; in fact, it is heretical.

What Christians around the world need is a new Edinburgh conference which impresses upon all believers and leaders that we must be missionary-minded. Africans, Asians, Latin Americans, Caribbeans, North Americans, Europeans must all see that we are responsible for the frontiers which surround us. The real question for Western Christians is, if they were to save their loose change every day, would they be willing to give it to a national group overseas, and not to "their" mission society? Are they willing to support Christian leaders who have the zeal, know-how, language, culture, etc., to evangelize, but do not have the means? And to all of us, are we willing to support nationals elsewhere with our prayers and with our pocket-books? We need to rediscover evangelism in the New Testament sense, that all of us are responsible for spreading the good news to the "ethne" where we are. It seems to me that the failure of mission societies is precisely the dependency they have created. We need to allow the Holy Spirit to move among the peoples and to then support new converts who will evangelize in the context of their home setting.

From John W.B. Hill, Canada: Anglican diocesan priest, Toronto

Donald McGavran's Giant Step in Christian mission reminded me of the "Hunger Project", recently described and assessed in the journal *The New Internationalist* (June 1985; see "Hungry for Converts"). Both the appeal and the weakness (of the two approaches) seem to me quite similar. The Hunger Project "seeks to create a context" in which world hunger can be eradicated by convincing a multitude of sincere people of the need and the possibility (without explaining *how* hunger will be eradicated); and thus it proposes to create a global "will" to eradicate hunger. McGavran's proposal attempts to generate massive funds for evangelizing the unreached. Is it true that money and ignorance are the only real obstacles to global evangelization?

McGavran's article does recognize (almost in passing) that existing mission strategies may be unsupportive of this thrust or even hostile; the article does *not* recognize that there are historical, socio-political, and sometimes even theological reasons for this resistance. And the resistance is amongst *us*, the needed agents of the mission. Is money really the resolution of this problem? I am sceptical. His article likewise fails to recognize the potential, in such a marshalling of popular support, for a renewed Christian imperialism, rooted even more deeply in chauvinist prejudices.

In saying this, I do not wish to imply any criticism of those truly evangelical frontier ministries. Indeed, a more widespread aquaintance with the spirit and strategies of such ministries could well be a greater source of the enthusiasm that McGavran covets than any amount of sheer information about the scope of the challenge. For I believe that a truly evangelistic passion for the peoples of the world will cost us dearly in terms of our cultural, political, economic, and unecumenical complacency. Our hearts will be more truly challenged, I suggest, by stories of those who have been prepared to pay the price and so have demonstrated the power and grace of the regenerating Spirit.

The concluding comments of the above-cited article name the real danger of the "Hunger Project"; and I suggest that those comments also apply, *mutatis mutandis*, to the Giant Step project: "While it may be harmless in itself, the uncritical attitude it engenders diverts attention from the real and difficult choices that we face. Where it undermines our ability to make such choices, it is more likely to postpone the abolition of hunger than encourage it."

From Edward R. Dayton: senior vice-president, World Vision International

It is obviously biblical that every local congregation should be missionary in its outlook. What McGavran is challenging us to do is to work this out in practical terms. Essentially he is calling us to recognize that mission structures, like all human structures, need to be continually revitalized. Most of our missions efforts are now in the hands of agencies which are following "traditional" patterns: not traditional in the sense that this is the way we have always done it, rather traditional in the sense that we are operating under the naive assumption that we now know how to do "it" by calling for new local initiatives. We are also asking for renewal that comes with breaking of traditional ways of doing.

To what extent McGavran's call for a Giant Step in Christian mission is appropriate for all congregations everywhere probably needs to be debated further. However, it would be my observation that local congregations that are challenged to mission are also challenged to self-renewal.

From Anton G. Honig, Netherlands: missionary and professor of missiology, Kampen

What is the real urgency? How do we look at the three billion "unreached people"? Are they "lost" people unless we preach them the gospel before they die? Is that our motivation, when we say that in this generation everybody should hear the message of the gospel? Several movements in this century have chosen this device. Is mission participation in God's work of salvation and are people saved by faithful acceptance of the message of the gospel? Or is mission informative only, i.e. does it only inform people that they are saved by Christ?

In the Reformed tradition there has never been any hesitation as to the fact that the Holy Spirit is at work everywhere, also outside the church. The biblical message is so convincing in this matter. This is why missionaries time and again are astonished when they discern God's work in the people they meet. Our training course for missionary work often stresses: "Never forget that our Lord has been doing already something in the hearts of the people you will meet." And I have often had that deeply moving experience. But what is this "something" which God is doing in people's hearts? Should it be called salvific?

I think the answers we give to these questions are decisive for a choice between dependent evangelistic work or participation in the evangelistic work of local churches; decisive for "taking time" or not. It makes a big difference whether I consider others to be lost, or to be saved, but not conscious of it, so that they have to be informed about their salvation. Let us listen to Vinay Samuel and Chris Sugden: "Through reading *Kids and the Kingdom* by John Inchley, a scripture union children's worker of vast experience, we are realizing that it may be more biblical to regard children as persons who belong to Jesus until they reject him, rather than as lost souls who need to repent as soon as possible."

I think we all agree that a person is saved by faith and not *ex opere operato*, i.e. by the fact only of Christ's work of salvation in his death and resurrection. That makes it urgent to preach the gospel, in order that people may be saved *sola fide, sola gratia*. And when billions of people have died in the course of twenty centuries without having heard the gospel, Christians should feel guilty when it happened through their laziness and lack of love for others. But when it happened because we simply could not reach them all, we should not be nervous about what happened to them. They have fallen into the hands of a merciful God.

That gives us room for "taking time" in the sense that we should do our evangelistic work as it should be done. Careful strategy according to the best criteria is better than overheated hurry. Too much harm has been done already; too many people have been repelled already rather than attracted. With our uncareful approaches *we* have been too often already a stumbling block — not the gospel nor our Lord, who was not even met by the people. I think our hurry has more to do with Western nervousness than with devotion to the gospel.

This makes it important to consider the importance of the moratorium debate. It is useful to listen to the statement on mission and evangelism made by the central committee of the World Council of Churches in July 1982: "Moratorium does not mean the end of the missionary vocation nor of the duty to provide resources for missionary work, but it does mean freedom to reconsider present engagements and to see whether a continuation of what we have been doing for so long is the right style of mission in our day."

The Lausanne Covenant noted that "the reduction of foreign missionaries and money in an evangelized country may sometimes be necessary to facilitate the national church's growth and self-reliance and to release resources for unevangelized areas". "There can never be a moratorium on mission, but it will always be possible, and sometimes necessary, to have a moratorium for the sake of better mission," concluded the WCC statement.

From J. Verkuyl, Netherlands: missiologist

I hesitated to participate in this reflection because of my age, but my consolation was that Dr McGavran is still older than I, and that he is also still deeply interested and involved in the task of world mission.

In the first place I would like to express my deep gratitude for the fact that an attempt is being made to try to build a bridge between "ecumenicals" and "evangelicals". From both sides there are symptoms of rapprochement and communication.

In the second place I would like to express my gratitude for the attention given to the unfinished task of world mission. The great conferences on mission and evangelism from the past decade have always stressed the theme of the unfinished task for world mission: the world mission conference of Bangkok (1972), the congress of evangelicals in Lausanne (1974), the Roman Catholic bishops conference in Rome (1974), the conference of the Eastern Orthodox churches in Bucharest (1974), etc. But there has been a growing distance between the theoretical acknowledgment of the unfinished task of world mission and the practical work in that area.

May I finish with a proposal to McGavran? We had in 1980 two world mission conferences: "Melbourne" and "Pattaya". Should we repeat such separate world mission conferences? Is it not possible to organize a world mission conference together and could not McGavran or one of his successors take an initiative in that direction? I have the impression that it is time to meet and to cooperate "for the sake of the kingdom". Thousands in "evangelical" circles and in "ecumenical" circles hope and pray for such a meeting and such a breakthrough in relations.

December 1985

32

RESPONSES TO McGAVRAN — CONTINUED

From Seppo Syrjanen, Finland: Evangelical Lutheran Church Mission Centre, Helsinki

Dr McGavran's definition of "unreached" people is questionable. According to him, "an 'unreached' *ethnos* or segment of society is not one in which individuals who are Christ's followers are perceived by their fellows to have 'left their own people and traitorously gone off to join another people'". In other words, "unreached" people may have been reached with the gospel, but as long as Christ's followers among that people are not socially powerful enough (the extent of which is defined by the psychological attitude towards Christians of those who have not accepted the gospel), the people still remain unreached. The whole matter of "reachedness" then hinges on the success of the local Christians to form such relationships with their compatriots so that the Christians are no more considered an alien element in their culture. If this should be so, one only wonders how much North American missionaries and mission societies can be of help. How much can rich American missionaries help local Christians in Asia and Africa and elsewhere to create an impression that Christians in their various localities have not traitorously gone off to join another (very rich and different) people? Isn't it exactly here that the local church, which McGavran totally bypasses, comes into the picture? Therefore it is surprising that when McGavran gives an example of a reached people, it is Guatemala. The question asked, however, is: "Are you an evangelical?" (Not: "Are you a Christian?") In the treatment of an "unreached" *ethnos* theological questions such as the unity of the church and ecclesiology in general do not seem to matter at all. Cultural anthropology over-rules theology.

From Charles van Engen, USA: Western Theological Seminary, Reformed Church in America

McGavran's Giant Step proposal presents us with a new goal of mission. Within each "hidden people" the goal is to bring about the existence of a group of believers in Jesus Christ whose presence in their mosaic is seen as a positive force for the welfare of the entire mosaic — even by the unbelievers within the same cultural group.

It is important to give serious thought to this purpose as a goal of mission. How it coincides with McGavran's earlier "harvest theology" is unclear, for it does not give us an idea of quantitative measurement, but rather speaks of radical cultural indigeneity, the element of having "favour with all the people" which is stressed in Acts 2:47. Just how this goal of mission might be evaluated biblically is unclear, since the scriptures seem to stress faith as a relationship between humanity and God in the context of the kingdom. The horizontal and cultural dynamics of conversion whereby there is "neither Jew nor Greek" (Cf. Gal. 3, Eph. 2, Col. 1, 2 Cor. 5:20) would seem to be within the faith community, not as an evaluation from the non-Christian population. McGavran's Giant Step proposal sets before us a goal of mission which is broader than saving individual souls, and broader than multiplying churches. It goes significantly further than the boundaries of the church, and asks about salvation and conversion in relationship to the non-Christian's perspective of the newly-converted member of his or her own mosaic. As a goal of mission, the proposal includes cultural sensitivity precisely within the incorporating and evangelizing activity itself. And yet we must also remember that "conversion" involves more than just church participation: it also involves a radical reorientation of one's world-view towards the presence of the future kingdom and a call to participate in the transformation and reconciliation of each social mosaic.

McGavran's proposal calls for revitalizing the "missionary structures of the congregation". It opens up a vista for the ordinary church member to concentrate on a practical and do-able mission objective. It directs the local congregation beyond its own boundaries in a stepping towards the world, and thus assists the Christian in that movement which overcomes the "ecclesiastical captivity of the church". The proposal also gives us a new option for the old "church-mission" problem. The creation of the societies mentioned is *not* outside the church, *per se*; it does not create another "sodality". Rather, the missionary structure proposed arises out of the concerns and activities of the members of the congregation. It is *one* concrete expression of the life of the local congregation. Finally, the proposal changes our way of relating "sending church" to "receiving church", since the idea involves individuals from congregations of *both* sending and receiving churches who gather together to pray, strategize, and work towards reaching a third group of people — a "hidden people", normally outside the relational and cultural boundaries of *both* the sending as well as the receiving churches.

And yet the proposal raises many questions. Once consciousness, energy, personnel and money have been raised in a local group of believers, how do you give legs to that interest? How do local Christian groups from a North American denomination, for example, relate to the local Christians of an African church to reach a given "hidden people" without involving the denominational structures of each church? How do these congregations bring about the proposed new thrust without creating yet another "mission agency" alongside of (and possibly in competition with) existing denominational and independent agencies? How do such new agencies, formed for that new thrust, relate to the existing global Christian ecumenical and cooperative agencies with agendas which may be diametrically opposed to that of the new agencies? And when does the new "hidden people" mission agency know that it has achieved its goal? The proposal needs that "fierce pragmatism" which the church growth movement has so often requested. If the proposal is to be accepted as a legitimate goal of the missionary structures of the congregation, we must find a way of refining the definitions so that they can be biblically and theologically accurate, holistically kingdom-conscious, practically reachable, empirically verifiable and statistically measurable. Having done that, we may embark on a new thrust of mission outreach beyond the boundaries of our congregations and churches to the millions who have not yet responded to the good news of forgiveness and reconciliation in

Christ. It looks like McGavran's proposal has given many of us a lot to think about, and much to do.

From Johannes Aagaard, Denmark: missiologist, University of Aarhus

Let me affirm some of the important sentences in the appeal of our senior colleague Dr McGavran:

1. There is a gigantic unfinished task. Large numbers of humankind are "out" in relation to the Christian gospel.
2. These "lost sheep" are not considered by the sheep in the flock, be it in the flock of the Western churches or the flock of the churches of "the colourful world".
3. Existing promotional schemes are tied to existing mission structures, controlled by the churches "in power".
4. Millions/billions of people are in fact locked out and locked away from the gospel and the Christian faith.
5. Well-trained, well-equipped, lifetime task forces are most needed. Short-term missionaries cannot do the job which has to be done today.

What I want to add are the following points:

1. The hard fact is that the great religions and their billions of adherents are as a whole hardly reached at all. Christian missions have always tended to evade this issue, today more than ever. The religious dimension is neglected and on purpose. Secular realities tend to absorb all our mission interest and all our energy. To change this we have to equip our people intellectually, but also socially so that they can cope with cultural and religious differences.
2. While we have been ignoring the religious dimension for two generations, in the same period the incredible invasion of Eastern religions has taken place in the whole world, also in the part of the world which was once called "the Christian world". This invasion still takes place practically unnoticed by the churches and with practically no resistance, in a number of cases even with "tolerant" support by important segments of the churches.
3. While the whole world is threatened by global dangers coming first of all from warmongers and racists, a movement of retreat has taken place in the churches: "return to the pews" and "return to individual piety" and "forget about the world and its problems".

The call to take the Giant Step cannot be just a quantitative leap, it has to be at the same time a qualitative leap forward. If the new move still turns away from the great world religions, if the new move still forgets about the incredible counter-mission coming into our own congregations today, and if the new move becomes a part of the retreat from the world of reality, then the Giant Step can become a giant betrayal.

From Archbishop David Penman, Australia: Anglican Church, Melbourne

The concept of new "frontier missionary fellowships or societies" being encouraged in every congregation to study one Unreached Peoples group, to pray and to raise funds by, say, giving the price of one meal each week, is an exciting idea.

They would need to be developed in addition to existing denominational and other missionary societies; otherwise established societies will feel threatened. One way forward would be to encourage newly founded fellowships to raise finance for existing societies and earmark it to be used only for frontier evangelistic work being done by those societies. This could become a real incentive to established societies opening up new work among Unreached People groups.

Another way forward would be to ask existing societies to form *within their own networks* "frontier missionary fellowship societies".

One of the difficulties will be to establish what is and what is not primary evangelistic work. To take an example, the recent work of the Rev. Jo Hogarth in Tanzania with Church Mission Society in developing theological education by extension has a very important frontier spin-off further down the line as it eventually trains African evangelists by training Africans to train Africans, but it appears to be just "supporting a young church", to use McGavran's phrase. The article presupposes a sense of urgency. In many, perhaps most mainline Australian congregations, there is little or no sense of urgency about this matter.

From John Brown, Australia: Commission on World Mission, Uniting Church

I appreciate the enthusiasm of Dr McGavran for Christian mission. Clearly many churches see mission as something peripheral to their life and the call to see it as central to the being of the church is important. However, I have some concerns about the Giant Step in Christian mission.

The use of vocabulary in the statement is revealing. We read that new churches have little power... there is discussion of strategies... thousands of ambassadors... millions of dollars... establishing beachheads... and concern about the effectiveness of outreach. All this terminology derives from an understanding of mission as a strategy planned with large resources. How can we engage in mission in this way without distorting the very gospel to which we bear witness? The earliest disciples were sent out without resources except their faith and the vision of the kingdom to which they bore witness? How is the power of this mission to be reconciled with the weakness of Christ?

My other concern is with the lack of ecumenical perspective and the lack of any connection between the unity of the church and its mission. I have just been reading an interview with a leader of the church in Burma where church growth is occurring rapidly. But one of the problems faced in Burma is the fact that many of the new missionary organizations and para-church groups create havoc and do their own individualistic thing without any relationship with the church which is already there. I shudder at the thought of thousands of new missionary organizations from the United States of America particularly sending their ambassadors around the world to do mission.

I am interested in what sort of a gospel it is that whole nations are going to believe and accept. According to Jesus, the gospel is a sword which separates person from person, and it creates division. What kind of a gospel, then, is it that is going to be so acceptable that whole nations will be discipled?

From James C. Dekker, Venezuela: American missionary

Donald McGavran assumes that a people is "reached" or evangelized when X percent are Christians. Thus "the evangelical churches... in Guatemala are working and praying that by 1990 half the entire population will be Bible-believing, Bible-obeying Christians". "Africa south of the Sahara will soon be as Christian as North America." Is North America Christian because more than 40 percent of US citizens say they believe in Jesus Christ as their Lord and Saviour? The US continues to be one of the most self-centred and violent lands in the world. Even famine relief efforts for Africa are done with a hooray-for-generous-us-hoopla. Is Guatemala "25 percent Christian"? Have violence, injustice and suffering been reduced by 25 percent during the civil war of the last decade (the time of the greatest evangelical growth there)?

These are not capricious questions; rather, they attempt to put some ethical content into the term "Christian". I would suggest that to qualify as Christian, a nation or people should be measurable both in numbers and in demonstrable qualities such as Paul's "fruits of the Spirit" (Gal.

5:22) or Micah's canons of justice (6:8). Quantifying can be helpful, but it can be an easy way to avoid profound evangelization by only doing what comes naturally. If quantifying Christianization becomes programmatic, it could give statistic-happy Americans and mission bureaucrats licence to ride roughshod over the rest of the world's Christians who are just as seriously involved in world mission as they are.

Third, while McGavran does not dismiss national churches' discipleship efforts, he does minimize their importance for mission. Why? I think because he does not consider ecclesiology and kingdom as significant in frontier evangelization. He assumes that a group of persons who accept Jesus constitutes a church; a denomination is a group of such groups. That, though, is a weak ecclesiology not based on Christ's claimed authority (Matt. 28:18 ff.) and Lordship (Eph. 1:20-23; Col. 1:15-20; Phil. 2:5-11). Authority and Lordship gave the first small group of frightened Christians a missionary impulse, even though in the Roman empire such a doctrine was treasonous and cost many their lives, including St Paul's. Frontier missions today have to be based on the same doctrines as the early church's frontier missions were. If they are not so based, we are not involved in the same mission as the early church was.

Of course, McGavran is more interested in technique than content; that has been his major contribution to world mission for more than thirty years. But while a technique that does not integrate proclamation of God's extending rule can still develop many churches, it will be at the expense of the church and kingdom faithfulness.

The churches that McGavran projects in a "giant step" have been developing for years throughout the world. Guatemala has more than two-hundred different evangelical groups. Often these churches are personal fiefdoms of fractious leaders who individualistically confess Jesus as their Saviour, but who fail to witness to Jesus' Lordship over their and all human associations. As a result, "churches" grow by schism, but not in moral influence. Many become Christians, but the witness from evangelical churches to Christ's Lordship and God's rule in Guatemala is almost mute. Church members do not recognize Christ's Lordship as a doctrine that should unite them to stop the violence that kills more than 50 people weekly. In that context, the figure of one-half of Guatemala's population being Bible-believing, Bible-obeying Christians by 1990 means little more than saying that Latin America is Christian because 90 percent of its people are automatically Roman Catholic from birth.

If McGavran's proposal can be combined with hard mission content and be carried out with a spirit of humble service and partnership, it will indeed be a giant step.

From Theodore Ahrens, Federal Republic of Germany: Northelbian Centre for World Mission and Church World Service, Northelbian Evangelical Lutheran Church

It is precisely because I am committed to the task of world mission that I do have a number of questions and concerns which I raise without any implicit "we-do-know-the-situation-better" attitude. I shall dare to draw on my missionary experience in Papua New Guinea and express my foreboding that this new crusade to reach the unreached may in effect reach very few "new tribes", but only many local congregations of second — or third — generation Christians. One only needs to define someone as "unreached" or as "dead wood" to provide oneself with a quasi-legitimation to draw up maps of whole countries where "Christianized" people are mapped out as inhabitants of unevangelized fields! Papua New Guinea, for instance, Christianized basically by five or six "big" classical missions up to 1960, is hosting an ever-increasing number (now more than 150) of missions, many of whom work with some "unreached ethne" concept. For the sake of our ecumenical well-being and missionary credibility, I do hope that all who commit themselves to a missionary call are ready to credit those who claim to be Christians with that basic dignity of Christian belonging.

There is one more reason why I hesitate to bypass the missionary witness of the "small and the weak". I have seen time and again local preachers communicate the gospel in more acceptable ways and maybe also in more digestible doses than are often handed out by strong-willed and determined expatriate missionaries. Those local missionaries seemed to be "effective" because they could reconcile within themselves their new faith in the Good Shepherd with their inherited sense of self-respect. I am personally so deeply indebted to some such teachers and preachers that I would always want to seek their guidance first if I felt a call to serve in their neighbourhood. If there are parishes which are "dead wood" — and there are — then there are also such men and women who, together with their people, stretch out for a renewal of their life through the Spirit of Christ. How can we encourage them?

Can we assume that God speaks at all times and all places? Are there not times when we do not hear his voice? Do we not know of long periods of fervent and dedicated missionary service where, as far as we could see, there was no response of faith, and ours as well as other people's patience was stretched to the utmost and sometimes beyond? We may be in a theological position to share some pertinent insights about the arrival of faith — but what can we say about the non-arrival of faith as responses to the gospel? Many, though reached, remain unreached. God alone knows why.

From Floyd Howlett, Canada: Prairie Christian Training Centre, United Church, Saskakoon

I think we need to be much more humble in our approach to mission. I find McGavran's attitude extremely triumphalist — as if we have the whole of truth and that we can share it merely by proclaiming the word. I hear no word of challenge to the unjust structures and systems, many based in our own Western nations, which are oppressing the marginal and unreached people of the world. Unless this is also part of our mission we may hear Jesus' words: "You travel over land and sea to win one convert; and when you have won him you make him twice as fit for hell as you are yourselves." I have learned from my own experience that people will only listen when you begin to take on some of their burdens, to join with them in tackling the real life issues that are facing them every day. When that basis of understanding and trust is built, then we can begin to share. And always this needs to be a two-way communication — they have something of truth to share with me, and I, if I am faithful, may have something of faith to share with them. I have found that in those situations the Spirit does work in most unexpected ways.

McGavran also mentions the hope that by 1990 half the population of Guatemala may become Bible-believing, Bible-obeying Christians. I do not know what his interpretation of Bible-believing and Bible-obeying Christians is but I do know that certain of those who have called themselves such are among those who have supported the military dictators who have been decimating the population of Guatemala. Unless something more is done in the US to put an end to the support of the military in Guatemala, half the population will not be living by 1990. I find a much more authentic kind of Christianity in the hundreds of thousands of base communities to be found in Latin America. These are the groups we should be praying for and helping in ways we can. These are the very ones who are bearing the brunt of the persecution in our time.

From Dietrich Mendt, Democratic Republic of Germany: pastor, Zittau

Here in our country the kind of model McGavran suggests could not be applied, for two closely related reasons.

We cannot speak of "unreached peoples" and disregard the situation in the German Democratic Republic. It has become clear that here in our own country and in our own parishes a great many "unreached" people live — though up until 1933, or even 1945, we still thought of ourselves as a "Christian" country. That is not the fault of the communists (though we blamed them at first because that was the easiest thing to do). It is the result of a long process in which a once lively community developed into a Volkskirche, an established church, to which one automatically belongs. People demand nothing more of the church and the church demands nothing more of them. But it was in the public interest, and hence also in one's private interest, to belong to the church. The communists simply showed up the situation as it really was. Suddenly it was no longer of public or private interest to be a Christian — and the church was left to be the church. Only apathy has kept more than 50 percent of our people from leaving the church since 1945.

In our country, perhaps even more than in most industrialized countries, because of the Nazi period from 1933 to 1945, the written and the spoken word have lost much of their power and that process has not stopped at the church door. People are only prepared to listen to words that are clearly backed by the life of the person speaking them. The credibility of a sermon depends on the life led by the preacher. A congregation's witness is only worth something if people can "live" with it and in it. This process has rendered methods such as evangelism campaigns largely ineffective because no personal relationship, beyond the words, is possible. Here we therefore set great store by such things as Bible study groups, congregational gatherings with the children when we have meals together, social evenings, group weekends and retreats, and also worship prepared in groups.

A few weeks ago I spent twelve days with a group of over a hundred people — Christians, not-quite-Christians, non-Christians, members of different confessions. We call this a "family retreat" but, of course, everyone is welcome — singles, old, young, intellectuals, workers... The programme is not very strict: a children's party, a social evening with entertainments, film shows, discussions about churches. We end the retreat by gathering together round the Lord's table, with open intercessions. This time everyone who wanted could bring a stone or a flower, or both, and with the flowers we made a "cross of thanks" on the floor, and with the stones a "cross of intercession". As they placed their flower or their stone in the cross people said, quietly or aloud, what they were giving thanks for or what they were asking. In this way some people joined in a fellowship of prayer who had probably never prayed before. As we parted many people were in tears (not all that common among us Germans!). One participant said: "It's been like twelve days in the kingdom of God." And I think that is exactly it: during these family retreats we "live" God's kingdom because we live together in such ideal conditions, sitting at one table, under the same roof, sharing our leisure. So for twelve days everyone has help at hand when they need it, someone to laugh with or to cry with, children and parents and brothers and sisters, even if otherwise they have no-one in this world. We always try on one of the evenings to speak about this and think how we can transfer this model situation to the everyday life of the congregation, where basically it should also be possible, though conditions are more difficult.

From J.N. Kudadjie, Ghana: Department for the Study of Religions, University of Ghana (This represents the views of a group of basically evangelical people who are members of the Interdenominational Church on the university campus in Legon.)

Dr McGavran's proposals, if implemented, will definitely lead to a giant leap in the realization of the goal of making disciples of all nations. "Africa south of the Sahara will soon be as Christian as North America," he says. One may say, it will even hasten in the parousia, since the Lord's return seems to hang very much on the condition that the gospel is preached throughout the world to all humankind and that those who hear accept the Lordship of Christ and live pure and holy lives.

A truly Giant Step! All Christians cannot but say amen to this vision.

There are, however, some observations that must be made. First, one is not at all clear who the "unreached people" are in the context. Is it peoples (*ethne*) who have not heard the gospel preached? Those who may have heard but are not Bible-believing and Bible-obeying? A people some of whose members have become Christians but have left the ethnic fold and are not making the effort to bring others into the faith?

Whoever the unreached people are supposed to be, McGavran clearly does not think they are in North America. For sure, we in Africa need the help of our brethren in North America in our effort to bring the gospel to our own people. But we would encourage our American brethren not to look so far afield, to the uttermost parts of the world, as to forget to witness to Jesus Christ in Jerusalem and Samaria also! People in North America have the Bible, commentaries and electronic churches. So they cannot be regarded as unreached in the first sense above. But in the second and third senses, millions of them are yet to be reached. If everyone who has merely read or heard the gospel or goes to church is regarded as reached, then not many believers in Africa will earnestly desire the era of the new frontier movement. Some of the money and missionaries must be spent to make America Christian — in personal life-styles and attitudes as well as in national policies. We African Christians see much that is not particularly Christian in Americans. The great commission is to make disciples and not just make the word available.

Secondly, one also thinks the proposal makes the wrong assumption, that if you send out millions of dollars and thousands of American missionaries, then automatically you will reach people in the sense of making them disciples of Christ. This is doubtful. There are some other conditions to be fulfilled. For example, will all those thousands have been truly sent by the Holy Spirit?

Thirdly, how will the monies be used? By sending "missionaries" from America? Or funding individual Africans who have studied in the USA and have drawn up ambitious plans for "evangelization of their pagan countrymen"? Experience shows that such "direct" missionaries and solo effort of freelance evangelists (even if indigenous people) are tolerated but not particularly liked. I have found in discussion with a few evangelicals, some of them very mature and involved in outreach work, that they do not think that the proposed frontier mission movements should sponsor "direct" or solo missionaries, or even new movements in the "unreached" countries.

Admittedly, some of the big churches here are not particularly given to disciple-making; they seem satisfied with growing numbers of church-goers. But that is not true of all congregations. Therefore, it is wrong to rule out all churches entirely, and work through only foreign missionaries and indigenous freelance evangelists. After all, must people not be converted and nurtured in a church, a fellowship, an ekklesia?

It will be far more effective if the frontier missions in North America fund and work through identifiable existing mission-oriented groups in the various nations who are breaking into unevangelized people and bringing them into the church. It will also be profitable to use some of the loose change to train local people for this most urgent task. In the author's own country, Ghana, there are a few of these outreach groups already endeavouring to reach the unreached; but their most crippling handicap is finance and transportation, since Ghanaian Christians have not yet learned, unfortunately, to give sufficiently for the Lord's work; and partly because many do not, in fact, have much. In this, we shall welcome help from frontier missions efforts. Maranatha.

From Keith Jamieson, India: Canadian lay missionary engineer in tropical sanitation and rural development, Bombay

Following Dr McGavran's "thinking big" in the positive sense, I believe that it is very important to recognize that the total activities of the church, of the real body of Christ, are much more than the sum of the activities of all the "institutional churches". That is, the living church is made up of people, whose witness as expressed through their daily lives is much greater than the witness expressed through the activities of the institutional churches alone — important as these may be. All Christians, clergy and laity alike, are called to be "living witnesses" at every moment of the day according to their gifts. Not all may have the special gifts or the opportunities to witness through word, but certainly all will have the gifts to witness through action.

In recent years, the most exciting "church" work that we have seen in India has often been that initiated and directed by dedicated lay people — unhampered by the bureaucracy of the institutional churches. Literally thousands of lives have been influenced positively — caste barriers broken, people informally educated, women liberated, children nurtured — simple, ordinary folk accomplishing miracles by working together and treating each other as human beings. No, there have not been conversions in the accepted sense — not, I believe, because the above-mentioned dedicated people have not been doing their work conscientiously but rather because neighbouring Christians have not done theirs in a complementary fashion. That is, because the divisions, squabbles and bickerings of so many members within and without the institutional churches, much of the creative work has been nullified.

Maybe what we need now is the kind of community repentance and renewal such as occurred in the time of King Josiah (2 Kings 23:3) after the reading of the hidden book. If we, individually and corporately, could only begin to live at all levels the life of love and fellowship which we profess (Mark 1:15), then I am sure the Holy Spirit would joyously complete the evangelistic mission.

From John Watson, Britain: Centre for the Study of Christianity in Islamic Lands, Kent

My thinking, writing and above all praying is dominated by my daily mail and contact with Christians in Islamic lands. I believe that I am a Christian who is being saved by God. I also believe in telling anyone I can reach about Jesus the Christ and what he has done for me. But Dean Emeritus McGavran cannot be serious when he writes: "Africa south of the Sahara will soon be as Christian as North America." As I read him, he really seems to think that America is Christian. In the real world, Africa south of the Sahara is soon to be Islamic or Marxist. The world of the church — I do not mean denominations — is a world of irreconcilable differences. J. Spencer Trimingham in his *History of Islam in West Africa* says that "the North African church died rather than was eliminated by Islam, since it had never rooted itself in the life of the country". A primary reason he gives for the rapid conversion to Islam is "Christianity's failure to claim the Berber soul". In the light of the proposed Giant Step which will generate $100 million per annum, it is worth noting what Trimingham says: "The primary Islamization of the negroes was almost entirely the work of Berber merchants." T.B. Irving seems to me closer to the mark than McGavran when the former writes: "Africa itself, with over 300 million people, is an Islamic continent (1968) since the clear majority, 180 million, are Muslims." It is important to record that many of the "unreached peoples" have become the "unreachable". In Saudi Arabia a church building is not permitted, in Egypt permission to build Coptic churches has long been withheld.

I have lived in three countries which were foreign to me — in a little Malay village, a town in Pakistan with a "secret Christian" and in a tin shack in Australia's outback, a contemplative living near the "unreached" Aborigines. You see, McGavran and I do not live on the same planet. We need no plans for tomorrow for, as we hear the sound of the approaching hoofbeats of the four horsemen of the Apocalypse, we know that American management is the last thing to advance the gospel.

From Simon Barrington-Ward, Britain: Church Missionary Society, London

Today the most effective missionaries are those who can demonstrate in their whole person, being and style that the gospel is not a Western affair, as is believed by most Muslims, Hindus, Buddhists and many of the African intelligentsia. We in CMS would only be too glad to join in with prayer, with money and with people in a world church initiative led by African, Asian and South American church leaders. I have received strong *negative* impressions of the impact of certain kinds of "go-it-alone" North American initiatives, often aggressive, insensitive and uncoordinated in the very areas and among the very people we would hope to "reach". Such initiatives make the ultimate task harder.

It is urgently necessary that this appeal be conducted in such a way that it may really and effectively fulfill its ultimate purpose. We need also to pray for a worldwide movement of the Spirit and for a genuine Ephesian "fellowship of the unlike" in this one urgent cause: namely the spreading of the gospel, humbly, sensitively, imaginatively, internationally, multi-racially and *always* in a context of *long-term loving*, social and corporate as well as individual.

February 1986

33

It is my turn to say my piece on Dr Donald McGavran's "A Giant Step in Christian Mission"! Since Dr McGavran started the ball rolling, I feel he should have the last word.

Of the 145 written comments on the McGavran proposal, 38 have been published. I made the selection on the basis of representativeness, geographically and content-wise. The published responses do give a representative picture of the total. The whole exercise, of course, is not a scientific survey of world opinions on world evangelization. I am sure no reader will take it that way. The subject matter is obviously too complex and the reasoning too multi-faceted for that kind of treatment. Perhaps what I would like to claim is that the responses may well reflect the thinking of the readers of the monthly letter. I am glad that one-third of the responses come from readers who identify themselves as evangelicals and are recognized as such. And their views cover the whole range. The debate therefore is not one of ecumenicals versus evangelicals. It is a debate across the whole spectrum of Christianity, a debate within the Christian church.

I am gratefully aware that my response has benefitted from your responses. Receiving your responses, reading them, often more than once, assessing them, trying to understand them from where you are, has been a spiritual journey for me.

McGavran's invitation to a Giant Step "includes me out". I do not understand the terms "Bible-believing, Bible-obeying Christians" or "congregations of biblical Christians..." These must have a special meaning to an exclusive religious group believing itself to be "Bible-believing and Bible-obeying". As for me, I understand myself and many fellow Christians to be very much like the father of the possessed boy in Mark 9:24 confessing to Jesus: "I do believe; help me overcome my unbelief." McGavran's language and its theological assumptions leave me on the outside. They leave me cold.

Still, I cannot be indifferent to the good doctor's concern for world mission and his proposal for its implementation. If the churches, and the WCC for that matter, have a task, it must be the task of sharing the gospel with the unbelieving world. And, when it comes to planning and taking action, I must say I have little problem with "thinking big", certainly not while I am sitting in Geneva, as part of the *World* Council of Churches. "Small is beautiful" is beautiful only when the small can be multiplied, and that means numbers, quantity, statistics. And that means, behind the numbers, individuals, persons, people with whom God can work wonders! For me, the issue is not whether there should or should not be a world mission strategy or strategies. The human reality is such that if we do not have good strategies, we have bad strategies. The issue is whether the strategizing is totalitarian or participatory, and whether or not the strategies faithfully reflect the gospel of Jesus Christ.

Reading the Giant Step, I cannot but feel that it is chauvinistic. That it is not intentional, which I fully accept, only points to its deep-seatedness. That it was written for an American audience explains a little but not all, given that the article first appeared in a periodical called "*International* Journal of Frontier Missions" (italics mine), before it was offered for reprint and discussion by the Monthly Letter on Evangelism. Besides, one would have thought that one American writing to fellow Americans would feel more free to be self-critical than, say, in a more international setting. At least, that is what we Chinese tend to do.

I was recently in the USA for a meeting on evangelism. My colleagues from other parts of the world and I took time out to visit the churches. We were encouraged and excited by their near-unanimous commitment to evangelism. We were overwhelmed by the abundance of material and spiritual resources they have. But frankly, we were scared. We asked our hosts: "What sort of Christians are you producing, or hope to produce?" I must confess that in my case I did not so ask primarily out of my love for America or for its churches. I asked primarily out of my concern for my part of the world. Sooner or later, what happens in the USA affects the rest of the world — the dollar, the soldiers, the tourists, the big companies, the press services and the news magazines, TV, music, and of course the churches, their members at home and missionaries abroad. Well, I exaggerate, but not much. Anyone who sees such power and the thousand and one possible chauvinistic uses of such power will have reason to be scared.

What then is the issue, especially as it touches on world mission? The issue is deeply theological: can a person, a missionary society, or a church, indeed a whole people, who holds human power over others, truly evangelize? I think not. If I hold power over others, I can feed them, I can protect them. I can impose my will on them or manipulate their will. I can instruct them. I can lead them. I can even offer my life for them. But I cannot challenge them. As long as I have power over others, I cannot challenge them to repent, or to stand up and walk, or to take up their cross and follow Jesus. I can say these words all right, backed by the power I possess. But if I am not blinded by chauvinism, I could not reasonably hope for any response other than reciprocal manipulation. Or I am simply playing games with people's souls. As long as I hold power over others, I cannot share the gospel of Jesus Christ with them and expect an authentic response. There is no evangelism. There is only proselytism.

These are harsh words. But in a way, I guess I am saying something similar to Jesus' observation on how hard it is for a rich man to enter the kingdom of heaven (Matt. 19:23). It is not impossible, but it is very very hard. It is hard for a person in a position of power over others to share the gospel with them. Doubly hard, to put it kindly, if that person is absolutely convinced of the righteousness of his or her power, and of its exercise being a divine mandate. America is an issue for world mission. McGavran's *A Giant Step* compels me to ask theologically: "Can American Christians evangelize beyond their border?"

I have neither the power nor the certainty of conviction to say to the American churches or McGavran's frontier missionary societies to stay home (although I constantly dream of a five-year moratorium on all US foreign mission efforts if it can be done across the board). Besides, to go back to Jesus' comment about the rich man, the biblical answer to my question whether American Christians can evangelize beyond their border seems to be quite clear: it is hard but not impossible. Jesus said that "with man this is impossible, but with God all things are possible" (Matt. 19:26). God has to be at work in the heart of the rich man. Likewise, in the case of sharing the gospel with the unbelieving world, God has to be at work in the heart of the evangelist, the missionary. Or the missionary task is an impossibility.

What does the religious language of "God working in the heart of the missionary" mean in this discussion of who can evangelize? I think it means exactly what it states — there is this person, formed and informed by his or her world, and there is God coming into that person to deal with him or her. I am speaking of the need for an encounter in the same person between the cultural-ideological and the religious. I am referring to the dialogue within oneself of gospel and culture. I suspect all this is part of the conversion, or born-again, experience, or should be. It was Paul's surely. And mine and many other first-generation Christians, particularly in the non-Western world. But this cannot be taken for granted: our theologies, whether liberal or conservative, in their different ways, seldom encourage this internal dialogue. (No wonder Christians, wherever they are, find it so difficult to have dialogue with people of other cultures and faiths. But that is a different story.) Its absence makes personal faith hard to take root and blossom. In the case of the Christians who feel called to cross-cultural mission, the absence of an internal dialogue of gospel and culture becomes down-right deadly. How can an American Christian (or a European, or a Japanese, or a Korean, or a Chinese or any other) share the gospel with others from another land and attempt to plant churches there, if he or she never attempts to find out what part of his or her belief is American or Christian? And worse, if he or she is convinced that it makes no difference? In the final analysis, this is my biggest quarrel with McGavran's *A Giant Step*. This is the reason why I feel compelled to raise this seemingly offensive theological question: "Can American Christians evangelize beyond their border?"

To be sure, *A Giant Step* talks of the need for "well trained, well equipped life-time task forces" to reach the unreached. McGavran in the article twice urges American Christians "to study one or more of the very numerous unreached pieces of the mosaic of mankind". In the studying and the training and the equipping, sensitivity to local people would be given due attention. Of that I have little doubt. Anthropological studies of different parts of Asia, Africa and Latin America rank high in importance in evangelical mission schools in the USA. But is there any training and equipping of the missionary so that he or she can have an internal dialogue between gospel and American culture, between gospel and the American Dream? And when keen Christian people from the suburban congregations of southern California gather in "frontier mission fellowships" to study "an unreached people" and to pray for their spiritual deliverance, is there any studying of their own situation in the light of the gospel and with the sharp tools of anthropology? Is there an awareness of the need for a dialogue with one's own culture and ideology, a readiness to engage in it, within the American missionary, within the American missionary society, indeed, within the Christian community in America? Surely such internal dialogue is not irrelevant to the formation of the missionary's character, world-view, understanding of others and of the missionary task, indeed their understanding of the Christian faith. I detect no such readiness in *A Giant Step*, and no awareness. The US Center for World Mission, led by Dr Ralph Winter, which provides data and ideological support to the movement of reaching the unreached, engages in intensive study of Unreached Peoples across the globe. There is no study there of what constitutes the USA as the context, the source and the moulder of American mission policy and personnel. As if the subject were irrelevant to world mission. But unless this internal dialogue between gospel and one's own culture is seriously taking place within the missionary and the missionary societies and fellowships, all claims of Bible-believing and Bible-obeying must be suspect, and all claims to sensitivity to and respect of other cultures and peoples become, at best, no more than methodology and technology.

Finally, with all the arguments and all our passion, the McGavran challenge remains. What of the unreached? Or, to use the language I prefer, which points to not exactly the same thing, what of the unbelieving world? If churches and missionary societies have failed to keep this central task constantly in the forefront of their mission understanding, then it is right and proper that we should be reminded by McGavran. If we find the McGavran strategy wanting in theology and abounding in chauvinism, what is our version? What do the WCC-related churches and missionary societies present in all corners of the earth have to offer? The question is only fair.

Here, I derive much strength and hope from the readers' responses. Reflecting on them, I detect elements of common purpose and methods and a cohesiveness which point to the possibilities of a strategy or approach for sharing the gospel worldwide. You see, my problem with Dr McGavran's strategy is not only theological. It is also, if you like, technical.

Will it work? Will it result in masses of people coming to faith in Jesus Christ? The strategy of reaching an Unreached People's group one at a time is basically a projection of the method of personal evangelism. Reaching people one by one. Presenting the Christian faith so that it makes sense to one particular person, and then another. On the personal level in the life of an individual Christian, mine certainly, I think this is the only way to go. But the same is not necessarily the case where one considers evangelism worldwide. Here, the larger issues (but not necessarily more important or more profound) of influencing the forces which lead to individual decision-making have to be considered. Our emphasis must go beyond individual salvation or the reaching of a particular Unreached People group. If we are really keen about sharing the gospel with the largest number of persons possible, in the long run, we must also put our evangelistic emphasis on influencing the world in such a way that individuals and groups would be more inclined to respond positively when confronted with the claims of Jesus Christ. I fear that without this evangelical concern for the macro, the strategy of personal evangelism and reaching the unreached one by one would prove self-defeating even in terms of numbers. We may succeed in drawing several known persons to Christ but risk alienating unknown hundreds and turning them away. In order to reach the largest number, one does not attempt only to make sense of Christianity to one or a group of "targeted" potential believers, one must also attempt to make sense of Christianity to the whole unbelieving world towards the goal of a better world and, in that journey with others, for a chance and the right to share explicitly and personally the gospel of Jesus Christ. For authenticity and for effectiveness, the church must be meaningful not only to those who are in it as well as those who are aspiring to be part of it, but it must stand for something even to the unbelieving world. I fear that the church growth strategy, which McGavran has so powerfully represented, would find itself as running a few battles and yet losing the war.

This is where the insistence in many of the responses for justice and peace and solidarity with the poor and the oppressed comes in. This is where the churches' public commitment on matters of poverty, hunger, racism, human rights violations and totalitarianism becomes necessary for world evangelization, indeed, part and parcel of it, even in McGavran's terms. With such public commitment, the church stands for something in front of the whole world. The church makes sense to the masses of unbelievers, even to those who are hostile to such commitments, because they would have to ask "why?" and cannot remain indifferent. That is why I believe the WCC's Programme to Combat Racism is one of the most significant and effective evangelistic ministries for Africa. This, I believe, is the way to wage war for millions upon millions of human souls and, may I add, for the soul of the church.

So I join my voice with that of many respondents that the churches beware lest we win a few battles but lose the war. On the other hand, it is absurd to talk about winning the war if one engages in no battles. Without the local engagements, the church's witness on the macro level, in short any level other than the grassroots, is at best an exercise in influencing public opinion. Not a bad thing, but not enough.

Despite these my generally critical remarks about *A Giant Step*, I suspect, or hopefully suspect, that nothing I have said so far is basically unacceptable to McGavran. My comments amount to saying: "Just hold it. Look closer home. Examine your basics and your strategies. Your Giant Step may well defeat your giant purpose." At the same time, I am aware that I have not directly responded to the "how" of reaching those who are geographically and culturally locked out from existing mission efforts. The questions of *who* can share the gospel and *what* the good news is are so important to me that I am reluctant to go into the *how* question by itself, and I do not apologize for that. Content must dictate methodology. And methodology must reflect content. Jesus Christ, God Incarnate, is both the substance of the good news as well as the means of its communication.

At this point, let me share with you two chosen foci in my ongoing reflection on world mission, partly stimulated by this discussion.

The first is the missionary role of the established churches in world evangelization — the denominations, the synods, the districts, the dioceses, the parishes, the congregations, and the people in them. I think McGavran is chauvinistic about them, especially those in the third world, but I do not think a careful reading of *A Giant Step* would show that he intends to bypass them in his world mission proposal. But if the evangelicals are guilty of giving the brush to the churches, the ecumenicals are no less so. The former have their para-church organizations, evangelistic associations, and now the frontier mission fellowships; the ecumenicals have their networks, the action groups, and a whole range of ecumenical bodies. From both come much rhetoric about being servants and partners with the churches, yet from where I sit, the churches seem to remain second fiddle. Not that some churches do not deserve that, but that is a different matter altogether. My present reflection on the subject inclines towards a different direction: perhaps instead of creating new structures and new ways of engaging in mission, which both the ecumenicals and evangelicals have been doing all these years and still are, the older and younger churches and their mission apparatus should have stuck with each other long enough to work through the ties already established but in a new spirit of interdependency and mutual challenge for the sake of spreading the good news. Perhaps if we give these ties time to mature and grow and develop, the more traditional structures and ways may yet prove to have a longer and deeper mission reach. Perhaps!

My other reflection focus has to do with the scriptural basis for world mission. It is clear to me that for most Christians, including McGavran and probably even most of his critics, it is what is commonly known as the Great Commission of Matthew 28 with an emphasis on authority, on teaching and global reach. There is nothing wrong about this, of course, except that, given that human nature is what it is, we, especially when we have a certain amount of power, would always tend to get it wrong. But there is nothing wrong about Matthew 28 as a basis for world mission. The problem is Matthew 28 is not the only scriptural basis, and therefore cannot provide a complete biblical understanding. For me, and I am very grateful to be given this hint,* there is also Jesus' new command of John 13-17 which is equally world-mission-and-evangelism-oriented, indeed, glaringly so.

At the time, Jesus was acutely conscious that his days on earth were drawing to an end. He still had a lot to say to his people. And he said, repeated in different ways: "A new command I give you: love one another. As I have loved you, so you must love one another. All men will know that you are my disciples if you love one another" (John 13:34-35). And he prayed: "My prayer is that all of them may be one, Father, just as you are in me and I am in you. May they also be in us so that the world may believe that you have sent me... may they be brought to complete unity to let the world know that you sent me and have loved them even as you have loved me" (17:21). Note that Jesus is stating categorically here that Christians loving one another, in unity, is capable of proving to the world that Jesus is God, and that Christians belong to Christ. This new command of Jesus is therefore not primarily an internal policy of the church. It is meant as the church's mission policy. Christian unity, is Jesus' strategy for world mission.

There is a lot more work to do. I am not quite clear yet how Christian unity can actually evangelize. But that is what I would like to work on. I long for a world mission understanding and methodology based on Jesus' new command in John 13-17 with its characteristics of love, dying for others, suffering and joy. Then, maybe, the unbelieving world may be more willing to listen.   *April 1986*

---

* I owe this to Bob Lupton, urban missionary in Atlanta, Georgia, USA.

34

RESPONSE TO THE RESPONSES

Donald McGavran

First, let me congratulate those who wrote the responses. Many of them saw the undone task, they heard eternal God's command to Christianize all the peoples of the world (Rom. 16:25,26), they recommended many additional steps. They also saw many problems which the Giant Step certainly entails. The vast enterprise of world evangelization has many facets. Most of these were not even mentioned in the Monthly Letter. It is quite impossible to cover all facets in one thin article or even one fat volume. Effective evangelism among the highly organized homosexuals of San Francisco is substantially different from what it is among the Masai tribe in Kenya or the highly educated segment of the South Korean population...

If a missionary conscience can be aroused in all congregations in all nation-states throughout the entire world and if the resulting activity is directed to effective evangelization among the unreached segments of society, *at home* and abroad, tremendous church growth will result. That in turn will bring substantial improvement in the social, economic, and political realms. If we want a just world, Christianize all segments of the world's population. If we want a peaceful world, multiply soundly Christian congregations. If we (all Christians everywhere) want a brotherly world, make sure that every *ethnos* in the world is at least 30 percent genuinely Christian.

Second, *A Giant Step in Christian Mission* was written for a magazine read almost exclusively by American Christians. Consequently, it spoke about arousing a missionary conscience among North American Christians to reach the unreached.

However, the article also indicates that this same Giant Step ought to be taken by Christians in all continents. The article called for missionary action by all congregations throughout the world, east and west, north and south — the formation in each of a local missionary group or society...

Hundreds of thousands of new local missionary groups or societies must arise in the Eastern as well as Western lands. The publication said this but did not emphasize it. This seems to have caused some misunderstanding. I emphasize this because as an aftermath of the break-up of the imperial era some people mistakenly think of missions as a European and

North American enterprise. In their mind the missionary is always a white man or woman. Possibly my proposal should have made clear in the very beginning that what I was proposing was that every congregation in every continent should form a missionary group or society whose purpose was to carry out Christ's clear command to *matheteusate panta ta ethne* (Matt. 28:19), that is, disciple all segments of society everywhere. These Greek words in Hindi have been correctly translated as *sab jatiyon ko chela karo*. This means, "incorporate in my body, the church, all the castes, tribes, and classes". These are the segments of society in India.

Thus my second response to those who criticized the proposal on the basis that it looked like Western imperialism. No Western imperialism can be deduced from a careful reading of the article. Rather a vast new obedience to Christ was called for. That there are today maybe 17,000 and maybe 100,000 unreached segments of society is the main point. These unreached segments exist in every nation. Great sections of France are by the Roman Catholic Church called mission territory. In the great city of London east of the tower I was assured by a Christian sociologist that 98 percent of the whites never attend Christian worship anywhere. A German Lutheran pastor told me that in his parish were 4,000 people. Of these, 100 attended church and with 300 more he had some contact. With *three thousand six hundred* he had no contact at all. In the United States every state of the union has unreached segments of the population. Some of these are blue-collar populations and some are white-collar. Some are uneducated and poor; others are highly educated and rich. The proportions are different in every nation-state in the world. But unreached peoples exist everywhere.

Let me assure all readers that what *A Giant Step in Christian Mission* calls for is an aroused conscience on world evangelization. What it demands is that Christian men and women in every congregation throughout the entire earth form *local* groups, whose purpose is to pray for, give to, and reach the unreached, discipling all segments of society. From these local groups (in the Pacific islands, Africa, India, Scandinavia, Russia, Japan, the United States, and *every other nation*) will go a steady stream of missionaries to proclaim Christ and multiply his congregations in some unreached segment in their own or some other nation. Some of these missionaries will be brown, white, black, yellow. Some may even be purple! I trust that this will help those readers who saw in the article a revival of Western imperialism to join the great multitudes of earnest Christians, making every effort to carry out Christ's command.

Third, I am grieved that so large a percentage of those who read *A Giant Step in Christian Mission* interpreted my proposal to arouse a missionary conscience in every congregation of every branch of the church in every nation/state in the world as a naive, stupid, and outmoded case of white imperialism. When three-fourths, rapidly becoming four-fifths, of the world's population is not even nominally Christian, these responses must also grieve God our Heavenly Father.

However, these indignant, strident attacks on Western imperialisms of all sorts have one redeeming feature. They clearly indicate that the missionary conscience needs to be aroused. If the unreached hundreds of millions in Europe and America as well as the rest of the world are to inherit eternal life, this tremendous angry frame of mind in so many people, West as well as East, must be overcome. The facts are clear. Most of the blue-collar workers in England remain outside of the church. At least 100 million in the United States have no contact at all with any church. Only 1.06 percent in Japan are Christians of any sort. In many districts in India Christians number less than 5 in 1,000. Many other illustrations could be given. Any Christian, seeing these facts and believing that no one comes to the Father but by the Lord Jesus, must ardently work for an aroused missionary conscience in his own congregation. I pray to God that this exchange of opinion will help many to see that white imperialism is now dead. The missionary conscience of every congregation in every continent must now be aroused.

But can it be? Can the poor congregations in any part of the globe really evangelize their fellows? Of course they can! Multitudes were discipled by fishermen and day labourers, as recounted in the first chapters of Acts. Poverty-stricken Irishmen who called themselves Perigrini (wanderers) surged out from that island between A.D. 500 and 800 to evangelize North Europe. In India practically all the great movements to Christ have been carried out by ardent Christians who belong to the landless labouring castes. One thinks at once of Ditt, the Chura of Punjab, and other leaders of the great caste-wise movements to Christ. A missionary conscience is God's gift to every believer who accepts Christ as his Saviour and the Bible as his rule of faith and practice.

Fourth, some of my readers are engaged in increasing justice and brotherhood in the world and are devoting their lives to urging Christians to be more Christian; this certainly must be done. However, we can never forget that while the Bible tells us that in Christ "there is neither Jew nor Greek", it also goes on to say "neither slave nor free". Yet in the entire New Testament there is not a single word calling on the Roman empire to free all slaves. Indeed, Paul commands slaves to obey their masters. When populations are Christianized, they will work to obey the clear commands of Christ and the Bible to behave in accordance with God's law and the leading of the Holy Spirit. However, this process may take time. It was 1863 before four million slaves in the United States were emancipated, and even longer before slavery was outlawed in some other nations. Much economic slavery still exists in all countries but particularly in India. By all means let us work for social justice. Let us also remember that the longest single step towards social justice is taken when segments of society (people groups) become soundly Christian. Each such group is, then, by its own leaders, highly motivated to act justly. No group moves towards justice as rapidly as you, dear readers, or I would like. But they all do move.

Fifth, some of the respondents refer to the nation-states of Europe and North America as Christian countries. I must sharply dissent. There are no Christian countries in the world today. Christians everywhere are a minority. A tidal wave of secularism has spread across the world.

Sixth, the comments from Dr Bosch and his associates of South Africa do not speak directly to the Giant Step proposed but lash out vigorously against any recognition that mankind exists in the form of many segments — tribes, castes, classes. My respectful reply to this would be that the Bible itself records scores of segments. The Bible recognizes that mankind is a mosaic made up of many segments. It frequently mentions Hittites, Amalekites, Perizzites, and on and on. Anthropology reveals thousands of separate tribes in Africa. England is sharply divided into the intelligentsia and the labouring population. In the American city of Philadelphia over fifty minority populations can be identified, and among English-speaking Americans there are many segments. Even in South Africa the population is sharply divided into descendants of the Dutch, the English, the Indians, and many African tribes.

All major advances of the Christian faith during the past nineteen centuries have occurred as Christward movements swept through segment after segment of non-Christian society. When Ireland became Christian, it did so as tribe after tribe (127 in all) turned to the Christian faith. The church in the New Testament first spread exclusively among the common Jewish people. The priests stayed out of the church until a great number of them became willing to become Christ's followers (Acts 6:7).

Evangelization which calls on people to leave their economic, educational, financial, or ethnic standing to join a church which refuses to recognize any segments of society experiences very slow growth — if any. Even Zulus in South Africa like to join a Zulu black church. This is both understandable and reasonable. Evangelization which encourages people to become followers of the Lord Jesus while remaining ethnically, culturally, economically and educationally themselves will experience rapid growth.

The battle for brotherhood must certainly be fought. I have fought it. My wife and I were for some years the only white members in a black church in the United States. We are for justice, brotherhood, equality. However, we insist that striving for brotherhood must not be substituted — repeat, substituted — for effective evangelization.

It is my hope that with this clarification of meanings Dr Bosch and his associates will find it quite possible to take the Giant Step in missions. Let them establish in every congregation in every tribe, every community of Indian descent, English descent, and Dutch descent in South Africa a band of men and women committed to, working for, and praying for world evangelization...

April 1986

Chapter 7
Perspectives on Proselytism

35

With this letter, I propose to begin a series reporting and reflecting on the issue of "proselytism". "Proselytism" used not in a positive sense, but in a negative one, to mean sheep-stealing and coercive and improper attempts to get others to change their religious convictions and affiliations.

Proselytism, understood negatively, has been condemned by almost all Christians, indeed by almost all religious bodies. But there is no working or workable consensus at all as to what constitutes sheep-stealing or coercive and improper attempts to convert. Part of the problem is that while there are constant outcries against proselytism, there has been much less willingness, or ability, to talk about proselytizing circumstances. This makes discussions of a general and theoretical nature of limited value. We need to know what is actually happening.

Some months ago, I asked readers to send descriptions of specific situations where proselytism has happened. They have given me the biggest editorial headache and heartache ever! The headache has to do with finding ways to communicate the complexity and sensitivity of the issues involved. What is involved is not just religious affiliation, but also other equally important things of life — the freedom of the individual, the dignity of the family, the integrity of the nation or tribe and, let us not mince words, power and politics. I shall strive to be fair. But I know the very selection of material itself is interpretative. So I ask for your indulgence and the benefit of doubt.

The heartache has to do with reading passages like these: "The other day, an Orthodox bishop, who is a dear friend of our family, once again urged me to come back to the fold. My God! After 145 years, our church

is still told that it is illegitimate!!" Or: "Despite good will and cooperation, I know Western missionaries today still assume that Orthodox
Christians who have a personal faith and who diligently work at the
scriptures, will find it difficult to remain in the Orthodox faith." And
much more.

Adding to the editorial difficulty is the desire for anonymity. Of the
42 entries, 18 will not let me use names and specific references. Some
would not even let me quote directly. There is the fear that the cause of
Christian unity and common witness might suffer, indeed, a fear for
communal peace and personal safety in some cases.

In the circumstances, I cannot simply publish what has come to me
and then add a reflection towards the end. For the sake of communication
and understanding, I shall let the entries speak for themselves whenever
possible, use my own words when appropriate, and provide descriptions
and explanations when necessary.

Let me start with a statement on proselytism from the Holy Synod of
the Ethiopian Orthodox Church, followed by a story of the faith journey
of two sisters.

From the Ethiopian Orthodox Church, General Secretariat of the Holy Synod, October 1987, Addis Ababa

PROSELYTISM IN ETHIOPIA

1. Introduction

Christianity was introduced into Ethiopia in the era of the apostles. In
the fourth century the church was organized at bishopric level. The
Ethiopian Orthodox Church was one of the five Oriental Orthodox
churches which rejected the decisions of the council of Chalcedon (451
A.D.). Until the middle of the sixteenth century, there was only one
church in Ethiopia and this was the Ethiopian Orthodox Church. In the
tenth and sixteenth centuries non-Christian religious groups had carried
on proselytism against EOC.

2. Some historical experience of proselytism against EOC

After the sixteenth century, first the Catholic and later the Protestant
missionaries slowly started coming into Ethiopia and began large-scale
and aggressive proselytizing work on the EOC. Slowly the religious
disputes became the cause of much bloodshed and turmoil in the country.

Between 1607 and 1632 the foreign missionaries who combined their
religious work with the tasks of colonialism wanted to impose on the

people by force their objectives of proselytism. This generated a counter-force among the clergy and laity of the Ethiopian Orthodox Church against the missionaries. The clergy and laity of the Ethiopian Orthodox Church defended their church and their country through bitter struggles and big sacrifices.

Proselytism in the nineteenth century: In the second half of the nineteenth century, that is, during the period of the European scramble for Africa, other Protestant Christian missionaries began to arrive in Ethiopia. They too followed a policy of hostility towards the Ethiopian Orthodox Church and on several occasions attempted to advance their cause to the detriment of the Ethiopian Orthodox Church.

The 1944 state regulations governing missionary activities in Ethiopia recognized Ethiopian church areas and open areas where the inhabitants are predominantly non-Christian. The regulation restricted missionaries from establishing themselves in the Ethiopian church areas for the purpose of proselytizing, although they were permitted to establish hospitals and non-denominational schools therein.

Proselytism among the Orthodox youth — a recent incident (1970): In the late sixties, the urban Orthodox youth was the target of proselytism by a wide spectrum of foreign Christian missionaries. They attacked the Ethiopian Orthodox Church and dislodged some youth from their mother church. They filled them with muddled thoughts and conceptions with bits and pieces drawn from the Holy Bible. Slowly, these youth became socially destructive and lacked even the elementary standards and norms of Christian morals and behaviour. Through a series of seminars and discussion sessions arranged for the urban youth, the EOC was able to withstand the proselytism then in action.

3. Forms of proselytism against EOC

Proselytism against our church is carried on in a variety of ways. The following are some of the methods used by other churches to induce the followers of our church to abandon the faith and practice of our church with the ultimate objective of winning them over to their congregations.

Infiltration of EOC institutions: There are several attempts made by the agents of proselytism to infiltrate EOC institutions with the purpose of weakening or diluting their influence. The main target of this infiltration is the Sunday school. There are at present over 4,500 properly function-ing and adequately organized Sunday schools within the Ethiopian Orthodox Church. Some children or youth who belong to other churches infiltrate our Sunday schools in a deliberate plan to undermine the position of the Sunday schools and to dull the enthusiasm of the children in their Orthodox faith and education. On the other hand, they pose as the most authentic alternatives in the service of the Lord.

Vicious campaigns: In various platforms, in groups or at individual level, opportunities are not missed to agitate against Orthodox Christian faith and practice. With differing nuances but with the same theme, the traditional administration of the EOC and the clergy are falsely made the objects of attack and even of ridicule. These are done to blur the perspectives of the members of the church and to reduce their confidence in and love of their church.

Blurring distinctions: Where infiltration of EOC grassroot institutions and organized campaigns become counterproductive or where the laity of EOC are tenuous and resilient, they resort to a more refined and subtle approach. There is no lack of rhetoric to persuade others to believe that there are no real differences between the Orthodox faith and the other denominations. To prove this they imitate our ceremonies and practices. They try to appropriate for themselves the historical and liturgical tradition of our church. These are in fact all masks to hide their actual work of proselytism.

Buying over converts: Prominent EOC members are sought after in the endeavour of other Christian denominations to proselytize EOC congregations. Where, much through material inducements, success is achieved in winning over a convert, he is provided all the possible platforms and occasions to carry on a vicious campaign against his church.

Proselytism through famine handouts: The Ethiopian Orthodox Church has throughout its history consoled the distressed and supported the needy. Recently it embarked on an organized and sustained effort of relief and a rehabilitation programme, in the face of the recurring drought and famine of the last years. The other foreign-based Christian denominations with better resources and organization have performed very commendable relief and rehabilitation operations in Ethiopia. They have operated also in predominantly Orthodox Christian areas. There are frequent attempts to make the famine-stricken population abandon their Orthodox faith. This is done more through the stomach than through the brain. The acceptance of the new faith is sometimes made a precondition for a sustained programme of assistance. There are historical precedents for such actions. During the great Ethiopian famine of 1888-92, a Catholic priest said: "The Abyssinian is in dire poverty. The Protestant dangles his gold in front of him. But he will not give it him until he sells his soul to eternity."

4. Facing the challenge

Education of laity: The Ethiopian Orthodox Church looks with some concern at the proselytism as practised by some missionaries in Ethiopia. She arranges seminars and discussion sessions, depending upon the nature of the problem, to explain the basis of her faith and practice. In July 1987, a one-month refresher course was arranged for the clergy of the Addis Ababa diocese with proselytism as the main theme of the seminar. Here, once again based on our own historical experience, the current specific national form of proselytism was discussed and methods and approaches of combat against this pernicious weed were forwarded by many participants.

Strengthening ecumenical cooperation: Proselytism stands in opposition to ecumenism. In the ecumenical movement, which is the hope and plan for the eventual union of all Christian churches, the Ethiopian Orthodox Church makes all efforts for the realization of this goal.

a)   Ecumenism at the national level (local ecumenism): The EOC participates at the national level in common prayers with those religious groups who think of her positively. She organizes and invites others to a platform of action of common interest. Recently, in the face of the serious drought in Ethiopia, besides her own separate effort, she took part in a joint relief programme with other Christian charity organizations.

b)   At the international level: The Ethiopian Orthodox Church has always attached great importance to contacts and collaboration with the rest of the faithful world. Ethiopian (Orthodox) faithful have been observed in Jerusalem in the very early Pentecostal celebrations (Acts 8:26-40).

The EOC is a founding member of the World Council of Churches and a staunch supporter of its ideals. She maintains through the WCC bilateral contacts with and pays friendly visits to other churches around the world. She collaborates specially in religious education with the Eastern Orthodox churches. As the non-Chalcedonian Orthodox churches together maintain a single doctrinal, canonical and liturgical unity, the EOC gives special significance to relations with these churches.

The EOC is a member of the All Africa Conference of Churches and is represented in the general committee of this continental organization. Besides, the EOC participates in the programmes of the Christian Peace

Conference. The EOC, as much as she strives to cultivate good ecumenical cooperation with other Christian denominations, also expects similar attitudes and efforts from the other Christian denominations. The World Council of Churches should work towards goals and measures to avoid proselytism among Christian denominations which has now become a major obstacle to serious ecumenical brotherhood and cooperation.

From two sisters, Addis Ababa*

We have heard that you are interested in hearing from people like ourselves. So we gather courage in our hands. We wish to share the story of our walk with Jesus Christ with you and your readers. We are two sisters in our early thirties, a teacher and a bank officer. Each of us has a family, and children of our own. Had it not been for the fact that we have always been very close, having no secrets between us, we would not have stayed firm in the faith of our Lord Jesus.

We could have said we are still Orthodox Christians. But that would not be very honest. Today, we belong to the family of the Ethiopian Mekane Yesus Church (Lutheran). The church has protected us and nurtured us. Her arms were open to us when we were in doubt. She took us in in our suffering.

Our family has always been Orthodox. Our father and mother brought us up Orthodox. We did nothing and wished for nothing other than Orthodox. So the one thing that our father asked of us before allowing us to choose our own way was never to use bad words about the Orthodox church. He was in deep pain: "If you pour scorn on the (Orthodox) church, you pour scorn on me and on your people." We knelt as we gave our promise. Please do not ever think it was an easy thing to leave the church we were born into. We did not leave the Orthodox church "in order to have fun with young men". We did not do so in order to "sing immoral Western songs in a dark room". It was not easy to convince our father of the joy of speaking to Jesus and to his spirit. It was so hard to face the priest, his pleas and admonitions, and the malicious gossip of neighbours.

Our walk with Jesus began in the last years of secondary schooling. Several classmates invited us to join a Bible study group at the home of a

---

* An edited, composite version based on a series of correspondence. The writers asked not to be named and that specific references be removed. Some background material, provided by persons with first-hand experience, has been inserted for the benefit of readers unfamiliar with recent development in the region.

European medical missionary. She opened our eyes to the word of God. We were all girls, sitting on the floor in her simple, comfortable room, sipping a cold drink. We shared our ideas, our dreams, our difficulties. Then we turned to the Bible and together sought the will of the heavenly Father. "What is God saying to us today through this text?" What a simple question! When we first heard it, it came as a big spring gushing out into an arid land. It sounded so strange and yet so immediate. Then we learned to use commentaries and other reference material. There was so much to learn. Every piece of Bible learning thrilled our mind. We took turns to prepare and lead the meeting. We cared for each other with the help of the word of God. Later on, we two became part of a puppet road show, and we enacted gospel stories in orphanages and old people's homes. All this time, we remained faithful Orthodox. We followed the faith of our fathers. We were happy.

Then a great spiritual revival swept the land. Two of our friends in the Bible study group began to speak in tongues. In our school, the same thing happened with many girls. Outside in the streets, new songs were being sung and heard. They came from bus boys and shoe-shine boys. They were singing the Lord's song at their work. They preached in street corners wherever they could. They were infecting the city with song and joy. One of us was in training college then. Life went on as usual for us.

Then in a Bible study meeting, the Spirit eventually caught up with us. A leader of what was then informally known as the Full Gospel Movement who was a young mathematics teacher asked for our repentance. Immediately we fell on our knees. Tears wet our faces and we received the Holy Spirit. It was a turning point in our lives. Now it was not possible not to change. All our time outside of our studies was dedicated to learning more about the Spirit, through prayers, Bible studies and preaching. The weekends were spent in missions to the countryside. Like the early disciples, in twos and threes, we carried the message of the good news to homes and villages. We went wherever we would be received.

Then things changed. Many of our leaders were picked up by the security police. Some priests were helping the authorities. It was a dark period. We were frightened. We sought all the more the guidance of the Spirit. Many of us left the city and fled to the countryside. Some of our most beloved brothers and sisters in the movement were picked up. We could no longer meet.

We are sure that our parents at the time were suffering with us. One evening, my father came home with our priest. We tried to talk to one another. But we could not make him understand. There was no turning back. The Evangelical Church Mekane Yesus was open to us. She was ready to take us in, even in our thousands.

April 1988

36

From Ms Annette Daum, Department of Inter-religious Affairs, Union of American Hebrew Congregations, New York, USA

In seeking a different dynamic for effective evangelization of those lost to the church, careful consideration needs to be given to the impact of such a campaign on the special relationship between Christians and Jews.

Historically, especially in Europe, no matter who the initial targets were, missionary campaigns inevitably deteriorated into intolerance and coercion resulting in persecution and massacre of Jews — a sad history still largely unknown to many Christians. Any upsurge in enthusiasm for Christian evangelism, then, becomes cause for alarm in the Jewish community. While the Joint Working Group of the Vatican and the World Council of Churches denounces coercive proselytism, little guidance is provided regarding specific techniques, overt or subtle, which may be regarded as unethical or offensive, especially when approaching the Jewish community. The following examples of tactics used by aggressive evangelizers which trouble American Jews might be helpful in determining the limits beyond which evangelism becomes proselytism.

Jews are most offended when they are singled out as special targets for conversion by Christian missionaries. They are particularly incensed by the deceptive tactics of high-pressure proselytizers who distort Jewish symbols and rituals, giving them a Christological interpretation to confuse unsuspecting Jews into believing that they can be both Jewish and Christian. Calling themselves "Hebrew-Christians", these Christian evangelists target only Jews. They cover the gospel message with Jewish music and Israeli dance to make Jews feel comfortable culturally while converting them to Christianity. They treat Jews as merely another ethnic group, denigrating the essence of their identity — their connection to their religion — Judaism.

Jews are particularly incensed by the tactics of groups like Assemblies of God, which is creating a network of "messianic synagogues" attached to their churches, designed specifically to attract Jews by conducting worship services which appear to be Jewish, but which actually parody traditional Jewish rituals and prayers recited in the name of Jesus Christ.

These so-called "synagogues" are promoted as another way to be Jewish, developed and defined as a new movement by Christian missionaries which they call "Messianic Judaism". Every authentic branch of Judaism — Orthodox, Conservative, Reconstructionist and Reform — rejects this movement as illegitimate from a Jewish perspective. They resent this blatant attempt by Christians to redefine Judaism in a way that threatens to destroy Judaism and decimate Jewish peoplehood. Over-zealous missionaries have also been attending Shabbat services at legitimate synagogues, taking advantage of the hospitality provided to evangelize Jews at worship on their holiest day.

Evangelists also need to address the ethics of informed consent and the appropriate age of consent when considering religious conversion. These questions are raised when youth ministers systematically gain entry to public schools without identifying themselves as Christian clergy, to recruit children sometimes no more than twelve years of age. These ministers approach youngsters to join "social clubs" which also conceal their religious affiliation in an effort to hide their missionary intent.

The consequence of these aggressive, deceptive tactics has been increased tension between Jews and Christians in communities where missionaries engage in such practices, reinforcing the suspicion among some Jews that Christians have a hidden agenda in promoting inter-religious dialogue and fostering coalitions of concern on social, economic and human rights issues.

Jews are also withdrawing from contact with churches which cooperate with or support "Hebrew-Christian" missionaries. In some instances, these coercive techniques are bringing Jews and Christians together in a cooperative effort to denounce such tactics.

Since mainline Protestant denominations are beginning to acknowledge that Jews remain eternally in a covenantal relationship with God, this may be an appropriate time for evangelists to consider that Judaism's continuing vitality is part of God's plan by rejecting approaches to the Jewish people which denigrate Judaism, preventing Jews and Christians from joining in common witness in the creation of a just and peaceful society.

From the Rev. Robert W. Pirtle, Division of Home Missions, General Council of the Assemblies of God, Springfield, Missouri, USA

I want to thank you for writing and giving us the opportunity to reply before you print the statement from the Union of American Hebrew

Congregations. It was gracious of you to invite us "to respond officially or facilitate other forms of response that you think appropriate for publication". I will limit my remarks to general observations on some of the criticisms, and a specific response to those directed against the Assemblies of God.

The Assemblies of God does not view evangelism as the seeking of "those lost to the church", but rather the seeking of those who are lost to God. Our official position on evangelism is simply an echo of the biblical teaching: "Since God's purpose concerning man is to seek and to save that which is lost... the priority reason-for-being of the Assemblies of God as part of the church is: (a) To be an agency of God for evangelizing the world (Acts 1:8; Matt. 28:19-20; Mark 16:15-16)...."

As you wrote in one of your letters on evangelism: "Christians owe the message of God's salvation in Jesus Christ to every person and to every people." Understandably, there are those who believe otherwise, and we need to be sensitive to their beliefs, without denying our own.

We believe that there is a special relationship between the church and the Jewish people. Unfortunately, the church has often not understood or accepted the biblical presentation of that relationship, turning instead to actions that violate its own identity and integrity. We agree that it is important for Christians to learn about this frequently tragic aspect of Jewish-Christian relations.

It is not, however, true to state that "missionary campaigns inevitably deteriorated into intolerance and coercion resulting in persecution and massacre of Jews". That was often the case when: (1) prevailing doctrines replaced Israel with the church, individual repentance with cultural uniformity, and faith in God with subservience to man; and (2) the church and state were joined in unholy alliance. It was never the case when the church held fast to its New Testament identity.

The New Testament church was the most missionary-evangelistic church ever, but it did not engage in coercion or persecution. There are similar, modern, Western examples of such genuine missionary evangelism. For example, the Great Scottish Revival was immediately preceded by the sending of evangelistic teams to the European continent to share the gospel with the Jews, but it brought neither coercion, persecution nor massacre. The Wesleyan revival in England and the Great Awakening in the United States are other examples of times of fervent evangelism that were faithful to the New Testament. Both, in the good they brought to society, are bright lights in human history.

The New Testament context is Jewish. Initially, the church was composed only of Jews. They did not think, speak or write of themselves as anything other than Jews. They claimed that being faithful to God meant accepting Jesus as the Messiah, the King of the Jews. They met in the temple, in synagogues and in homes. They spoke the various languages of their fellow Jews of the time — whether Hebrew, Greek, Latin, or the languages of the countries where they lived. Believing in Jesus changed their hearts but not their culture or heritage.

It is the New Testament itself which gives "a Christological interpretation" to the symbols, rituals, holy days, and lessons of the Old Testament. Those Jews who believed in Jesus naturally understood the history and the faith of Israel as the New Testament explained it. Those Jews who did not believe in Jesus understood their history and faith in different ways. The real question was, and remains "Is the New Testament true?" which is another way of saying "Is Jesus the Messiah or not?"

The most divisive issue that the early church faced was whether or not *only* Jews could be Christians. There were those who maintained that non-Jews had to become Jewish in order to be Christians, by submitting to circumcision and the covenant of the Law given at Sinai (cf. Acts 11 and 15, and Gal.).

Some Jews who believe in Jesus today call themselves "Hebrew-Christians", "Messianic Jews", or other terms designed to present clearly the Jewish nature of their faith in Israel's messiah. Likewise, they often call their congregations "Messianic Synagogues".

The Assemblies of God is not engaged in "creating a network of 'Messianic Synagogues'". We know of two groups in the United States that are creating such "unions"; perhaps similar in form to the Union of American Hebrew Congregations. Some of those affiliated with the Assemblies of God have established Messianic Synagogues. Some of these are involved with one or the other of the Messianic Synagogue groups. Others are not involved; and others have different types of work. We have no policy or practice of encouraging or discouraging such involvement or expression of faith.

The Union of American Hebrew Congregations statement says: "Every authentic branch of Judaism — Orthodox, Conservative, Reconstructionist and Reform — rejects this movement as illegitimate from a Jewish perspective." To paraphrase, "Messianic Judaism is not an authentic branch of Judaism because the authentic branches say that it is not".

Three points should be made: (1) The definition of what is not "authentic" is circular. (2) It is normal for existing groups to view new movements as illegitimate. This was the case with the Roman Catholic Church and the Protestant Reformation. Which of the four "authentic" branches of Judaism were considered authentic when they first appeared? (3) There are Orthodox groups who reject the Conservative, Reconstructionist and Reform movements as illegitimate.

We are always open to fruitful cooperation with other religious bodies on issues of mutual concern but, in general, the Assemblies of God is not involved in "promoting inter-religious dialogue and fostering coalitions of concern on social, economic, and human rights issues". Recently, representatives from one national Jewish organization approached us for the purpose of dialogue. We have been glad to meet with them several times, and remain open to further meetings.

To the best of my knowledge, the Union of American Hebrew Congregations has never contacted or expressed its concerns to any official of the Assemblies of God, or any Assemblies of God Jewish worker. I appreciate the opportunity here to give this response to some of their criticisms

Letter to the editor

You ask your readers for concrete data on alleged cases of proselytism. In view of the statement of the Ethiopian Orthodox Church, general secretariat of the Holy Synod, October 1987, on "Proselytism in Ethiopia", it is proper that the subject of proselytism is taken up for serious discussion. It touches upon a crucial theological problem which should be treated in a theological manner and not in the language of naked polemics.

Of course, in the statement of the general secretariat neither the Ethiopian Evangelical Church Mekane Yesus (EECMY) nor any other church is mentioned by name, nor are we as individuals official spokesmen for the EECMY. However, to avoid any possible misunderstandings among the readers of the WCC *Letter on Evangelism*, we should like to make a running commentary as to the role of the EECMY in the context of mission activities in Ethiopia.

— The only Protestant missionary organizations which were operative in Ethiopia in the latter part of the nineteenth century were the Chrischona Mission with its base in Switzerland, and the Swedish Evangelical Mission. Neither of these mission organizations had the intention of proselytizing Orthodox Christians.

— EECMY had no part in the proselytism among Orthodox youth in the late sixties which is hinted at in this paragraph. In fact, on many occasions it took up and discussed critically the implication of certain immature approaches to evangelism. Furthermore, to maintain that the entire youth involved in this wave of alleged proselytism lacked "the elementary standards and norms of Christian morals and behaviour" is not true.

— The EECMY has never been involved either directly or indirectly in the Sunday school activities within the EOC.

— Far from conducting any "vicious campaigns" against the EOC, the EECMY has supported the participation of the Ethiopian Orthodox Mission in the activities of Radio Voice of the Gospel. One of its supporting missions, the Church of Sweden Mission, still supports the evangelistic efforts of the EOC in various ways.

— The document reads: "To prove this they imitate our ceremonies and practices. They try to appropriate for themselves the historical and liturgical tradition of our church. These are in fact all masks to hide their actual work of proselytism." Our question is: To whom do the words *the* and *their* refer in this accusation?

Here it would have been proper to mention the specific church or mission organization in question. As far as the EECMY is concerned, none of her orders of worship build on the liturgical tradition of the EOC. But one can also say that the appropriation of the vernacular and the liturgical tradition of a given country in the proclamation of the gospel has precedent in the activities of the early church.

— Material inducements have never been used to attract members of the EOC to the EECMY or to its precursor, the Evangelical Church of Eritrea (ECE). We shall provide evidence in support of this view later in this document. Two prominent scholars can, nevertheless, be mentioned in this connection.

Alega Taye Gebre-Mariam, an Orthodox Christian from Begemder (today's Gonder), who by conviction found common cause with Evangelical Christians, became a scholar of great renown. He was selected by the Emperor Menilek for the prestigious task of teaching Geez and Amharic at the Oriental Institute of Berlin University in 1905-07. Yet, he was subjected to ostracism and a year-long imprisonment for his convictions which were based on a thorough knowledge of the fathers of the church and the wisdom of ancient theologians of the EOC. He was *not* drawn to the evangelical cause by any material inducements. The same pertains to Halega Tewolde-Medhin Gebru, a prominent Bible translator and writer from Tigrai.

— The statement of the General Secretariat maintains: "There are frequent attempts made to make the famine-stricken population abandon their Orthodox faith." What concrete evidence is there for such a charge? We do not know of any.

— What does the expression "...the current specific national form of proselytism..." imply?

— We can only rejoice that the EOC takes part in joint relief programmes with other Christian charity organizations. The EECMY takes an active part in such activities.

Gustav Arén's book *Evangelical Pioneers in Ethiopia* (*Studia Missionalia Upsaliensia* XXXII, 1978) describes the origins of evangelical mission in Ethiopia. It shows that Protestant missionary activity primarily aimed at evangelizing non-Christian peoples. Political unrest prevented an immediate outreach to such peoples. While tarrying on the Red Sea coast, the Swedish missionaries received Orthodox clergy and laity who were excommunicated because they belonged to something of a reform movement in the EOC on the highlands of Eritrea. These Orthodox Christians were not only eager Bible-readers but also took exception to certain Orthodox practices. Among these one can mention the practice known as "tezkar" (a commemorative feast for the dead) and the belief in the mediating role of the saints. These people became the nucleus of the ECE. It was the ECE which realized the original missionary vision of an outreach to non-Christian peoples.

Through their messengers, Qes Gebre-Ewostateos Ze-Mikael and Ato Onesimos Nesib, an evangelistic enterprise was initiated in Wollega where their followers remained members of the EOC till the end of 1938, at which time they were excommunicated and denied baptism and church burial.

This eventually led to the founding of the EECMY which became officially recognized on 13 February 1969. The EECMY is a member of the Lutheran World Federation, the World Council of Churches and the All Africa Conference of Churches.

We grant that there has been a widespread lack of knowledge and respect for the historical and doctrinal roots of the EOC which go back to the ancient creeds and liturgical documents of Christendom. Many members of the EECMY, however, realize the values of the history and spirituality of the EOC, whose baptism and clerical ordination the EECMY has always recognized.

Uppsala, Sweden, 15 June 1988

Ezra Gebremedhin, D.Th.
General Secretary
of the EECMY 1963-66

Gustav Arén, D.Th.
Missionary in Ethiopia
(EECMY) 1945-85
November 1988

From John Watson

Moussa was born in Upper Egypt. In the South there are many Christians. As a baby, only days old, he was baptized. The priest who administered the sacrament was a Coptic Orthodox Christian. There was a strong feeling that there was something extra in this baptism. It was concerned with a feeling of "nation" or "blood". Moussa was being baptized a Christian. He was also being baptized as a Copt. From the earliest years he heard that he was one of the "sons of the Pharaohs". The Copts were the real children of Egypt, predating the Arab Muslim invasion of the seventh century and, in some sense, predating the Christian era. Moussa was made a Coptic Christian. From childhood the pure body and precious blood were spooned into his mouth and the long history of Coptic suffering and bitterness was poured into his ears.

The child grew up and became a man. Moussa received the sacraments, attended classes and confessed his sins. He enjoyed the feeling of "belonging". He felt accepted. He often travelled north to Cairo to attend the amazing lectures given by the Coptic pope in St Mark's cathedral. He loved his religion. He understood that there were, in lands beyond the Mediterranean and the Atlantic, Christian nations whose public life reflected their faith. In those lands a Christian had a chance; a chance no Copt had in Egypt. Copts like Magdi Yacoub, the heart transplant surgeon, left Egypt because they could only achieve recognition in Christian Europe or America.

The man went to university and obtained a good degree.

"Are you a Copt?" an American doctor asked. "Of course," Moussa replied. "Have you accepted Jesus Christ as your Lord and Saviour?" The American often asked this question. It was the first of a dozen conversations. The American said: "Pope Shenouda preaches salvation by works, but you must be born again."

"We will take care of you."

"The evangelicals are the only real Christians of Egypt. Coptic Orthodoxy is merely the ritualism of the Old Testament."

"Nationalism is not Christianity. Egyptian Christians who really love Christ join the Evangelical Christian Mission. We have many Christian ministers who were Copts."

The Egyptian said: "Shouldn't we both be converting Muslims?"

Can Muslims become Christians in a Muslim land?

Moussa accepted the Lord Jesus Christ as his Saviour at 5 p.m. on 20 September 1981. Just before that event the Coptic pope was imprisoned by President Sadat. Just after that event Sadat was executed by some fellow Muslims. No evangelicals were involved in either. Moussa was satisfied that he understood what to render to Caesar. Moussa was baptized by an American visiting preacher. Moussa adopted the name of Bobby.

Bobby left Egypt in December 1984. The Coptic pope was still in prison. A new president ruled. Bobby thanked God that Christ's kingdom is not of this world.

I met Moussa in October 1987. He has found no Christian nation. He has not known a sense of community for years. He has lost the intense feelings of 1981. He is a sceptic. He is cynical. He is repaying the money lent by Christians in America who wished to help a brother converted from mere ritualism and tradition.

June 1988

37

Guillermo Cook, who is studies coordinator of the Latin American Evangelical Centre for Pastoral Studies (CELEP), sent in the following from Costa Rica:

The urge to evangelize, and to proselytize, is very strong among Latin American Protestants. One important aspect of the problem is our inability to listen and to dialogue with people who are different from us, as the following anecdote will illustrate.

A small group of church workers were gathered in a Baptist campground to discuss Christian communication. Divided into study groups, we went out into the village next to the seaside camp to learn as much as we could about the situation of its inhabitants, then report back to the entire body. The next morning, at prayers, we found an unexpected guest: a gnarled old villager. The worship team asked us to converse with him about his life situation. This was to be our worship experience. Suddenly, a pastor (he was the camp manager) blurted out: "Sir, are you a born-again Christian?" When the peasant looked puzzled, and mumbled an unconvincing reply, the pastor pulled out his Bible and began to preach, urging upon our bewildered guest a decision for Christ.

After his embarrassed colleagues managed to quiet him down, the group leader turned our attention once more to the halting story of our unexpected guest. We learned that for many years he had been a fisherman in a village of self-sustaining fisherfolk. What had happened to the fishing? we asked. "Many rich city folk have come here and taken over all of our shoreline and dirtied our water, so we no longer have any place to fish," he told us in his thick brogue. At some point, someone thought to ask our visitor what he knew about the place where we were meeting. "I don't really know," he said. "Lots of city people come here. We hear singing coming from inside and we know that they are called 'embangelicals', but that's all we know about them... because I've never been invited to come in." Not even to fish? "No." As we stared past the bowed head of an embarrassed Baptist camp manager to the beautiful beach beyond, it slowly dawned upon all of us that this place where we were supposed to be learning about communicating the gospel was, in fact, physically standing in the way of the gospel in its fullest sense, at least for the people in that small village.

This experience taught me, a conservative evangelical, that when Christian witness is done in a spirit of vulnerability, service, and openness to others, it is evangelism. The people who respond to this call often come from churches (Catholic and Protestant) where the message is proclaimed in a self-serving manner, or already have turned their backs on the church.

Proselytism, in contrast, is motivated by a spirit of churchly pride which goes against the grain of the gospel. Proselytizers are often overbearing. They assume that only they possess the truth and that it is therefore the duty of the unregenerate to accept it without question. They usually do not take the time to find out where their hearers are. And because they are not vulnerable, they miss the chance of being evangelized by others.

Dario Alampay, a pastor of the United Church of Christ in the Philippines, from Manila, has this to report:

Proselytism in the Philippines today is more than just a sheep-stealing issue among the scandalously divided churches. If it were merely sheep-stealing the shame and sin of proselytism could be forgivable. As it is now practised, it has taken an ideological dimension such that not only are churches being divided, but even the social and political structures of the people are being destabilized. Contemporary proselytizers are using the gospel as an antidote to godless communism and the cult of satanism; their unbiblical and untheological message is, "Jesus is the answer and the only alternative to communism and satanism". Communism is made to appear as the main source of all evils that plague our country and the world. Evangelistic crusades conducted every now and then by supposedly internationally known Christian evangelists coming mostly from the US have only this message to proclaim: "Join the crusades. Be a part of it. Fight communism and satanism. Be healed and find peace and happiness." What is most unfortunate about these so-called evangelistic crusades is that people who believe this kind of preaching see "red" at anyone who disagrees. A good number of ultra-conservative ministers worked against the ratification of our new constitution because some of the constitutional commissioners were perceived to be communists, and these ministers urged their members to reject the constitution. In a good number of churches today, especially churches organized by para-church organizations, only members who display the spiritual badge of born-again Christians are considered to be true Christians. Those who are not are considered godless, idolaters and, worse, communist. The Philippines today is gripped and being divided by this communist hysteria. More than any political group that is encouraging and spreading this communist hysteria are para-church organizations, international evangelistic crusaders, fundamentalist "Bible-believing" sects, and a number of other charity organizations using the name of Christ.

A supposedly well-known evangelist with a Bible school in San Diego, California, USA, established an office here in Manila for the purpose of conducting evangelistic meetings and seminars for ministers and lay people of the various churches in the Philippines. The office is located in the Hilton Hotel. A minister of the United Church of Christ in the Philippines was hired to coordinate its programmes and activities. One of the attractions of this study programme is the opportunity to go to the United States. Except for the travel, everything is free during the period of study.

A good number of ministers and lay people who went to attend the school did not return. It was used as an opportunity to stay illegally in the US.

When the ministers and lay people who attended the training program-mes start implementing what they have learned, they cause a great disservice to the life and unity of the church, because they become very dogmatic in their evangelistic methodology. Their dogmatism alienates some members of the church. In some cases those who attended the seminars and participated in the evangelistic meetings form their own separate congregations or join other groups.

Another contribution from the Philippines, this one not necessarily on proselytism, in my opinion, is highly relevant to our concern all the same. The name of the writer is withheld.

Let me mention four events in the Philippines. The first was a chance meeting with a couple on a bus. They told me they had been working for a month with "Youth with a Mission", an organization in the US. They had decided not to return to the US and were living in a rather poor section of Manila in a hotel. They characterized their work as evangelism among the poor. They were frustrated, however, that they knew no Tagalog. They were also considering taking Bibles (English language) into China as part of a vacation there. (Apparently their work with "Youth with a Mission" had been among college students who speak English; they mentioned "Bible Camps".) They were also planning to witness in China but admitted they knew no Chinese.

A second encounter was with three middle-aged gentlemen who had come from Seattle (sponsored by a local Methodist church). They wished to find a cheap place to stay so they could witness and give out Bibles to the poor. Again — they had no prior language training and they were equipped with English Bibles.

Both of these groups showed an interest in learning Tagalog — but were dismayed at the cost of a course. Neither had extra money for such training nor any source of support and guidance in the country. The first mission had already failed to some extent. Although I do not know the outcome of the second you will perhaps excuse my assumption that it stood little chance of success. The following two examples represent what one might call cooperation missions between American and Filipino groups. But these particular Filipino groups — because of their class and overseas education — were perhaps as far removed from the Philippines as any American.

The third event was sponsored by the Full Gospel Businessmen's Association. Over three months they sought to establish a Friday Bible study/prayer group to include young adults and college students.

Mrs B.E. was a well-respected leader in her church which was a frequent forum for her announcements. Nonetheless, after three months she had not recruited a single student (pagan or Christian). The reason was quite simple. The Bible study was held in the Hilton Hotel and few of those she recruited could afford a cup of coffee in such a place. Some frankly could not dress well enough to enter. The Bible study was in English. Although the targetted students could speak English, they invariably conversed and discussed in Tagalog. I found they had great difficulty sharing thoughts and feelings in English.

A fourth event was the distribution of the film *Distant Thunder* by the Campus Crusade for Christ. It made the round of Protestant youth groups in Manila until it came to be shown in the "Abot-Kamay", an evangelistic fellowship which met outdoors and tried to attract non-Christians to listen to evangelical sermons. The film was in English, but it still attracted a collection of squatter children, the clients of the church's social welfare programmes. It is based on Hal Lindsey's works. What is bizarre in this depiction (made in 1972) is that it so clearly focuses on the fears and worries of middle-class Americans. What was tribulation in this film seemed paradise to most of its viewers. Indeed the point was lost even on the better educated (and fed) members of the group. Even those who showed it were a bit embarrassed in the end. The squatter children stayed for sandwiches, then faded into the night.

The Bible Society had available very cheap Bibles and tracts in all the Filipino dialects — but none of these groups I have mentioned used them.

Finally, some observations on proselytism from Bishop Michael J. Nazir-Ali, Pakistan.

1. While recognizing that there are still many independent groups engaged in evangelistic activity, the local church is often the primary agent for mission in its locality these days. Has this reduced the danger of cultural insensitivity and of unworthy incentives for conversion?

2. In the Muslim context it is clearly understood that the ummah (or community of faith) has a responsibility for the material as well as the spiritual well-being of a convert to Islam. In Christian churches, however, such responsibility is often shirked on the ground that it may be regarded as proselytism. Can a distinction be made between a legitimate (and necessary) concern for the material as well as the spiritual welfare of new Christians and unworthy inducements to people so that they may become Christian?

3. The Roman Catholic and Orthodox churches are right to express concern about the activities of certain "proselytizing" missionaries in areas where these churches are dominant. Two observations, however, need to be made here:

a) the process of evangelization is a continuous one and the baptized continue to be evangelized by the gospel. Some traditions call this sanctification, others refer to it as discipling. Whatever the terminology, the gospel continues to change and to shape the life of Christians everywhere. In the past, separated communities of Christians often came into being when the dominant tradition refused to have Christians who have been "renewed" in one way or another in its midst. In some so-called "Christian" countries, the dominant Christian tradition has allowed, and sometimes even encouraged, repressive laws to be framed by the state against Christians of other traditions.

b) The Roman Catholic and (to a lesser extent) the Orthodox churches often have vigorous "proselytization" programmes of their own. In the early 1900s, the RC Church in the area which is now Pakistan constituted just 4 percent of the total Christian population. In the 1980s it constitutes fully 40 percent of the total Christian population! Much of this increase has been due to "proselytizing" activities.

Parents of school children, for example, may be required to become Roman Catholics if their children are to be admitted to schools, employment is made conditional on church membership, low-cost housing is used as an incentive for conversion to the church and so on.

4. While much progress has been made within the ecumenical movement on a common recognition of baptism, certain denominations continue the practice of rebaptism or conditional baptism. A newer phenomenon is that "charismatic" churches, even within "mainline" denominations, sometimes practise rebaptism of those without "charismatic" experience, whether they are from their own or another denomination. This raises a whole number of questions about the place of baptism within denominational structures.   *August 1988*

38

From Thomas F. Stransky, Paulist father, New Jersey, USA.

During my thirty-one years of priesthood, seldom have I not been instructing and counselling a small group or individuals who intend to become Catholic or are seriously "inquiring". Who are they?

Very few are *un*churched in the sense that they have had no previous direct relation to a Christian community of faith. Fewer still are those who are committed, church-going Christians already with a clear-cut creed, moral code and piety, and who now seek what they believe to be their fulfilment of Christian vocation in the Roman Catholic Church. Almost all inquirers are *de*churched; they had been relatively active church members some time in their lives and still bear a Christian memory, good and bad, either of nostalgic joy or of bitter hurts.

I doubt if my experience is unique. I wager that 95 percent of those who swell church-growth statistics in the USA churches are *de*churched — former Methodists, Baptists, Episcopalians, Catholics, etc. Here in New Jersey, for example, the fastest growing church is the Pentecostal Assemblies of God, and a leader of that church tells me that 40 percent of the new members are former Catholics.

Overall in the USA, evangelism seems in fact to be the Christian exchange of pews, collection plates and parking lots, as well as "the faith enhancement of the penitent returnees" who found it again but elsewhere. The truly *un*churched, those never before evangelized, the folk with no previous Christian experience or none of any religious tradition — alas, that far more difficult challenge is avoided. That is for future evangelists at a later date; it is "out of season" now (but see 2 Tim. 4:2).

Back to my instructing and counselling "non-Catholics". I joyfully try to give authentic witness to my Roman Catholic faith in God and God's workings among us all. Yet I can be tempted to distort that witness. I have not yet quenched every urge to proselytize, despite my ecumenical sophistication and, yes, despite my participation in the very drafting of the two WCC/RCC study documents on common witness and proselytism (1970 and 1981). How so?

First of all, I can easily manipulate the person with previous bad, at times downright hurtful, experiences in another church. I can be more concerned with gaining a new Catholic than with helping that person patiently to heal those memories, to correct distortions and prejudices now projected on the previous church, and to test the conscience in discerning if it is truly informed and free, *even if* the result sometimes leads the now healed and better informed one to return to that church.

Secondly, I can be tempted to lay aside my ecumenical learning, to de-emphasize the common gifts of Christ we Christians share "in real but imperfect communion", to be silent on the convergences in the dialogues (e.g., BEM), and to resort to simplified "we Catholics"/"those others" language. With clever mind and glib tongue, it is too easy to overgeneralize with memorable stereotypes, or to offer only the weaknesses of other churches over and against Catholic strengths.

Or worse, to list Catholic *ideals* alongside the *practices* of some others: "Unlike the conservative Baptists, we Catholics acknowledge both absolute sobriety *and* the moderate drinking of wine-for-the-stomach, even a highball or two. But I know some Baptist drunks." The list of more subtle examples is longer, e.g., "we celibate priests are freed up from family responsibilities for total service to the people (our ideal), and too many Protestant ministers are divorcing, or skiing with their spouses too much". By such convert-techniques I am building up *my* case, not the Lord's, at the expense of others and of truth.

Witness or proselytism? How to test myself? I use my imagination! Last Lent, towards the end of a four-month programme for inquirers in a nearby Catholic parish, I led two sessions on "The Catholic Church Looks at Other Christian Churches". In front of me were, among others, a former Episcopalian couple, a former Missouri Synod Lutheran, three former Christian Reformed, and a former Presbyterian (we are blessed, and cursed, with twenty-two denominations in this rural township). As I tried to describe "the others", I imagined sitting in the back row all the clergy of the local ministerial association who were listening with careful ear. If I would change my presentation, always done in their absence, but now in their "out-of-season" presence, I most likely would not usually be witnessing with that topic but proselytizing.

"Not bearing false witness against one's neighbour" remains the most violated commandment in interchurch relations. "Speaking the truth in charity" (Eph. 4:15) is never easy, yet isn't that what witness is about?

From Carol E. Beyer, pastor, Delaware, USA

The best response I can give to this discussion on proselytism is to share my own faith regarding the ministry of the gospel of Jesus Christ. I am a United Methodist pastor serving three churches, and while I always rejoice when someone comes to know Christ as his or her personal saviour while in fellowship with the churches I serve, I also recognize that there may be those who may be led to Christ by others and feel led to join a different fellowship of believers. Only God knows what or who an individual will respond to when led to a saving knowledge of Christ.

For me, while I have no clear definition, proselytizing is when individuals use something they themselves do not understand to persuade others to their own way of thinking. An example: I have had discussions with people who have been approached by others who cannot accept women in ministry and "use" this as a means to persuade them to "come out from among them" into the truth! I am thinking of a young couple who had a visit by two Baptists from a neighbouring town. I had been counselling with the wife for some time because of distortions of God's word that were responsible for her hospitalization on several occasions. It is a long story. While in the hospital on one occasion she met a young woman from a Baptist church and agreed to allow her to ask someone from her church to visit with her. I received the husband's urgent phone call right after this couple had been visited by two men from the Baptist church. As he seemed very agitated, I responded immediately. In the course of attempting to persuade this couple to attend their church, the men told them that the church they were attending would fall because there was a woman pastor and God does not condone women preaching! Now, this is what I call proselytism, and of the worst kind! This young woman was already tormented with doubts and fears as to her worth as an individual to receive the grace and forgiveness of Christ. The damage the visitors could have done, were it not for the quick thinking of her husband, would have been traumatic. I am happy to say that she continues to attend the church I serve, even though she continues to struggle internally regarding her salvation. I am also happy to report the steady growth of the church.

From G.J. van Butselaar, general secretary, Dutch Missionary Council, Amsterdam, the Netherlands

Proselytism is not an issue for the churches and Christians in the Netherlands. I am curious, though, to find out what happens when a person changes confession and that not by marriage, as often happens, but out of conviction.

In the fifties we had some Roman Catholic priests who became (Reformed) pastors and also some pastors who became priests. It created then, in those pre-ecumenical times, strong reactions. Those who came to us confirmed our truth, those who went to others created the difficult question how in the world it was possible to abandon the truth! However, no real contact between Protestant and Catholic churches emerged out of these frontier crossings.

The question became more tricky when in the sixties one of the royal princesses, Irene — whose family name, "van Oranje" (of Orange), was linked up, sometimes even identified, with Reformation history in the Netherlands — became Catholic and was re-baptized. But out of the complicated political and religious debates following that act, something good resulted: official agreements were made between major Protestant and Catholic churches recognizing each other's baptisms; even a cardinal visited a Reformed synod meeting at that time...

Since then, no news in this field. Secularization made religion a private affair. No need any longer to have public debates on what someone believes, stops believing or starts to believe. Until recently, when two Reformed pastors announced their decision to enter the Roman Catholic Church in our province. A remarkable step, not so much for dogmatic as for church-political reasons. In the last ten years, Rome has replaced, one by one, the rather progressive Dutch bishops by more conservative ones, a move which is almost completed. This change has caused immense tensions within the Catholic community: where a few welcomed the new-old orientation, many others had difficulty to see their future in the church. The entry of some Reformed pastors at this very moment, therefore, created some astonishment in our country. What was going on? Proselytism?

With one of the pastors concerned, the Rev. Martin Los (41), I discussed this question. He indicated how he had got himself, without any help or pressure from Roman Catholics, the insight that he needed to change his church membership. In the turmoil of the sixties, when every tradition in the church was challenged, he had searched for the meaning of the church, for the meaning of ministry. On that road he became interested in the Jewish tradition, but he did not find the answer to his questions there, although the experience was helpful. He then concentrated on the early church and found himself safe and secure with the church fathers' writings. After long hours of study, he contacted a Catholic bishop who, at first, rather dissuaded him from becoming a Catholic! After repeated requests, however, the bishop helped Los to find spiritual guidance. Before the decision of this pastor to leave his present ministry and to become a Catholic was made public, there was a brotherly contact between the cardinal of Utrecht and the moderator of the Reformed synod. Los's choice was respected by both. No hard feelings could emerge, no plaint of proselytism could be justified.

Perhaps the only problem created by this change was for the receiving Catholic church itself: the problem of ordination. Los, who became Catholic, especially since he was attracted by their doctrine of ministry, could he be ordained priest? The former pastor is married and has five children... Those pastors who changed in the fifties all received ordination – but then celibacy was not an issue. Today, in the Dutch Catholic church, the lack of (unmarried) priests is becoming disastrous. In the parishes many of their functions (apart from the sacerdotal ones) have been taken over by so-called "pastoral workers", mostly married, often with a fine theological education. Many priests, who decided to marry, were forbidden to fulfill any priestly functions. The rules of Rome are clear. Now, in this situation, can you ordain a newly-converted, married man, and a former Protestant minister?

So, for Holland, proselytism is out, good ecumenical relations are in. We are suffering far more from our lack of creative evangelism!

October 1988

39

It is now time to bring this discussion to a close. When I first introduced the series, I thought out loud if it was at all a good idea for a WCC evangelism letter to give so much attention to proselytism. Looking back, I think what happened, and readers' reactions to it, justified the effort. And two events during this period have further persuaded me that those who care about evangelism should not shun the issues of proselytism.

One was the appearance of a full-page cartoon on the back cover of a serious Christian magazine dedicated to the promotion of world evangelization.

I reproduce the cartoon here [see p. 214]. It is sadly self-explanatory.

The other event, much happier, came with World Vision's Policy on Evangelism. The statement ends with the following paragraph: "Whenever the ministries of World Vision are offered on the condition that people must be willing to listen to a message, or to leave one particular expression of the body of Christ and join another, proselytism has taken place. All forms of proselytism reduce the gospel and misrepresent the person of Jesus Christ. World Vision will not proselytize, nor will it work with those who insist on proselytism." *

In radically different ways, these two events demonstrate the need to view charges of proselytism with the utmost seriousness in our evangelism effort, local and global.

It is when stories and reflections are most concrete that they prove to be most helpful. Probably the most helpful ones are the pieces carrying the perspectives of the converts themselves. Such inputs have been too

---

* "World Vision's Policy on Evangelism" in *Together,* October-December 1988, pp.11-12.

few. Bishops, general secretaries and theologians debate the subject of proselytism. The debate will be that much more fruitful if the leaders would listen to the new converts first — people who have recently left their church and people who have recently joined it. Having read the letters and reactions received, I have the distinct impression that this kind of listening seldom happens. This is not to say that whatever a recent convert believes to be his or her new journey is necessarily right. Or that I am assuming that the destiny of an individual person always supersedes that of the corporate entity called the church. All I am saying at this point is that church leaders had better find out what their church — their missionaries, pastors and evangelists, their synods and parishes — has been doing with thousands of human beings within its sphere of influence. Proselytism is an interconfessional problem, but it is first and foremost an internal matter for the pastoral and missionary ministries of every single church.

I would like now to describe several sets of circumstances which have most easily given rise to charges of proselytism.

A. *History:* Probably the most bitter charges of proselytism have been the ones made by and between some Orthodox communities and the Uniates. The term "Unia" dates to sixteenth-century Europe when some

clergy and large minorities of lay Christians left the Eastern and national churches, both Byzantine, non-Chalcedonian and Nestorian, and came into communion with the holy see in Rome. With local variations, the reasons were largely political, financial and ecclesiological. The need for foreign protection for Christians was the chief motivation. During the days of the Austro-Hungarian empire, large parts of the Ukrainian population entered into union with Rome. They severed their canonical links with Orthodox churches, but retained their Orthodox faith, liturgy, rites and ceremonies and a married priesthood. Throughout history, the movement has created schisms from the ancient churches of eastern Europe, Asia Minor, Egypt, Syria, Ethiopia and India. Much of the wounds and bitterness remain even today. The historical circumstances which have given rise to the Unia are not likely to repeat themselves.

B. Power: Another set of circumstances often lending itself to alleged proselytism is much more modern in origin and widespread geographically. It is found in many parts of the third world, in situations where a church is perceived to be exploiting the weakness of the people it is reaching out to.

Orthodox in the Middle East have accused Protestants of proselytizing through relief, hospitals and youth camps. (Hindu and Muslim groups in India charge Christians of using schools and orphanages and their guitar-singing groups in similar fashion.) And in some parts of Africa, Christians and Muslims criticize each other in such terms. The situation is exacerbated by the fact that much of this modern missionary diakonia in the third world is financed by wealthy Protestant and Roman Catholic churches from the economically and politically powerful West.

On the whole, there is not much evidence nowadays of Protestants and Roman Catholics using diakonia as a proselytizing means. The Christian desire to share with people in need is an attempt to help and not to exploit. But the fact of obviously unequal resources among churches does have its logical consequences, independent of intention and motivations.

Here is a realistic scenario of what commonly happens:

Somewhere in the Middle East is a township whose Christian population is predominantly Orthodox. There are two congregations. The Orthodox congregation is served by a lone priest in his late sixties who has been there for some forty years. Every morning, without fail, the holy liturgy was celebrated. Then the priest would visit the sick on foot and show himself in the market place. Once in a long while, a church van would come to show films with a biblical theme to the children. Otherwise life goes on as it always has. The other congregation is Anglican. It has a younger man as priest, with a university degree from abroad. He has an assistant, a dynamic young woman who goes around visiting schools and homes on a motorbike. There is a well-equipped nursery in the church, a medical clinic which opens two days a week, a Sunday school, and a group of guitar-playing young people.

From time to time, the congregation receives visitors from abroad and there are special activities. In summer, a team of clean and shining young people arrive from Britain or the US to help with evangelistic youth camps. There is, I know, no proselytizing intention, but neither is there any doubt which congregation the young people of the town will be attracted to.

C. Laity: A third set of circumstances which has contributed to large numbers of people changing their confessional affiliations has to do with the dramatic increase in the involvement of the Christian laity in mission and evangelism. This is not the only explanation for the substantial inroads made by Pentecostals into Catholic Latin America, but it certainly is an important one. (There are other factors too which are in themselves downright unworthy.) Every major Pentecostal congregation in the big cities of Latin America has a plan for the total mobilization of its people for outreach. Teams of lay evangelists fan out into the mountain areas. Among the indigenous people, whole communities, traditionally Catholic, have been known to convert to some form of Pentecostalism through the work of itinerant preachers. A common scenario is a village of Indians, isolated geographically and by war, cut off from priests and catechists for long stretches of time, severely deprived and frightened, responding to the message the visitors bring.

In North America and Europe, charges of proselytism are seldom very loud. People moving from one Christian confession to another is common occurrence. Much of the evangelism ministries of churches and groups are in fact ministries among people who have left or are about to leave their own church. But we should not be cynical about it. In a culture where the world is becoming more "churchy" and the church more worldly, the recovery of personal faith and discipleship rightly takes precedence over wrangles about who is proselytizing who. Once again, as in Latin America, it is primarily lay Christians who, in their daily witness in their homes and in the market-place, are the main carriers of the thrust.

The present situation

These are three sets of circumstances where proselytism is often alleged to have happened in different parts of the world. Confining ourselves to proselytism as an interconfessional matter, I do not think we are talking about big numbers worldwide. The vehemence with which some Christians talk about proselytism, and its global spread, sometimes gives the impression that the churches are facing an immediate issue of enormous dimension. That is not true. True, there is no shortage of fundamentalist missionary groups who have no qualms about proselytizing other Christians. But their words are louder than their acts. There is of course no cause to be complacent. And I am aware that most Protestants, given our history, tend to be slightly nonchalant about the cross-over. When the subject of proselytism comes up, there is a tendency among Protestants to view it as an ethical issue. Orthodox Christians, however, see it very much as a theological issue, and more — at stake is personhood, familyhood, nationhood, indeed the blood and soul of a people and their church. Still, there is no reason to be alarmist. Some Protestant churches are growing in predominantly Orthodox lands (as in Romania), and some Orthodox churches are growing in predominantly Protestant lands (as in Finland). Even if some cannot see it as a good thing, and many Christians can and do see it as a very good thing, the situation is not critical. The Christian churches have time to work things out.

In the course of organizing this discussion on proselytism, I have come to know of a number of areas where, I believe, churches should be talking to one another seriously and soon. It is possible to turn a situation of potential mutual incrimination into a tremendous opportunity for effective mission together.

I feel a sense of urgency, say, for the situation in the USA, particularly in the south. Thousands upon thousands of migrants from Mexico and other parts of Latin America have crossed the border. The flow is not going to stop. Most of the newcomers are Roman Catholic, desperately in need of protection, jobs, housing, health services and, no less, a spiritual home. The Catholic church in the region is aware of the problem. Valiant efforts are being made. But the dimension of need is so great it boggles the mind. At the same time, Protestant and Pentecostal churches have redoubled their efforts at church-planting in the sun belt, with particular emphasis on minorities. Conferences on outreach to ethnic groups have been held and strategies formulated, and all the time apparently unaware that the "ethnics" they are trying to reach out to are mostly Catholic Christians. This is the case not only with evangelical and Pentecostal churches, but denominations with strong ecumenical commitments too. Ecumenical officers seldom talk to church development officers of the same church and vice versa. Given the supermarket that the USA is, where one simply picks from the shelf what one wants from among a thousand items, without the slightest need to bother or to talk with another person, this is perhaps the way things are. And I can imagine some Catholics sighing with relief at the Protestant and Pentecostal effort, given the magnitude of need among the new Hispanic population. But surely there must be a better way. At the moment, charges of proselytism have not hit the headlines and probably never will, but the noise is bound to grow louder. And what a great opportunity churches in the United States will have missed in engaging in mission together.

I feel a similar sense of urgency too with the situation in Eastern Europe, particularly between the Orthodox churches and the Baptists. The opening up and the restructuring of socialist society will in all likelihood benefit all Christian churches and their mission activities. But it is probably the Baptist churches who can best take advantage of the situation for growth. I refer to their tradition of flexible polity, of emphasis on lay involvement in evangelism, and of their international ties which are real even to the level of the congregation. Alongside other more historic churches, Baptists in Eastern Europe exude a comparatively "modern" look, largely through their music and evangelistic style which, rightly or wrongly, seems to be in tune with the "look West" thrust of that part of the world today. This development may well lead to tension in places where Orthodox communities constitute an overwhelming majority of the population. In Romania and the Soviet Union, for instance, Baptist churches, substantial Christian minorities, are increasingly confident, spread out, and vocal. I feel an urgency that churches there should begin talking to one another on all levels and not just at the level of the top national leadership. The commitment at the top for mutual respect and refusal to proselytize must be shared by the rest of the church. If it doesn't happen, the real victim will be the cause of the gospel in these lands. The Soviet Union and Eastern Europe face a *kairos* today. It is also a critical moment for the Christian churches in their quest for unity and common witness.

I could go on identifying situations of potential proselytism conflict which seem to invite urgent attention. But I must stop. And there are cases which it would not be prudent to disclose.

Five observations

Finally, I would like to make five observations on how churches and mission agencies can begin to deal with the question of proselytism. These are random thoughts that have come to me and they apply to different levels of this sensitive subject.

1. The present overall WCC approach to the problem of proselytism remains sound. Spelled out in a document on "Common Witness and Proselytism" (1970), the WCC has underlined the importance of common Christian witness rather than the religious freedom of individuals and churches. This is not to downplay the concern for religious freedom in our ecumenical commitment. That remains vital. What the WCC is saying is that our basic concern is witness to God's redemptive work which provides the rationale and the energy for churches to come together. This approach, in my opinion, makes good sense and should prove useful internationally and locally.

2. With common witness, in this instance as a policy to deal with the problem of proselytism, it follows that the part of the church which has the biggest role to play must be the local congregation. Each local congregation must be equipped to nurture its people in the faith (so that they do not go astray), to evangelize (and not to proselytize), and to join with other Christians for common witness. The strengthening of the local congregation, all local congregations in a given location, must therefore be a major ecumenical concern, especially in dealing with the problem of proselytism. But it is precisely at this point that the present way of resource-sharing among churches is the weakest.

The ways Western churches and their agencies share their resources — money and missionaries — are not meant to strengthen local congregations, and seldom do. Western Christians send money for relief, social service and development projects. Churches in the third world then set up new structures whose sole purpose is to receive and to use the money. And then to ask for more. Or Western Christians send their missionaries, in most cases to work in para-church organizations or new evangelistic projects, with some involvement of local people. In neither case is the local congregation, much less all local congregations in the community, supported and strengthened. There are of course happy exceptions. And Roman Catholics tend to do much better. Within WCC circles, there is a growing awareness of all this. But by and large, the present ways of resource sharing among churches, both on the ecumenical and evangelical scenes, are not geared to local congregations, particularly in their pastoral and evangelistic needs. It is of course extremely difficult to do the right thing in sharing money and mission with local congregations on an international scale. But if we set the goal and work at it, something might happen. The goal of common witness on the local level is far too important for the ecumenical movement to ignore.

3. From the reports and stories I have received, almost all Christian confessions have sometime or other been accused of proselytism. And yet all these confessions have publicly committed themselves to an anti-proselytism position. This of course has to do with the difficulty of differentiating between proselytism and evangelism. Our discussions are not going to resolve that. But there are many questions Christians can properly and legitimately ask one another. There is a lot of room for theological and missiological clarification which will be mutually helpful. So let us start the questions.

A question to some of my evangelical friends involved in international and cross-cultural missions. I have in mind particularly friends associated with some of the largest missionary societies and fellowships operating in Asia, Latin America and the Middle East. "Your organizations send out many missionaries to these parts of the world. Your literature shows no anti-Catholic, no anti-Orthodox, no anti-mainline Protestant language. In fact, working with different Christian groups for missions is your stated policy, and you do so publicly and I can see this in your reports. I know of occasions where your people in the field did work closely with other Christians and churches. So, I do not quite understand what exactly you are saying in your description of a missionary situation. I quote: 'Egypt, a country with a significant national Christian population, over one million of whom are thought to be evangelical.' The same I find in your description of your attempt to reach out to the whole of the Philippines and the major cities of Latin America. In both cases, you talk about mobilizing existing churches there. And then in no time you start lamenting the dearth of evangelical congregations and state your desire for planting one thousand evangelical congregations or one in each community within a given number of years. What exactly, my friends, are you saying theologically about Roman Catholic, Coptic and other Protestant churches? And what are the implications for your missionary goal and programme?"

A question to some of my ecumenical friends involved in some of the largest Christian funding agencies in Western Europe. I have in mind agencies which channel vast amounts of money to churches in the third world. "You have recently met with representatives of churches from an African country which has been devastated by natural disaster, civil wars and religious strife. People have been starving, homes burned, and Christian churches destroyed in large numbers. In the round-table meetings you responded positively to the requests for help in all kinds of ways except one. You responded very clearly and negatively to the request to help with the churches' evangelistic ministries. I am aware that there are technical, bureaucratic and legal factors which contribute to the refusal. And I am with you completely, that you must avoid, like the plague, the slightest possibilities of being seen to make 'rice Christians' of the people you seek to serve. My question to you is theological. In the ecumenical movement, what you do is regarded as Christian mission and rightly so. Christian mission is more than inviting people to believe in Jesus Christ. What I do not understand is how your work can be considered Christian mission when you have categorically rejected evangelism from your understanding? And I am nervous as to what your decision is going to do to the churches in that African country. This is, as you know, not an isolated case. I seek clarification."

4. Proselytism, given its multi-faceted complexities and accompanying intensity of emotions, looks set as a problem defying human solution. And it probably is if we lay out the whole problem and analyze it. But at a very human, day-to-day level, and that is the level where the pain of proselytism is genuinely experienced, I am convinced that most practical situations are open to prevention and to a simple solution. Except in cases involving extreme fundamentalist or the most intractable arrogant minds, all it takes for proselytism not to occur, and for evangelism to happen, is for the Christians involved to exercise basic human decency in mutual relations. That is, to inform, to listen and to consult. The burden of making the approach rests with the one from the outside or the one who wants to take the outreach initiative. There is no reason why different Christians in any given locality cannot come together to share ways of awakening faith. When a young man in the Middle East experiences conversion and renewal, there is no reason why Orthodox priests and Protestant missionaries cannot come together to listen to his testimony, and together discern what may be best for him and his community. In this way, trust is built, advice given, wrongs confessed, mistakes corrected, and the body of Christ is built up.

5. Last, let me offer a way towards the problem of proselytism which I believe is both practically useful and theoretically promising. I refer to the apostle Paul and his dealings with the Corinthian church. There were deep divisions and quarrels in that church. Paul was visibly mad, at one

point so much so that he responded with a chiding challenge: "Is Christ divided? Was Paul crucified for you? Were you baptized into the name of Paul?" And he ended with some kind of a personal aside. The apostle referred to himself: "Christ did not send me to baptize, but to preach the gospel — not with words of human wisdom, lest the cross of Christ be emptied of its power" (1 Cor. 1:17). For me, this side remark is pregnant with meaning for this discussion on proselytism.

Suppose Christians today follow this Pauline advice, given, relevantly for us, in the situation of a divided church? Suppose Protestants, Catholics, Orthodox, Pentecostals in our churches go out and preach the gospel in homes, offices, in the market-place, in small groups and large crowds, and do not worry about others becoming or not becoming members of our denomination or confession? Suppose Christians preach clearly, like Paul, the message of the cross — the crucified and risen Christ — among our neighbours in the nominal Christian West, in religiously Catholic Latin America, the religiously Islamic Middle East and large parts of Africa, and in the Asian heartlands of Hinduism and Buddhism? Suppose Christians simply preach this message, and not the message of why and how our neighbours should become Baptist, Presbyterian, Catholic, Orthodox, etc.? The chances are the gospel will be preached throughout the lands. The world will have listened much better. And there would be no proselytism.

Of course, Paul did baptize (his claim was he was not *sent* to baptize). And Christians today should not forget that. But baptism, the statement on *Baptism, Eucharist and Ministry* tells us, is primarily an act of incorporation into the body of Christ. It is not primarily a membership due paid to an organization called a Christian denomination. This understanding of baptism, which has the support of all major theological traditions, ought to be able to take the churches a long way in dealing with the common problem of proselytism.

Such considerations lead us into very basic theological issues of tremendous consequence for Christian mission. Should conversion always mean visible membership in the historical church? Could conversion to Christ be developed within one's own cultural-religious tradition? The belonging of a Christ-converted person to a community of the faithful is not questioned. But what exactly is that community or communities? The problem of proselytism and our commitment to world evangelization invite this kind of exploration.

Let me close with a quotation from Bishop Lesslie Newbigin. He was thinking of proselytism. He referred to the story of the conversion of

Cornelius (Acts 10) which he suggested could also be called the conversion of Peter.

"This means that if we are faithful in mission we must recognize that Christianity is something that is always changing. I would not say, as has been suggested, that we have to 're-invent the gospel' in each generation, for the gospel is news of what has been done once for all. I would rather say that the Holy Spirit, through the faithful witness of the church to the gospel, teaches the church new things and brings it — through its successive missionary encounters — into the fullness of the truth. That is the promise spelled out so clearly in the fifteenth and sixteenth chapters of St John. Here is the real difference between proselytism and evangelism."*

January 1989

---

* L. Newbigin, *Mission in Christ's Way*, 1987, Geneva, WCC, 1987, pp.34-35.

Chapter 8

In the World Council of Churches

40

It is the season of advent, and the end of my first year in the WCC. I would like to share with you a few thoughts on evangelism and the ecumenical movement.

Let me start with Korea. The country has been featured high on the ecumenical agenda, largely because of the human rights situation there and the churches' responses to it. The Korean experience calls for international Christian solidarity and opens up new ways of understanding mission. It is right that the human rights struggles of Korean Christians become a matter of deep ecumenical concern. But too often this focus is seen and understood by some of us as a Korean commitment over against other Korean Christian realities, for example, the phenomenal growth in the number of Christians and of congregations there. Many of us in the ecumenical movement tend to see the commitment to human rights as somehow inconsistent with the commitment to engage in evangelism. Let me illustrate, from a report of an ecumenical church-to-church visit to Korea:

> We attended the second of two services Wednesday night at the Young-Nak Presbyterian Church. When we got to the church, the parking lot was already filled with cars. The English material indicated that they have a membership of 50,000 with 19 ministers, seven Sunday worship services, and several educational programmes. The congregation seemed to enjoy the hymn-singing and sermon. The main role of the church seemed to be to provide a refuge for troubled people. What impressed me was that there were many well-dressed young people who were proud to be members of the church. *Contrasted to this** was the attendance at the Thursday prayer service

---

* My italics.

for the political detainees' families and their supporters in the chapel at the Christian centre. The WCC team was introduced to the 130 people in that ecumenical fellowship. The Rev. KIM Dong Won, of Inchon, Urban Industrial Mission, general secretary, preached. Through hymn-singing and prayer all participants shared, experienced and received mutual encouragement for life together as they carried this common burden of concern for oppressed people.

A fair-minded description. But is there any reason to put the two pictures of Christians worshipping and praying in a relationship of "contrast"? Is there any reason to suggest that they are incompatible with each other? From the description as it stands, none that I can see.

With this kind of thinking, I doubt if we could ever understand the Korean pastor who said, in utter frustration with some of us in the ecumenical movement: "But the big churches pray for the detainees and their families too!"

Of course, there are differing degrees of commitment to human rights among Christians in Korea, as elsewhere. And how the commitment should be expressed must have been a subject of fierce debate within the churches. But to cast the question as an issue between commitment to human rights and social justice over against commitment to evangelism and church growth would be a serious distortion of reality as Korean Christians see it. With this perspective, no one is served. Neither the cause of human rights there, nor the sharing of the evangelism concerns and insights of Korean churches with the rest of the world. We need to affirm the oneness of the churches and the need for mutual challenge and support as Christians try to be faithful to their calling.

I can't help feeling how many more allies the ecumenical movement could have made, and how much richer and stronger we could have become, if only we would have more clarity in our theological convictions and allow them to guide us as we seek the unity that is promised us.

December 1982

41

The latest WCC statement on "Mission and Evangelism: An Ecumenical Affirmation" is now available. If you wish to know what WCC consensus is on the subject, and areas of disagreements, for they are present too, this is the paper to read and to keep.

How has this paper come about? Who does it represent? Emilio Castro
puts it this way:

> In 1976, immediately after the fifth assembly of the World Council of
> Churches in Nairobi, the central committee asked the Commission on World
> Mission and Evangelism to prepare a document containing the basic convic-
> tions of the ecumenical movement on the topic of mission and evangelism.
> The central committee itself began to work in that direction by preparing in
> 1976 a letter to the churches, calling their attention to the confessing character
> of every local community. During the preparation of the world mission
> conference held in Melbourne in 1980 on the theme "Your Kingdom Come",
> CWME engaged in a long and fruitful conversation with churches of all
> confessions and regions, assessing the priorities for our missionary obedience
> today.
>
> In 1981, the central committee received this document, "Mission and
> Evangelism: An Ecumenical Affirmation", for a first reading; in the most
> recent session of the central committee in July 1982, this affirmation was
> approved and sent to the churches for their consideration, inspiration and
> implementation.
>
> The document summarized some central points which have been learned in
> the thinking and doing of mission and evangelism in the member churches of
> the WCC. The WCC is in a privileged position for this task because it is the
> meeting place of the Orthodox and Protestant churches. In addition, a serious
> and very constructive Roman Catholic participation is also a normal feature of
> CWME's life.
>
> As usual with ecumenical documents, the authority of the document
> depends on its content and is not binding for any one of the member churches;
> most of the churches have had an opportunity to contribute to the formulation
> of this document and will recognize themselves in many of the pages. In the
> Protestant family, people of different theological persuasions and not merely
> different denominations have been consulted and have participated in meet-
> ings in order to help prepare this affirmation.

A good way to tackle this ecumenical statement, I believe, is
suggested by Archbishop Edward Scott. In his moderator's report to the
last central committee, he was reflecting on the WCC as a context in
which churches can challenge each other as to their ultimate loyalty:

> This need (to challenge each other) I believe is reflected in our search for a
> consensus. I personally have a strong reluctance to making any human
> statement or structure "absolute" because I believe this step is very close to
> idolatry. When Moses felt the very deep call to go into Egypt to lead his
> people out of captivity — a call he wanted to resist — he asked for the name of
> the god who called him. The response was that incredible answer "I am that I

am" — or "I will be that I will be". A scholar with a good sense of humour put it this way: "I am that I am — but not always what you think I am!" So often and in so many subtle ways we forget this reality; instead of trying to understand at depth what it means to be made, male and female, in the image of God, we tend to make God in our image, in the image of our understanding of God which is always less than God. We need to live with that sense of transcendence, with that sense of judgment on our own views.

In our search for consensus I believe we are seeking a new and deeper understanding of the truth, "of what is", the truth that is large enough to comprehend the aspects of truth that have been a part of the heritage of each and every church. This does not involve giving up positions that are crucial or settling for a lowest common denominator, but a common quest into a deeper and fuller understanding. In this process we do not lose — we all gain!

To a very large extent, the statement and its evolution excitingly approximates this process. "Approximate", because we still have a long way to go in learning to learn together. For instance, the section on "Witness Among People of Living Faiths", paragraph 42, though what it says is true, is hardly "deep and full":

> The Word is at work in every human life. In Jesus of Nazareth the Word became a human being. The wonder of his ministry of love persuades Christians to testify to people of every religious and non-religious persuasion of this decisive presence of God in Christ. In him is our salvation...

I would have loved to remove the "our" in the last sentence and affirm "in him is salvation", or something close. But then, the same paragraph goes on to confess that "among Christians there are still differences of understanding as to how this salvation in Christ is available to people of diverse religious persuasions. But all agree that witness should be rendered to all." Over this fundamental issue, I hope the ecumenical movement can go beyond agreeing to disagree.

Well, I should not have prejudiced your assessment by singling out what I feel to be a weakness. It is an honest, self-confessing weakness in a statement which makes explicit the underlying convictions of the life of the WCC. These convictions have become very meaningful to me in my missionary commitment.

Let me share with you how, almost accidentally, I once put this statement to use. Some time ago, I was in a university town in south China during a short trip. A pastor asked me if I could share with the more active members of the congregation something about the development of the Protestant church outside of China in the last two decades. I readily agreed. As it turned out, almost three hundred people showed up. I was in a panic. The pastor too. He had not expected so many, and "most are non-Christians, probably having absolutely no idea what Christianity is about". How would I communicate? One option was to talk about the sociology of religion. That would be communicable. But I rejected that. Probably people living in a Marxist state could do that better than I can. So in desperation, I took out a draft of "Mission and Evangelism: An Ecumenical Affirmation" and simply ran through the lists of convictions, telling illustrative stories here and there — conversion; the gospel to all realms of life; the church and its unity in God's mission; mission in Christ's way; good news to the poor; mission in and to six continents; witness among people of living faiths. Believe me, I did that in forty-five minutes. The questions lasted twice as long. Apparently, I was getting through somehow.

Will you test-use this statement in discussion sessions with adults and young people in your congregation? Or use it as a catechism? Sermon focuses? I covet your help in getting these ecumenical convictions to the grassroots. They speak the voice of committed people throughout the world.

November 1982

42

I am going to do something I have hesitated to do for some time: share with you a few thoughts on the *The Reader's Digest* attack on the WCC. Whether you have read the August 1982 article or not, the title says it all: "Karl Marx or Jesus Christ?" Well, one of the reasons I overcame my hesitation is that during the last month, I received three separate anonymous gifts — reprints of the *Digest* article, two with USA postmarks and one Korean. Now, there can be different ways to read these gifts. I prefer, if you will excuse a mild dose of egotism, to see them as an interesting challenge: "Okay, what has the WCC evangelism secretary to say to that?"

Let me admit that my first reaction to the *Digest* article was somewhat of an exasperation. "Well, another agenda item from the USA. Let USA member churches deal with it. The *Digest* is a USA magazine. The attack is based on certain USA values and perspectives popular at the time. The whole thing is USA through and through. Why should the whole World Council of Churches spend time on it?" Well, that wasn't very ecumenical, or very Christian. To say that would make me as provincial as the *Digest* article is, to put it mildly.

So I sat down and went through the article a second time. Not so much to ask "which part is fact and which fiction? which truth and which lies?" No, not so much to ask that as to ask: "Even if it is full of errors, what can I learn from the *Digest* article? What can I learn from it, in the privacy of my morning devotional and in the fellowship of my colleagues?" I am not suggesting at all that the determination of facts is not important. Our Communication Department has put out a paragraph-by-paragraph official rebuttal of the *Digest* article which does exactly that. Besides, I have already done my own homework when I prepared a pamphlet explaining the WCC in Chinese. So, sure of the facts as I knew them, I decided to pose to myself the challenge: "Granted all the bad things about the article, surely there must be something one can learn from it." The conclusion has so far proved to be a big surprise to me. Bluntly put, there is simply nothing I feel I can learn from this *Digest* article. I can usually pick up something useful for my own enrichment from every situation, every encounter, including *The Reader's Digest* which I read on rare occasions, but not from this particular *Digest* article on the WCC.

The argument of the attack is crystal clear. That the WCC has turned from Jesus Christ to Karl Marx because today, of the 301 member churches, third-world churches number half ("only 28 are American"). Third-world viewpoints dominate the WCC. Third-world churches have moved the WCC from the concern for church unity to "secular ecumenism". In short, according to the writer, the WCC has become apostate because of the participation of churches from Asia, Africa and Latin America.

My friends, as an Asian, what should I say? What can I say? And, for that matter, what can you, whoever you are?

I can nevertheless say something about the Programme to Combat Racism, a special target of the article. Probably you are familiar with the pros and cons. I will therefore stick to the evangelism angle. Here I must confess that I find the PCR and its support of liberation movements in Southern Africa among the easiest to defend evangelistically. I see it as a risky expression of love for the unlovable. A direct reaching out, with no intermediaries. By "unlovable" and "respectable society", I mean as most of us in the churches see it and, at the same time, I do not use these terms with embarrassment and apology. To the uninvolved, people involved in liberation movements are neither lovely nor lovable. They are not nice. People who are committed to one thing, and are struggling to stay alive, have no time or inclination to be nice. They are not the kind of poor who stir up our pity and who affirm our own judgments. These we, and the *Digest* for that matter, have no trouble with. Those we have trouble with are the poor who demand our respect, and who are a judgment on our virtues. The PCR, as I understand it evangelistically, represents a serious attempt to reach out to these people. Most of our evangelism work, yesterday and today, has been a reaching out of the have to the have-not, both in absolute and relative terms. This explains our success which is also our failure. The PCR attempts to be one of the encouraging, concrete pointers to how we can learn to proclaim the good news on the basis of equality and mutual respect. Without this basis, evangelism will always be tainted with proselytism and cultural and economic manipulation. In preaching Christ Crucified, we also preach ourselves. And that is not very helpful.

One of the images the WCC likes to have of itself is that of the dialogue of cultures. People coming together with their cultures, telling their Jesus stories, enhancing each other's understanding of God, and putting the whole drama under the illumination and judgment of the scriptures. Such an image, I believe, calls upon each one of us involved in the ecumenical movement to examine if we do indeed do that. Do we embody the pain and the hopes of the people from whom we come? If we do, then the chance is good that we will be able to hear the pain and hope of others in this great dialogue. I propose that this become a major ecumenical concern.

At this point, I should perhaps insert a short reflection by my friend T.K. Thomas, who is publications editor in the WCC. He was concerned with the difficulties in ecumenical communication. But he also has something to say about embodying pains and hopes.

> There is always a "they" and a "we", whether we want it or not. They see us from a distance, from the outside. They are not in daily dialogue with us. They do not share in our worship. They read our statements; they hear of our involvement in struggles for the liberation of people and programmes of development. Liberation and development have ideological overtones and political implications. They conclude we have opted out of causes Christian, and adopted a set of secular priorities and secular activism. They are wrong, theologically as much as historically, but how do we prove it?
>
> This is the basic dilemma of ecumenical communication.
>
> We are concerned over what is happening in Lebanon. We agonize over the suffering of people. We commit to God the Jews and the Palestinians and the people of Lebanon. The stand we take and the statement we issue do not

make ecumenical sense outside the experience of shared worship. But communication takes place only at the level of reports and statements.

We are concerned over the anxiety of the Pacific people over the nuclear testing in their part of the world. We know some of the people who are affected; we share their fear and their anxiety, and we pray with them and for them. Our statements are often prosaic pieces. They express sorrow or indignation, and they condemn or demand. The ecumenical concern for a nuclear-free Pacific is much more than what the statement mediates.

South Africa. PCR grants. The dialogue programme. Militarism. Big-power politics and small-time dictators. Outside the experience of personal prayer and corporate worship, none of these can become ecumenical concerns. And when communicated without reference to that, they cease to be ecumenical concerns.

"They" and "we" are not absolute categories. There are "they" among us and "we" among them. That makes the problem of ecumenical communication all the more complicated.

I asked T.K. if I could knock off the last paragraph. He said no. He's right.

February 1983

43

What happened to evangelism at the WCC's Vancouver assembly? How fared evangelism at the sixth assembly? Here is one man's assessment.

In a very real sense, asking the question is like asking how the shark's fin tastes in a sumptuous twelve-course Chinese dinner. Wrong question! You do not single out one ingredient among the many for attention. No one dish is judged on its own. The shark's fin soup is part of that which goes before — an appetizer perhaps consisting of a few thin slices of roast piglet skin — and that which comes after — probably a light number such as steamed shrimps. They all go into one big, robust multi-flavoured meal. The same is true with the discussion on evangelism. By the way, proclaiming the good news and sharing a feast is no frivolous comparison.

Evangelism was certainly not an "every-minute" word in Vancouver in the same way as "peace", "justice", "unity" or "TV" (we received a daily sixteen-hour television coverage). It was probably an "everyday" word, not so much from the platform as from the plenary floor, in small groups, in programme hearings, and in the issue groups. However, it does not bother me that the word "evangelism" did not come booming out of the loudspeakers. (I would love to have heard a few such booms, though.) For me, the primary need for evangelism today is not more exhortation or strategies, but much sharper clarity as to what constitutes the good news. What is the Christian message? What are we, as Christians, committing ourselves to? What are we asking other people who do not know Jesus Christ to commit themselves to? As we share Jesus Christ, what are we sharing? In short, what is the Christian faith all about? If we deal with this concern, I believe we are dealing with the fundamental issue of evangelism today.

In this light, the assembly has been emphatic on evangelism. It has been persistent in trying to spell out the meaning and vision of the Christian faith as it bears on the world today. Take for instance the "churchy" statement on *Baptism, Eucharist and Ministry*. It became the focal point of the discussion on unity which so dominated the assembly. Going over it with deliberate attention, one rightly could regard it substantially as a gospel tract on what it means to be a Christian today. The assembly, I am happy to say, cared a great deal about the content of the Christian faith.

I would not have given this emphasis such importance evangelism-wise, had it not been for the way in which most of the evangelism discussions in the churches occur. In most of the church's concern for evangelism and growth, there has been very little interest given to the content of the Christian faith. Church people are urged to evangelize. Much effort has gone into research on strategies. But there is often very little interest in the content of the good news, that which we are supposed to proclaim. We say one-third of the world's people have not heard. We get ourselves busy talking about *how*, forgetting *what* it is we want them to hear. To our evangelistic efforts, I can hear many non-Christian people respond: "In inviting me to believe in Jesus, what are you inviting me to?" The assembly recognized this response and strove hard to give a reply in terms of unity and renewal, peace and justice, sharing and healing, learning and participating, on both the personal and the corporate levels of life. In this sense, the assembly has served the cause of evangelism. It has presented a fairly sharp and faithful vision of the Christian life to the world. To be a Christian today is to be such kinds of persons, to lead such kinds of life, to be involved in such tasks, and to build such kinds of world.

As indicated, many discussions on evangelism do not concern themselves with the content of the Christian faith. And too often, the vision of what it means to be a Christian that we offer to our neighbours boils down to no more than respectable behaviour and membership in a local church. Too often, the world vision projected by our evangelistic efforts is nothing more than this existing world except that everybody belongs to a church. In communicating the good news of Jesus, we proclaim the good news that Jesus came in order that everyone in the world would eventually belong to the church we go to on Sunday morning! As a good Baptist, I am not sure if I want to imagine a world populated by Baptist churches as we know them today — be they Hong Kong Baptist, Burmese Baptist, European Baptist, American Baptist or Southern Baptist. It may not be a bad scenario, but surely hardly one that qualifies as the kingdom.

Charles Colson of Watergate fame knows somewhat better. In the introduction to his book *Life Sentence*, he wrote: "I came upon a newspaper report of the latest Gallup Poll. One-third of all adult Americans, fifty million people, claimed to be 'born again'. Church attendance... was increasing. That was good news. Yet abortions were increasing, too, at a much faster rate, divorces were up, millions of couples were living together out of wedlock, pornography was rampant, avowed homosexuals sought the right to be ordained as clergymen, economic and racial discrimination continue record high ..." Some of us in the ecumenical movement would disagree with some items on the list, and add others of our own: "Yet poverty worsens, hunger becomes more rampant, human rights are daily violated, more and more people are marginalized within their own societies, war and the threats of war...".

The world as it is plus the proliferation of churches as they are cannot be what the Christian faith is all about. Vancouver had a much clearer biblical vision. It called the churches to examine what it is we should be proclaiming today.

That is the way I read the assembly in terms of evangelism. There are, to be sure, some clear and explicit references to evangelism in assembly official statements. "Life Together", the message of the assembly to churches, has a whole paragraph on the subject. Coming after renewal of commitment to Christian unity, and right before that to justice and peace, the assembly reports to the churches:

> We renew our commitment to mission and evangelism. By this we mean that deep identification with others in which we can tell the good news that Jesus Christ, God and Saviour, is the Life of the World. We cannot impose faith by our eloquence. We can nourish it with patience and caring so that the

Holy Spirit, God the Evangelist, may give us the words to speak. Our proclamation has to be translated into every language and culture. Whatever our context among people of living faiths and no faith, we remember that God's love is for everyone, without exception. All are invited to the banquet. Jesus Christ, the living bread, calls everyone who is hungry, and his food is unlimited.

The Programme Guidelines Committee recommended eight priority areas on the basis of assembly discussion. Evangelism emerges as a clear priority. The report explains that these priorities "are intended to provide focus and orientation for new initiatives to be undertaken by the WCC in the coming years. They presuppose the continuation of work in areas defined by the functions of the WCC, i.e. unity of the church, mission, service, education and renewal." On evangelism, the Programme Guidelines Committee states:

> *Evangelism* should undergird the work in all WCC programmes... The Council should assist member churches in their mission to proclaim Christ, the Life of the World, and in their calling of men and women to faith and discipleship. The implementation of this priority should have three dimensions. The WCC should:
> a) help member churches in developing an understanding of the relationship between evangelism and culture in respect of both the contextual proclamation of the gospel in all cultures and the transforming power of the gospel in any culture;
> b) seek to develop dialogue with evangelicals not related to the WCC on the meaning and methods of evangelism, particularly with concern for the relation between evangelism and the wholeness of salvation and the criteria for authentic church growth;
> c) help to clarify the distinction between evangelism, carried out in the spiritual freedom and power of the gospel, and proselytism in all its forms, particularly in view of activities, some of which evidence an arrogant disregard for people's cultural integrity...

It is much too early to tell how the message and the programme guidelines from the assembly will actually work out programmatically. That they provide the moral and thematic basis for a strong WCC emphasis on evangelism, there should be little doubt.

Then there is the statement on "Witnessing in a Divided World", one of the eight programme-oriented issues which engaged the delegates in the entire second half of the assembly. After several drafts, the revised statement was not accepted by a large majority of the delegates, returned to drafters, and finally, for lack of time, referred to the new central committee. It was obvious from the several comments from the floor which led to the vote that most delegates thought the draft on witnessing too weak, the Christology watered down. In that draft statement, "evangelism was portrayed as a problem", claimed a delegate. As things now stand, I feel I do not have an adequate handle on the statement on witnessing — its status, its meaning, and what it says about the assembly, and the WCC. The task of discernment will have to wait until a later date.

Let me end on a more personal note. The assembly experience has taught me a sobering lesson. On several occasions, I was shown portions of various kinds of draft statements from different assembly configurations. My opinion was sought. Every time I came across a reference to evangelism, I felt glad and I expressed approval. But soon I realized that on many occasions, my approving attitude was not shared by delegates involved in the same process. They thought the same references inadequate, incomplete and sometimes inconsistent with the rest. I was heartened by such clear manifestation of commitment to evangelism. I was, however, shocked by the difference in response, primarily my own easy-to-please way, which now appeared to be almost nonchalant. Soon it dawned upon me that I had been responding programmatically and bureaucratically. The presence of a reference to evangelism in an official statement ensures and strengthens the operational continuation of the evangelism programme in the WCC. (Although there is never any doubt about that at all!) Whereas the delegates had been responding theologically. They were less worried about organizational in-house matters than about the integrity of the faith and its expression in the world. That made them harder to please. A humbling lesson. I believe this experience will have much bearing on me as a Christian person and as an ecumenical staff person working on evangelism.

October 1983

44

I would like to use this letter to report on the most theologically polemic issue at the Vancouver assembly. It has a lot to do with evangelism. It has to do with Christology, with the claims of Jesus Christ in the context of other claims, especially the claims of other living faiths.

Let me start with the report on "Witnessing in a Divided World" which, when presented in the last plenary at the assembly, was heavily criticized from the floor and finally referred to the new central committee. In the intervening hours, some sixty written amendments were received. Now the official version is available. The controversial paragraph reads as follows:

> While affirming the uniqueness of the birth, life, death and resurrection of Jesus, to which we bear witness, we recognize God's creative work in the seeking for religious truth among people of other faiths.

This is significantly different from two previous drafts. The first went like this:

> We witness to the uniqueness of the birth, life, death and resurrection of Jesus, and precisely because of that we recognize and affirm the presence of God in the religious experience of people of other faiths.

Then it was amended in the following manner, which was also found wanting by assembly delegates:

> While affirming the uniqueness of birth, life, death and resurrection of Jesus, to which we bear witness, we recognize God's creative work in the religious experience of people of other faiths.

The three-stage genesis, in my opinion, does not demonstrate any logical progression, only the haphazardness of one thousand people having to make decisions under pressure at the final moments of an exhausting two weeks. The theological sentiment, however, is clear.

Six days previously, the same sort of sentiment was evident, at a more leisurely time. The Message Committee, charged with preparing a letter to the churches on behalf of the assembly, presented a draft for plenary approval. The text contained the following sentences in a paragraph specifying the assembly's commitment to mission and evangelism:

> Whatever our context, among people of living faiths and no faith, we remember that God does not love us more than others. We have no reserved seats at the banquet. Jesus Christ was given for the life of all. So he calls everyone who is hungry and his food is unlimited.

After debate, the final version read:

> Whatever our context among people of living faiths and no faith, we remember that God's love is for everyone, without exception. All are invited to the banquet. Jesus Christ, the living bread, calls everyone who is hungry, and his food is unlimited.

The polemic turned into open drama during the session to adopt the general secretary's report. At one point in his presentation, Philip Potter made a reference to "the way in which churches have been encouraged to carry out a dialogue with people of living faiths and ideologies and with those without faith". He stated:

> The nature of dialogue is as Peter presents it (1 Pet. 3:15). Even as we reverence Christ, so must we reverence those with whom we dialogue. In a profound sense Christ is present beside the other putting his claim upon us. Therefore, we must be ready to listen to the other to receive a word of judgment and promise, with the scriptures as our criterion, and be open to be renewed in faith as we pray that God's Spirit will do his own work with the other.

The Policy Reference Committee, which commended adoption of the general secretary's report, felt obliged nevertheless to comment:

> With regard to the general secretary's statement that even as we reverence Christ so we must reverence those with whom we have dialogue, as an encounter of life with life, we would understand that the use of "reverence" in the second part of this statement means holding those with whom we enter into dialogue in profound respect.

Here you have it, the highlights of the most polemic issue in Vancouver and its genesis during the assembly.

Some of my friends, a few from India, were visibly disturbed by the development. Is the WCC going backward in its theological understanding? Are the churches becoming increasingly parochial? What about the substantive work done by "dialogue" theologians and their efforts in all these years?

To answer these questions, it is best to go back to the famous Chiang Mai guidelines on dialogue with people of living faiths and ideologies. This statement, the fruit of an international consultation in 1977, was "received" by the WCC central committee. "Receiving" the statement means that "the central committee commended it to member churches for their consideration and discussion, testing and evaluation, and for their elaboration in each specific situation". The statement remains the most comprehensive guideline so far on dialogue from the WCC. Under the heading "the theological significance of people of other faiths and ideologies", the guidelines list "questions where agreement is more difficult and sometimes impossible but [which] we commend for further theological attention". First among these questions are the following:

> What is the relation between the universal creative/redemptive activity of God towards all humankind and the particular creative/redemptive activity of God in the history of Israel and in the person and work of Jesus Christ?

Are Christians to speak of God's work in the lives of all men and women only in tentative terms of hope that they may experience something of him, or more positively in terms of God's self-disclosure to people of living faiths and ideologies and in the struggle of human life?

Given the non-committal creative/redemptive format and the rhetorical form of the question that Chiang Mai chose to frame its theological concern, one must be hard put either to shout alarm or halleluja at what happened in Vancouver as part of ecumenical history. For me, the important thing is, however imperfect and clumsy the process, we now possess a clear record of an official debate on the theological significance of other living faiths, a reasonable measure of assurance that the churches care about this issue (after all, Philip Potter called Vancouver the assembly of the people of God, i.e. not dominated by hierarchy and professional theologians), and a few extremely carefully crafted statements which, whether you agree or disagree with them, embody the struggle of different schools of theological thought and experience present in the WCC. And, best of all, these statements are perfectly comprehensible. One of my biggest frustrations in my attempt to educate myself on dialogue issues has to do with my difficulties with the language of its proponents. Take the following crucial statement from one of the best and most powerful books in dialogue literature:

> The Christian, in recognizing, believing in and loving Christ as the central symbol of Life and Ultimate Truth, is being drawn towards that self-same Mystery that attracts all other human beings who are seeking to overcome their present condition.*

Obviously a statement of great theological importance. But what can one make of it? How does one ever begin to talk about it? Or to it? The rigour of the logic and the philosophical expansiveness may be admirable, but we are lost in utter unrelatedness. The statements from Vancouver are simply articulated. We can think about them, and debate with them. Now a dialogue on dialogue can begin. We can all participate.

November 1983

---

* R. Panikkar, *The Unknown Christ of Hinduism*, London, Darton, Longman & Todd, 1964.

45

I have now served five years in the WCC as secretary for evangelism. Time, I think, for a report on the state of concern for evangelism in the WCC organization. When I use the term "evangelism", here and in my work, I put the emphasis on the awakening and reawakening of faith, on the communication of the Christian faith so that others may move from no faith or nominal faith or other faiths to faith in Jesus Christ. This is not the whole of mission; only without it, mission is incomplete, and unholistic.

From my colleagues, I receive much trust, freedom, access and whatever resources I need to do the work assigned to me. I cannot, for example, think of any other programme desk within the WCC organization, and there are over 100, which enjoys the privilege and the resources for bringing out a monthly letter, through which a programme staff member can speak to the world church directly on a subject of his or her personal choice and invite participation. So no complaints here. The WCC organization does have an evangelism desk and does take care that it is a well-equipped desk within the existing framework.

But if one is to ask how strong the evangelism agenda is within the WCC's ecumenical agenda, my answer is "not at all strong". This is, in a way, a very puzzling thing. In my office is a file into which I put statements and reports of what member churches plan to engage in presently or within the next several years. And without fail, both for churches in the North and in the South, evangelism comes high up on the agenda. The Church of the Province of Southern Africa (Anglican), for instance, in 1986 lists five priorities for its life and work. Number one is "renewal and evangelism". Number two, "total opposition to apartheid", and so on. And I can name many more similar cases. Yet, evangelism does not appear on the overall agenda of the WCC apparatus nor is it a factor in the day-to-day development of its many broad concerns. Why is this so? Why is it that the evangelism agenda of member churches does not get reflected in the agenda of the WCC?

There are a number of plausible answers. I would personally opt for the following analysis. It has a lot to do with the churches' expectation of the WCC. Churches, or their representatives, simply do not have much evangelism expectations of the WCC organization. They have other expectations. To be sure, churches care about evangelism, but they do not necessarily see it as an ecumenical matter. To be sure, church representatives at the WCC would protest when they sense the cause of evangelism being shortchanged within the ecumenical movement, as they did loudly at the Vancouver assembly in 1983, but they do not quite see it in connection with the ongoing business of the WCC as an organization. Why is this so?

I cannot quite explain it, although I can come up with some fairly legitimate and common-sense reasonings. If your church is already doing well in evangelism, but has trouble with the government over religious policies or matters of human rights, it stands to reason that when you attend WCC meetings, you raise the matters where you need help. Or if your country is facing massive human needs of a material nature, obviously you want to make sure that that gets on the WCC agenda. Or perhaps, in your church, the WCC and anything that has to do with it are the province of the "foreign" or "world" department, as different from the "home" department. So it follows that your priority at home does not necessarily mesh with your priority abroad. Whatever the case, it remains that evangelism does not figure strong in the day-to-day, data-gathering and disseminating, decision-making, institutional life of the WCC. There is nothing anti-evangelism about it. Only that evangelism is simply not part of the WCC's ongoing institutional interest. Once in a while, especially in assemblies which occur every eight or nine years, someone would wonder out loud at the absence of evangelism on the agenda. However, for lack of ongoing institutional interest and preparation, and in the context of an agenda which does not expect it, "evangelism" would sound only too jarring, quickly become a "problem" after being worked over through a little discussion from all over. The lack of evangelism expectations from member churches, and the indifference to evangelism in the ongoing institutional apparatus of the WCC organization — they feed on, perpetuate and justify each other. The circle is now complete.

So we have a situation in the WCC in which there is much people-interest in evangelism but not institutional-interest. Does it have to do with the aura of the organization? With a certain ecumenical milieu? Or is it something much simpler? Or much deeper?

The director of the sub-unit on dialogue, in his most recent official report to the dialogue working group, surveyed the achievement of the sub-unit:

> In the early years, those who were suspicious of dialogue had put the sub-unit very much on the defensive, challenging it to define and redefine... its goals... [Now] we have been able to maintain that dialogue is not contrary to Christian witness or to mission, understood in a broad sense.

He went on to state what lies ahead:

> But what of evangelism? One of the questions being raised is whether Christians have the responsibility to invite, in all humility, persons of other faiths to follow Christ and to become members of an identifiable Christian community... hitherto we have been able to give answers in currencies of large denomination. Now people are looking for answers in small change! We should face this task with faith and humility, for we can never lose sight of the pastoral dimensions of these issues.

To those of us who are deeply involved in ecumenical circles, this would probably come across as a sober, clear, constructive and forward-looking statement, which invites similar kinds of response. That was the way I took it and I will be responding on the same level. I think it contains an honest, no-nonsense, useful description of evangelism, a description I am happy to work with. But if the statement is to be shown to any Christian person active in his or her local church, and reasonably schooled in the scriptures and Christian teaching, I believe the response would be one of deep puzzlement and shock. "What on earth is happening that a leader of the world's most representative church body is questioning the Christian responsibility to invite others to faith in Christ?" Or something like: "I know theologians are capable of saying all kinds of... things. But to hear this posed as a policy question by and for one of the WCC's departments...!" Or, it could be: "Holy smoke! I had thought all along that the WCC searches for Christian unity in order that the world may believe."

Such responses come from contexts different from that of the original, where my colleague's concern was the further clarification of the dialogue ministry. But the statement as it stands would create waves in any local Christian congregation anywhere in the world. And the writer fully knows it, hence the reference to the need for pastoral work. The point I am driving at is not that the statement is without merit. On the contrary, I value it and respect my colleague for articulating it. The point here is that within the WCC organization, a matter such as Christians inviting others to faith in Christ can actually become a question, raised as a matter of course, and causing not a single ripple.

December 1986

46

The WCC is developing four major programmes in these years which, in the words of Emilio Castro, "attempt to open up the imagination of

Christians for our missionary engagement in the world". Sharing of resources is one.* When the WCC was founded in 1948, one of the tasks member churches assigned to the organization was the coordination of interchurch aid and sharing. That task has continued and grown in scope with the emphasis on service and development.

I shall not bore you with the mechanics and the bureaucratic-institutional aspects of resource-sharing in the WCC. I cannot over-emphasize their importance, but the *Monthly Letter on Evangelism* is not an appropriate forum for this sort of technical and managerial discussion. My purpose is to reflect on why the resource-sharing discussion is important and urgent, and what contribution an evangelism perspective can bring to it.

First, the importance and urgency of the resource-sharing discussion.

1. In terms of staffing and budget, interchurch aid remains by far the largest single WCC programme. In addition, many WCC programmes engage in some channelling of resources. For many churches, the WCC, and the ecumenical movement for that matter, is no other than interchurch aid, or a funding agency or, slightly more accurately, a money broker. This image, in my opinion, is grossly unfair. But the perception is real, and does conform to certain aspects of our organizational reality. So it is time for a review, for soul-searching.

But the hope goes far beyond how the WCC channels fifty million dollars annually. This amount is only a tiny fraction of total church resources shared worldwide. The bulk is done bilaterally, and some through independent agencies such as World Vision International. The hope is that the ecumenical discussion on resource-sharing will lead to a commitment by churches to enter into a new relationship with each other; a relationship less modelled on the world's pattern as ours is now, but more expressive of the Christian faith as Paul expected of the churches in Asia Minor when he was collecting money for the mother church in Jerusalem.

2. Today, nearly all the churches in the third world are autonomous in their leadership and administration. Technically, the umbilical cord to their historic mother churches in the West has been cut. At the same time, many churches, hitherto severely restricted by authoritarian regimes, are finding more possibilities in building international ties. They are gradu-ally emerging out of imposed isolation. As these new autonomous

---

* The other three are "participating in mission in Christ's way; seeking unity; covenanting for justice, peace and the integrity of creation".

churches and older historic churches take their rightful place in the worldwide community of Christian churches, they also assume the privilege and responsibility of sharing. The ecumenical movement must then provide an understanding of sharing and of enabling structure(s) so that this can happen. To put it bluntly, what and how can churches share that do not happen to have hard currency?

3. The same sort of question is equally valid for churches who do happen to have hard currency. As a certain amount of money flows from churches in the first world to those in the third world, vaster resources are being sucked in the opposite direction through the smooth machination of an unjust international economic order. We may argue over what the money offerings of hardworking Christian people in the North have to do with the effective monopolistic economic behaviour of their governments and corporations towards the countries of the South. We may look into the more internal dynamics which contribute to the massive deprivation of the South. The much publicized international debt crisis does clearly show the injustice of it all, and that churches in the first world, if only for reason of their address, do have a case to answer. There is already much analysis and documentation. The whole thing came home to me when recently I learned of a lively denomination in Latin America which simply can no longer pay its regular minimalist bills. And this has been an admirable church whose autonomy, integrity, theological competence and mission commitment, by all reasonable standards, are beyond question. Now, after years of unceasing economic pressure, it finally buckles over. As its sister church in the North takes in the news and contemplates response (and I do not doubt there will be action), I wonder what sort of explication will be given to the headquarters board that decides on money matters, and to the pastors and lay people who must meet this need. I wonder what kind of prayer goes with the sharing.

I am convinced that for the sake of the ecumenical movement, if nothing else, we need this discussion on resource-sharing. What then can an evangelism perspective contribute to this process?

Evangelism does not have ready-made answers to a whole lot of problems, certainly not to the international debt crisis. But the insistence that the ecumenical movement must be faithful in communicating Jesus Christ as Saviour and Lord to every person certainly has implications for the resource-sharing discussion, including the debt crisis.

An evangelism perspective agrees that ecumenical resource-sharing has been shallow (too money-oriented), limited (almost exclusively North to South) and world-conforming (money means power and control). This is so primarily not because there are the donors and there are the recipients, and with that comes the evil of domination and dependency. There is some truth in that. But *primarily*, the reason is the ecumenical agenda itself, for which churches share their resources. You see, we do not just share resources. We share resources for a purpose. We share in order to do something. And this purpose, this something we want to do together, determines in a very basic way what resource is called for and shared, how the resource is shared, and the effects the sharing has on everybody concerned.

To put it simply, if our ecumenical resource-sharing is unholistic, it is because our ecumenical agenda is partial. If our sharing in the WCC perpetuates a one-way traffic from the North to the South, it is because the agenda by its very nature requires it. Of course we can tinker with the system here and there to increase the degree of responsiveness, participation and the protection of human dignity. And it is important that we do. But the logic is inescapable. The agenda determines what instruments are required. And there are only so many ways that an instrument can be handled.

Take, for instance, as a start, the two classical goals in the present ecumenical resource-sharing — service and development. They are important ministries. They require money, skill, technology and institutions for their functioning and maintenance. Churches in the North have these resources. Churches in the South do not have these resources, as is also the case with many Orthodox churches. With service and development prominently placed on the ecumenical agenda, the only basic pattern for sharing resources must needs be the North to the South one. The only basic role churches in the North can play is to give, or they are not serious. And for the churches in the South to receive, unless they opt out. As for the churches in the East, in Eastern Europe in particular, theirs is the role of a bystander, miserable or fortunate, depending on the point of view. Because of this ecumenical agenda, some churches who hitherto had no decision-making power over other churches now have some; and some who have never felt that they are poor in their own setting, and are not, now feel that they are indeed poor. And some have simply become irrelevant.

Let us now take the goal generally formulated as advocacy and solidarity for justice, which is emerging as a prominent item on the ecumenical agenda. This is an important ministry and, to me, a logical and biblical outcome of the Christian commitment to service and development. Advocacy and solidarity for justice also involve money, skill and institutions. But the one distinctive resource required in the implementation of this goal is power, specifically the ability to act vis-a-vis state and economic organizations. Which generally means, given our present global reality, power to influence the power centres in the West, whether governments or transnational corporations. Regardless of the forms of this power — lobbying, boycotts, organizations, demonstrations, civil disobedience, etc. — it is a resource to effect political change. And who have this resource, at least some of it, and are in the best position to exercise it? The churches in the North, naturally. Not those in the South. This is not to say that churches in the South have no significant role in the struggle for justice. All the evidence happily points to the opposite. But when it comes to *sharing* in the struggles for justice — and all WCC research and documentations have highlighted the international dimension of injustice — it is once again the churches in the North who happen to have the right sort of resources — power for political change — for the task.

This reflection is not a criticism of the ecumenical agenda of service, development and justice as such. It merely seeks to demonstrate that if we decide on a certain agenda, we are also deciding on what sort of resources we are emphasizing, which in turn spells out the roles and relationship of churches in the ecumenical movement. As it happens, this present ecumenical agenda, which clearly caters to the needs of the South, and is recognized as such by friend and foe alike, is in fact tailor-made for the existing institutional interests and patterns of the churches in the North, at least insofar as resource-sharing is concerned. So the real place to look in our reassessment of ecumenical resource-sharing is the ecumenical agenda itself. We need to put an item on our agenda the implementation of which requires the kind of resources that churches in the South do have and can therefore give and share in a protagonist role.

I am referring, of course, to evangelism. I am referring to the commitment to share the Christian faith with the hope that others may move from no faith or nominal faith or other faiths to faith in Jesus Christ. If there is one thing that can turn the ecumenical agenda towards becoming holistic, that churches in the South can share significantly out of their normal life and institutions, that keeps ecumenical sharing from becoming only a transaction between one church bureaucrat and another, that can help the ecumenical movement to become more real to men and women in the pews, and that can help all churches to stand equally tall, giving and receiving, it is evangelism.

I believe evangelism also offers a perspective that will open up in a new way the question of domination and dependency that the resource-sharing discussion must face. To the churches and the world, the question *service* asks is "where is the need?" The question *development* asks is "where is the potential?" The question *justice* asks is "where is the power?" And the question *evangelism* asks of the churches and of the world is "who are you?" The specific evangelism concern is not so much how many different kinds of power there are, or whether power is good or bad. Nor with giving up power and sharing power. Nor with the proper use of power. The question an evangelist has for the churches and for the world is "who are you who have no power?", "who are you who happen to have power over others?", "who do you think you are as you exercise the power you have?" I believe these evangelistic questions have practical consequences.

This is not an attempt to secure for evangelism a larger slice of the ecumenical money cake. In the first place, I do not believe that being holistic means splitting up the cake 50-50 between social action and evangelism. Secondly, I know that the prioritizing of evangelism on the ecumenical agenda would mean a bigger cake, not smaller slices. And thirdly, which is the real reason for me, it is not easy to share money internationally for evangelism without hurting the cause of the gospel. It can be done, but it is very very difficult. "Evangelism and money", the subject deserves a separate letter. The point of this entire reflection is to show how an evangelism perspective can help make ecumenical-sharing more multi-faceted, more multi-directional, less geared towards money, and therefore more capable of appropriating and sharing the different gifts and resources that all churches have received from God. In the process, there is a danger we must guard against: the danger that the concern for evangelism is used to spiritualize resource-sharing. That sharing in evangelism is non-material sharing, and therefore has nothing to do with money or with the discussion about money. This is nonsense. Nowadays, everything involves money, especially as the churches have decided to go international. Non-material sharing requires material facilitation. South-to-South sharing is often more expensive than sharing between South and North. Even interceding for each other requires money if it is to happen unceasingly, intelligently, and in a timely manner. I mean staying in touch, disseminating information, prayer letters, not to mention prayer secretaries and prayer congresses.

From my evangelism perspective, I feel that if the ecumenical resource-sharing discussion is to go anywhere, we must look critically at the ecumenical agenda as it is actually implemented in the WCC decision-making and programme apparatus. At the moment, and for a long time past, we have an ecumenical agenda for the South but not of the South. Not bad but not good enough. We have an ecumenical agenda which puts churches in the North in the protagonist role, and the churches in the South in a relatively minor role. The problem is not that the ecumenical agenda emphasizes service, development and justice. It is that it does not emphasize evangelism enough, if at all. In the literature which facilitates the WCC discussion on resource-sharing, and reports on numerous consultations, there is no reference to evangelism except one. And that one single mention, from Africa, happens to refer to evangelism as a problem, under the heading of "political issue". Feelings and theologies aside, surely, this is no way "to open up the imagination of Christians for our missionary engagement in the world".

August 1987

47

I have just come back from San Antonio, Texas, and the WCC conference on world mission and evangelism. This once-every-eight-year event sees itself as part of the series of historic missionary conferences dating back to Edinburgh 1910. Composed of delegates from member churches, councils of churches, mission boards and missionary societies, and practitioners at the grassroots, the conference provides some clear indications of where the ecumenical movement is at in its missionary thinking and commitment today.

With this letter, I propose to offer an initial and focused report on San Antonio. Initial, because a comprehensive report will be issued officially in book form later on. Focused, because I will not attempt to describe every aspect of the conference. Instead, I will attempt to answer the questions: What is the message of San Antonio? What major contributions do we see San Antonio making to the ecumenical movement? I am aware of course that mine cannot be the only available answer.

Overall, praying the prayer which is the San Antonio theme "Your Will be Done: Mission in Christ's Way", the conference has come to the conviction that Christians are called by God to proclaim the good news, to act with those who struggle for justice and dignity, to treasure the earth, and to seek renewal of missionary efforts and structures. Theologically I believe it is in the first part — that we are called by God to proclaim the good news — that the San Antonio message and contribution can be located.

This is what happened.

First, the statement "Mission and Evangelism: An Ecumenical Affirmation" was conscientiously supported and appropriated at San Antonio.

A San Antonio report entitled "Mission in the Name of the Living God" begins with this affirmation:

> At the very heart of the church's vocation in the world is the proclamation of the kingdom of God inaugurated in Jesus the Lord, crucified and risen and made present among us by the Holy Spirit.

Another, entitled "Witness in a Secular Society", leads with this recognition and plea:

> Everywhere the churches are in missionary situations. Even in countries where the churches have been active for centuries we see life organized today without reference to Christian values, a growth of secularism understood as the absence of any final meaning. The churches have lost vital contact with the workers and the youth and many others. The situation is so urgent that it commands priority attention of the ecumenical movement. (ME 37)

And the important chapter on "Witness among People of Other Living Faiths" bases itself on three sets of affirmations, in the order given:

> True witness follows Jesus Christ in respecting and affirming the uniqueness and freedom of others... such an attitude springs from the assurance that God is the Creator of the whole universe and that he has not left himself without witness at any time or any place. The Spirit of God is constantly at work in ways that pass human understanding (ME 41, 43).
>
> The proclamation of the gospel includes an invitation to recognize and accept in a personal decision the saving Lordship of Christ. It is the announcement of a personal encounter, mediated by the Holy Spirit, with the living Christ, receiving his forgiveness and making a personal acceptance of the call to discipleship and a life of service (ME 10).
>
> Christians owe the message of God's salvation in Jesus Christ to every person and to every people ... The wonder of (Jesus') ministry of love persuades Christians to testify to people of every religious and non-religious persuasion of this decisive presence of God in Christ. In him is our salvation... In entering into a relationship of dialogue with others... Christians seek to discern the unsearchable riches of God and the way he deals with humanity (ME 41, 42, 43).

San Antonio is built on the missiology of "Mission and Evangelism: An Ecumenical Affirmation". Secondly, San Antonio is explicitly emphatic on evangelism, to an extent unmatched in major WCC meetings since the New Delhi assembly in 1961. Herewith excerpts of the section one report: "Turning to the Living God". On the present situation:

> We have been made aware of a new and widespread interest in evangelism in communities linked with the ecumenical movement in the North as well as the South. The love of God for the world is the source for our missionary motivation and this love creates an urgency to share the gospel invitingly in our time. We recognize however with deep regret that some of our missionary endeavours may be attributed to impure motivations — concerns about declining church membership, subtle political agendas, and the like.
>
> Christians desire to "confess the life and work of Jesus Christ as unique, decisive, and universally significant" [the quotation is from the report of a January 1988 WCC consultation on mission and dialogue, held in Tambaram, India]; we therefore invite our churches to subscribe to the CWME aim, as endorsed by the Nairobi assembly of the WCC (1975) that the Christian community should be assisted to proclaim "the gospel of Jesus Christ, by word and deed, to the whole world to the end that all may believe in him and be saved".

On communicating the gospel in Christ's way:

> The faith evoked through the communication of the gospel needs nurture within the body of Christ. This nurture includes prayer, and the study of God's word in a language and cultural form which communicates without alienation and which facilitates the discernment of the contours of God's reign in all realms of life. We can and may never determine in advance the way the gospel will come alive in the life, context and culture of a community. We affirm true Christian communication to be an act of worship, a praise of God through the shared word and action of persons-in-community, reflecting the life of the Holy Trinity. Christ's mission to the world manifests the outpouring of God's love through the Son and the Spirit. The ground of unity of the church, the body of Christ, is the love and the unity eternally manifested in the life of the Triune God. The church as God's chosen instrument for proclaiming the good news of the kingdom is meant to embody and communicate values of oneness, reconciliation, equality, justice, freedom, harmony, peace and love. In the image of the Trinity, we must hold together this witness of the worshipping and serving community united in love, with that of its evangelistic task of sending forth persons to proclaim the word to those who have not yet heard or realized its fulfilling and saving grace.
>
> "The vicarious work of Christ demands the presence of vicarious people" (ME 25). We stand in awe in the awareness of the belief that God has committed to our faltering faith communities the message of his love and his reign. We witness to the humble power and servant lordship of the Crucified

and Risen, seeking to be faithful to him who called us into discipleship and into the ministry of witnessing to the living God.

As we seek to communicate God's image to others, we realize that our own lives and stories, as well as non-discursive ways of communicating through hymnography or song, iconography or symbol, movement and silence, may be more effective personal and experiential ways of sharing the faith than some forms of mass media. The church is also challenged to proclaim the gospel today in new languages, in both written and oral forms, and in the idioms and the symbols of the cultures in which it is carried. Many millions have not heard the story of Jesus, even in cultures where historically the gospel was common knowledge.

If the Uppsala assembly in 1968 introduced the language of social involvement into the WCC, San Antonio has reintroduced a new-found language of evangelism, making itself heard in the context of today.

These tremendous affirmations have, however, to be viewed in light of the present moment in history. In some parts of the world people face a total system of death, of monstrous false gods, of exploitative economic systems, of violence, of the disintegration of the fundamental bonds of society, of the destruction of human life, of helplessness of persons in the face of impersonal forces. We are called to exercise our mission in this context of human struggle, and challenged to keep the earth alive and to promote human dignity, since the living God is both Creator of heaven and earth and Protector of the cause of the widow, the orphan, the poor and the stranger. To respond to all this is part of our mission, just as inviting people to put their trust in God is part of that mission. The "material gospel" and the "spiritual gospel" have to be one, as was true of the ministry of Jesus (ME 34). Frequently the world's poor are also those who have not yet heard the good news of the gospel; to withhold from them justice as well as the good news of life in Christ is to commit a "double injustice" (ME 32). There is no evangelism without solidarity; there is no Christian solidarity that does not involve sharing the message of God's coming reign (ME 34).

Thirdly, San Antonio faces boldly the crucial mission issue of witness among people of other living faiths, and comes up with an understanding that represents a big step in the corporate, ecumenical discussion of the subject.

Probably the most noteworthy San Antonio statements on the subject are as follows:

We cannot point to any other way of salvation than Jesus Christ; at the same time we cannot set limits to the saving power of God. At times the debate about salvation focuses itself only on the fate of the individual's soul in the hereafter, whereas the will of God is life in its fullness even here and now.

We therefore state: (a) that our witness to others concerning salvation in Christ springs from the fact that we have encountered him as our Lord and Saviour and are hence urged to share this with others, and (b) that in calling people to faith in Christ, we are not only offering personal salvation but also calling them to follow Jesus in the service of God's kingdom.

We have paid attention to the complex debate about the relationship between witness and dialogue. We recognize that both witness and dialogue presuppose two-way relationships. We affirm that witness does not preclude dialogue but invites it, and that dialogue does not preclude witness but extends and deepens it.

Dialogue has its own place and integrity and is neither opposed to nor incompatible with witness or proclamation. We do not water down our own commitment if we engage in dialogue; as a matter of fact, dialogue between people of different faiths is spurious, unless it proceeds from the acceptance and expression of faith commitment. Indeed, life with people of other faiths and ideologies is by its very nature an encounter of commitments (ME 45). In dialogue we are invited to listen, in openness, to the possibility that the God we know in Jesus Christ may encounter us also in the lives of our neighbours of other faiths. On the other hand, we also see that the mutual sharing with people of other faiths in the efforts for justice, peace and service to the environment engages us in dialogue — the dialogue of life. We wish to commend this in recognition that all humankind is responsible before God and the human family.

In affirming the dialogical nature of our witness, we are constrained by grace to affirm "that salvation is offered to the whole creation through Jesus Christ" (Tambaram II). "Our mission to witness to Jesus Christ can never be given up" (Melbourne 1980). We are well aware that these convictions and the ministry of witness stand in tension with what we have affirmed about God being present in and at work in people of other faiths; we appreciate this tension, and do not attempt to resolve it.

These statements add up to two conclusions. One, Christians must share their faith with their Hindu, Muslim and Buddhist neighbours and invite them to be disciples of Jesus Christ. Two, Christians should be open to the possibility of God's presence and work in people of other faiths.

This second conclusion is a departure from the position arrived at at the Vancouver assembly 1983. San Antonio openly recognizes the possibilities of God's work in people of other faiths. It recognizes the tension between this position and our commitment to evangelize. It does not attempt to resolve the tension. "We cannot point to any other way of salvation than Jesus Christ, at the same time we cannot set limits to the saving power of God."

With this, the conference commits itself to the following acts of faithfulness, i.e. a commitment of the participants for a specific, account-able action:

a) We commit ourselves and challenge our churches to cooperate in witnessing to the millions of people who have not yet had an opportunity to respond to the gospel;

b) we affirm that witness does not preclude dialogue with people of other living faiths, but dialogue extends and deepens our witness;

c) we commit ourselves and challenge our churches to engage in dialogue, wherever possible, with people of other faiths and to work together with them for justice, peace and the integrity of creation.

The conference was not simply another ecumenical gathering. San Antonio was a legally required event mandated by the CWME constitution drawn up in 1961 when the International Missionary Council became part of the WCC. The constitution provided for maintenance of a CWME constituency and periodic world conference which has the powers to oversee the finance and programme of CWME.

Since 1961, organizational developments within the WCC and traditional CWME constituencies have rendered such provisions obsolete. Of the traditional CWME constituencies, many autonomous missionary societies have become the mission boards of denominations, and national councils of churches have developed into full-grown ecumenical bodies with comprehensive agendas of their own. On the other hand, since 1961 CWME has become more integrated into the WCC's accountability system, such as commissions, units and central committee, etc. Reality has outrun the "IMC" constitution of CWME.

At San Antonio, the constitutional anomaly was legally removed. CWME still retains its constituency. But the constituency will no longer exercise its powers through a periodic conference such as San Antonio, but through the regular structures of the WCC. For students in mission history, San Antonio marks the final step in the integration of the IMC with the WCC. At this point, it is significant to recall that in New Delhi in 1961 when the first step was taken, the assembly pointedly noted that "integration must mean that the WCC takes the missionary task into the very heart of its life, and also that the missionary agencies of the churches place their work in an ecumenical perspective and accept whatever new insights God may give". San Antonio brings the integration process to its logical conclusion. Has this strong hope of New Delhi been fulfilled? The findings of San Antonio are remarkably en-couraging.

I should add that what has most encouraged me is the people and the way the statements I refer to were developed and arrived at. The conference urges upon us an explicit and powerful emphasis on evangelism, on the commitment to invite people who have not heard of the good news and those who have not been moved by it, to be disciples of Jesus Christ. In San Antonio, this thrust was visibly led by delegates from Asia and Africa. Right in the first plenary, a Nigerian pastor and a bishop from Pakistan rose to put the classic concern "that all may believe" on the agenda. The conference was prepared for it. The first of the four sections entitled "Turning to the Living God" provided the specific space and support for corporate discussion on the subject. Thereafter, in section gatherings, in small groups and in plenary, delegates from churches and mission boards, from Scotland to Uganda, men and women, brought their concern for and experience of the direct communication of the gospel to the forefront.

From the vantage point of staff, I believe something important happened in San Antonio. A psychological barrier has been broken — the feeling that in WCC circles and meetings, one simply does not talk the language of evangelism, or that one does it only at the risk of confrontation, and that even if one does talk about it, one should so load it with qualifications ("balance" is the ecumenical word), that it no longer soars. In San Antonio, Christians committed to evangelism at home were able to express that same commitment with no hang-ups and no apologies. The openness that CWME deliberately created in the design of the conference, the working out of the ecumenical principle of participation, and the profoundly moving experience of daily worship must have something to do with such evangelical emancipation. Also the simple fact that nowadays there are more and more "ecumenical evangelicals" or "evangelical ecumenicals" in our member churches, both in the North Atlantic regions and in the third world. And these people are making their voices heard. In San Antonio, their voice found harmony with the Orthodox voice, certainly in areas such as evangelism, witness in secular society and in interfaith situations, but also over issues such as Palestine.

Finally, let me share with you an image that San Antonio has indelibly carved in my mind. The words are "the earth is the Lord's", the title for the third section of the conference. The picture is the brightly coloured globe which is the conference logo. The vigour comes from the memory of many participants at San Antonio from across the world, each with a story to tell and to share. And the scripture comes from John 3:16-17: "For God so loved the world that he gave his one and only Son that whoever believes in him shall not perish but have eternal life. For God did not send his Son into the world to condemn the world, but to save the world through him."

June 1989

48

For those of you who worry about the place of evangelism in the WCC's programme priorities and organizational profile, let me assure you evangelism is safe. The delegates at the Canberra assembly did not say or write anything powerful or creative about evangelism, yet they, or most of them, were very conscientious that evangelism must be clearly up front and visible. The forthcoming restructuring of the WCC Geneva office will make this clear. There is however no cause for complacency, as parts of this report will show. But, formally and officially, the WCC's commitment to evangelism is a matter of record.

This out of the way, let me hasten to say that I don't like this way of talking about evangelism as if it is a specialized ministry with an existence independent of other ministries and of the life of the WCC as a whole. We who care about the evangelism programme in the WCC also care about the WCC's theology and the WCC's body language. We have to. A commitment to evangelism does not mean everybody having to subscribe to one particular theology and one particular style. The commitment, however, does mean the acceptance that there is such a thing as truth, and that an assembly of churches and Christians must have the ability and the right to say: "This we do believe. That we don't believe." I know this is hard to achieve these days in an international, ecumenical setting. But it is the seriousness of purpose, and the mutual and public accountability in theology and communication, that I want to expect of the WCC.

With such a mindset, let me proceed with my reflection on the Canberra assembly. I propose to share what I personally experienced.

First, a few notes on methodology. It is very hard to have a firm grasp of the assembly. If you ask the insiders — the staff, the delegates — nine out of ten would say the assembly was awful. The more involved one was — those with committee assignments in particular — the more cynical one became. One of our presidents, commenting on the election of the central committee, told the press that "ecumenical politics stinks to high heaven". But if you are an outsider — the visitors, for instance, who came for the worship and some open sessions and a special programme — the assembly would come across as a most positive experience and a very significant ecumenical event. Of course both are right. And there is no reason why the insiders' view is necessarily better than the outsiders' view. What these two different assessments from Canberra participants point to is that the WCC makes for an inspiring gathering of Christians but as a theologizing and decision-making body it is in real trouble.

But even then, this may not be the most relevant thing to say about Canberra. This conclusion is based on the experience of those who were present, and rests on the assumption that Canberra is significant in so far as it has an impact on the WCC and on the participants. Perhaps this assumption is only of secondary importance. Perhaps a more important question is what Canberra does or will do to the churches and to the Christians who were *not* there. Here, we are concerned not so much with what came out of Canberra but with what the churches make of it. Transmission and appropriation are very different processes. What Canberra transmits and what the churches eventually appropriate could well be very different things.

With this broader and, I believe, more theologically appropriate perspective, I would say that the most important happening in Canberra has got to be the return to WCC membership of the churches in China through the China Christian Council. Some observers try to dismiss its significance by saying that membership doesn't mean a thing because it won't mean a thing to local congregations in the mainland. This is cynicism unworthy of our faith. The leadership of the China Christian Council had been struggling with the question of membership in various international Christian organizations for years, always stopping short of the final step with the hope of achieving a higher degree of internal consensus. Now a decision was made and formalized in Canberra. How would it affect the churches in China and their unity? How about relations with the state? These are long-term questions.

As for the CCC membership's impact on the life of the WCC, it will be felt, I believe, through "presence". CCC leadership has always admitted shortage of personnel for international meetings. This is likely to remain for a long while. But "presence" may well be enough. Speaking only of evangelism matters, the CCC contribution would most likely be evangelism through the daily witness of believers and the corporate worship of the churches, with no need for large evangelism budgets.

After I did a piece in these pages on "why radical Christians make ineffectual evangelists", I received the following in the mail from one of the most knowledgeable mission researchers on China. "As you know, the sermons in China are criticized by radical Christians on the outside because they neglect social issues. They aren't 'prophetic'. But these churches and pastors and Christians must be doing something right, the way the churches are growing. The sermons I have heard speak directly to the personal, spiritual needs of the listeners, drawing heavily on the Old Testament and the New Testament, and on testimony of the preacher. They are effective for these people and, I believe, would be for everyone else also. Moreover they are Christocentric. The Chinese preachers don't avoid mentioning Jesus Christ as Lord and Saviour." Such a message will be good for the WCC.

Let me move on with some Canberra experiences and personal reflections which I believe could help us understand the WCC a little better.

• The assembly was well covered by radio. The Australian Broadcasting Corporation had a permanent team on the site. With the Gulf war dominating the opening sessions, it naturally became the focus of the secular media. At the end of a long and sophisticated story, the commentator made this observation: "The World Council of Churches is not afraid of staking out a position different from that of governments." I think this is a most perceptive insight. Perhaps not many of us in the ecumenical movement have been conscious of ourselves in this light. Given the fact that all governments of whatever persuasion claim the right of having and speaking the truth, the journalist's observation is marvellously affirming and edifying.

However, this is not to say that the WCC has learned to proclaim to the nations. Proclaiming to the nations (peoples) is not the same as producing a piece of social and political analysis. It is to find the one word which cuts through historical contradictions and human ambiguities, in order to judge, to console, to bring hope, to rally, as the case may be. A reader's letter to the April 1991 issue of the *Observer*, the United Church of Canada magazine, shows how much we have come short in our attempt at public witness:

> Hamilton conference sent out a letter giving the United Church position on the Gulf war and Canada's part in it. As a member of Bruce Presbytery, I thought it sensible to bring the matter before our congregation.
>
> Before the meeting I handed out a summary and there was thoughtful discussion. The statement supports non-violent means, declaring that "war is

no longer an acceptable option for resolving political difference". I totally agree. Then came the vote — something like 70 to 7 for rejection. The statement does not follow the opinion of church members.

Unless our church courts start to reflect the thinking of persons in the pew, none of their statements will be taken seriously.

How this can be done, I don't know. Do I go to Presbytery and vote as I think, yea, or as our congregation thinks, nay?

Ruth Hunt, Mount Forest, Ont.

A case of being right and irrelevant.

• At a gathering of those with evangelical concerns, which met fairly regularly, and numbered close to a hundred, attention was drawn to Native peoples and their concerns. A bishop from Sydney was apparently unhappy with the way the assembly dealt with Aboriginal issues. He thought it was too one-sided. He called on a young woman, one of the only two Aborigines present, to set the record straight. I cannot exactly duplicate her words, but neither can I forget what she told us that day.

She said: I am an evangelical Christian, but sometimes I feel ashamed of the identification. Evangelical Christians claim to love us Aboriginal people, and you do want to share the gospel with us. But you seldom share our concern for our rights as a people and we get no solidarity from you in our struggles for our ancestors' land. It is the ecumenical churches and the Catholic church which lend us their voice, and give us the platform to speak. As for our rites and our spiritualities, don't you knock them. They are precious to us and they can be redeemed. We pastoral workers are very few in this assembly. Some pastors are not here because they don't want to be here. They don't want to be seen as part of the WCC. Some who want to be here can't, because they have not been invited. Canberra is expensive. Most of the WCC invitations go to the political people, those who struggle on the political front. If you want to talk to us Aboriginal pastors, you can find us in a corner in the tent. There are four of us. Please come. We can tell you a lot more.

The WCC has always looked for ways to be more faithful and more relevant. The answer is right here with people like her. She is a member of the Uniting Church. If we'd only look and listen.

• By now, you must have heard of Prof. Chung Hyun-Kyung's dance and lecture on the Holy Spirit theme. It was the one plenary presentation that got people excited. It was a powerful presentation, and the other plenary presentations were either incredibly dull in the name of theological tradition or amateurishly superficial in the name of "multi-media" communication. For me, Prof. Chung's presentation and the responses to it are most revealing of the churches' life together in the WCC. In this sense it is very significant. It reveals that we do not have enough trust among ourselves to do theology together. We use words to express ourselves. We do not use words to communicate. The charge of syncretism reveals only those who hurl it. To Protestants in East Asia, the last thing on earth to make that public charge has got to be Christian Byzantium with its ideology of intimate ties between church, state and Greco-Roman culture. It also didn't help when the general secretary chose to deal with it as a matter of human rights. Neither did it help when Prof. Chung, in exasperation, suggested that the days of old European male making decisions on theology are over, and that now it must be young third-world women's turn.

I don't think "syncretism" as a general category is useful any more for theological discourse. We have to be specific. With Prof. Chung's presentation, the specific question has to do with the relation between the Holy Spirit and the spirits. But the professor, having posed the question, treated the subject in a shabby manner. Referring to "the Han-ridden spirits who wander the land, seeking the chance to make the wrong right", she went on to assert that they are "agents through whom the Holy Spirit has spoken her compassion and wisdom for life". She concluded "for us, they are the icons of the Holy Spirit who became tangible and visible to us". Now, you can say many things about the spirits and the Holy Spirit. But you cannot say that spirits are both agents and icons of the Holy Spirit. An agent has an existence of its own. An icon doesn't. An icon reflects a reality outside of itself. An agent is active while an icon is passive. This is no nit-picking. Prof. Chung's subject was after all spiritual discernment. The discernment of spirits is a matter of life and death, certainly for those in Jesus' time who were possessed, and for many today.

Here we come to the heart of the matter. We come to the point which most disturbs not only Orthodox participants but many other Christians to whom the spirit world is real. Prof. Chung's unconditional and untroubled affirmation of the wandering spirits, and her contradictory delineation of their relationship with the Holy Spirit, suggest to many, myself included, a nonchalant attitude towards the spirit world which borders either on spiritual naivete or on manipulation and cynicism. Was she serious when she declared the auditorium holy ground and then proceeded to invoke a long list of spirits of people who suffered tragic deaths, and of the Amazon rain forest, and the spirits of earth, air and water?

For those of us to whom the spirit world is real, one does not invoke spirits, even benevolent spirits, lightly. Invoking the spirits has consequences. One does not invoke them in a gathering of thousands of strangers. One does not invoke spirits in the definitive time-frame of forty-five minutes. One does not, as Prof. Chung did, urge people to "prepare the way of the Holy Spirit by emptying ourselves" and then proceed to invoke a whole legion of spirits. What if the spirits do come? Do we know what that could mean? I don't think even our most radical imaginings could prepare us for the awesome presence, for instance, of "the spirit of Jewish people killed in the gas chambers during the Holocaust", of "the spirit of people killed in Hiroshima". If we have the slightest inkling of the reality of the spirit world, and of the frailty of our own spiritual fibre, our prayer would not have been "come, you spirits". It would be more likely "stay away, you spirits. But, come, Holy Spirit."

But Prof. Chung did invoke the spirits, a total of sixteen spirits. Could it be that they are not meant to be real spirits? That they are not meant to be supernatural beings as spirits are, but simply another way of talking about a remembrance that is good and significant and representative? An artistic way of saying things like "the spirit of the long march", "the spirit of the age" or "the spirit of Dunkirk"? In fact, a spirituality that is all style and no content, a spiritual theology without the spirit?

I am putting it bluntly partly because the whole controversy has been too easily portrayed as one between third-world theology and Orthodoxy. This is only partially true. The real truth is there were a lot more critical responses than reported. Particularly among Koreans and other East Asians who are familiar with the presentation's shamanistic gestures and allusions. To us, these are much more than innovative, artistic devices. They are, if taken seriously, rituals and rites with capacities for spiritual substance. But the religious press missed all that. They were too busy interviewing Orthodox and Europeans. Only one short comment from Asia — from India — appeared in the assembly paper which subsequent reports picked up. Even the reporting from Asia's ecumenical press followed thoughtlessly this European-centred way and missed the boat. Here then are a few comments from Northeast Asian delegates at the assembly:

> I take the spirit world seriously enough not to want to bother it. Prof. Chung should have heeded the advice of her Christian grassroots women activists in Korea. "Don't spend too much energy to call the spirit because the spirit is already here with us. Don't bother her by calling her all the time." That's in her presentation. *(from Korea)*

Yours

My conversion to Christ is a process of many years; part of the process is my liberation from the sort of spirits Prof. Chung invoked. I am not going back. I know this is true of many people in our churches... Maybe, two or three generations later, the church can take another look. *(from Taiwan)*

I am annoyed that there is no proper discussion of Prof. Chung's paper. It needs to be discussed. I am a Korean and a Presbyterian. I think such a presentation is impossible in any Korean church. Maybe in an ecumenical consultation. But that is the trouble, isn't it? We should not take the easy way out in doing theology. *(from Korea)*

The theology of the Holy Spirit is important for our situation. The church's number one concern in this area is spiritual discernment. Many Chinese people seek the blessing of the spirits. Many Christians too, particularly in the rural areas. Our theological emphasis is on the distinctiveness of the Holy Spirit as the Third Person of the Triune God. *(from China)*

• Midway through the assembly, we broke up to visit churches in various parts of Australia. With two others, I went to a beautiful little town called Orange. No oranges grow there, only apples. The name has to do with a Protestant brotherhood way back in Ireland. That Sunday, I visited four congregations — three Uniting Church and one Baptist. With the exception of one, which proudly proclaims itself ex-Congregational in bold stone relief (and that probably explains its problem), all three were full of people — old people, middle-aged people, young adults and many children. I heard no soul-rousing sermons or heroic testimonies of faith; but I came away strangely moved, reluctant to rejoin the assembly. The WCC would do well to make sense of itself to the people of Orange, and to build on such congregations everywhere.

June 1991